thirteen weeks

·····
·····
·····
·····
·····
·····

A Guide to Teaching College Writing

· ·

Irvin Y. Hashimoto
Whitman College

D0348434

Boynton/Cook Publishers
Heinemann
Portsmouth, NH

Boynton/Cook Publishers
A Subsidiary of
Heinemann Educational Books, Inc.
361 Hanover Street   Portsmouth, NH 03801–3959
Offices and agents throughout the world

For Marianne

The following have generously given permission to use material in this book:

Page 91: From chapter 9 of *The Smell Book: Scents, Sex and Society* by Ruth Winter. Published by J.B. Lippincott, 1976. Reprinted by permission of Ruth Winter.

Page 190: From "Putt-Putt Go-Go" by Bob Greene. Reprinted with permission of Atheneum publishers, an imprint of Macmillan Publishing Company from "Putt-Putt Go-Go" by Bob Greene in his *American Beat*. Copyright ©1983 John Deadline Enterprises, Inc.

Page 201: Excerpt from *Strictly Speaking* by Edwin Newman. Reprinted with permission of Macmillan Publishing Company. Copyright ©1974 by Edwin Newman.

Pages 261–62: From *Vic Braden's Tennis for the Future* by Vic Braden and Bill Bruns. Copyright ©1977 by Vic Braden and William Bruns. By permission of Little, Brown and Company.

Page 263: From *Georgia O'Keeffe: Art & Letters*, edited by Sarah Greenough, published in 1987. Reprinted by permission of the National Gallery of Art, Washington, DC.

Every effort has been made to contact those whose words and illustrations appear in this book. We regret any oversights that may have occurred and would be happy to rectify them in future printings.

Library of Congress Cataloging-in-Publication Data
Hashimoto, Irvin Y. (Irvin Yuiichi), 1945–
    Thirteen weeks : a guide to teaching college writing / Irvin Y.
Hashimoto.
        p.   cm.
    Includes bibliographical references.
    ISBN 0-86709-261-0
    1. English language—Rhetoric—Study and teaching.   I. Title.
II. Title: 13 weeks.
PE1404.H38   1990
808'.042'0711—dc20   90-2089
                                                                     CIP

Designed by Maria Szmauz
Printed in the United States of America
91 92 93 94 95   10 9 8 7 6 5 4 3 2 1

contents

part three

Essentials

part four

"Style"

acknowledgments

Of the people who had something to say to me about this book, I'd especially like to thank John C. Schafer, who laughed at my jokes and advised me to keep the original preface that finally got deleted in draft three; Susan Hubbuch, who reminded me that people don't have to agree with me; Margot Scribner, who read the first draft and liked it; Roberta Davidson, who read the third draft and liked it; Bob Boynton, who suggested in his polite way that I should write like a civilized, sensible person; Paul Hoornbeek, who read the first, second, third, and fourth drafts and advised me to keep all the jokes and complex arguments and kettle drums—even while I was deleting them and simplifying them after Bob Boynton told me to write like a civilized, sensible person; and Barry Kroll, who waded the Frying Pan River with me and helped me keep the academy in perspective. Finally, I'd like to thank my students, who every year teach me more about what I don't know about teaching and continually remind me that whatever I do learn about teaching writing ought to include them.

preface

People come up to me all the time and ask unfortunate questions like "How do *you* teach writing?" or "How can you stand teaching writing?" or "Do you think you'll ever want to teach something interesting like Shakespeare?" I usually mumble something about "doing the best I can in an unfair world" and quote Dale Carnegie to myself: "If you want to gather honey, don't kick over the beehive." I hear my voice, or something like my voice, saying something stupid like "Well, ahem . . . I . . . I don't know . . . it's, well, it's complicated . . . and we all have a job to do, don't we? . . . don't we all?" or "Well, ahem . . . I sweat a lot and suffer a lot and cry a lot, har har har."

Or I go away and pull weeds in my backyard and think about all the good things I could have said if I had a fast mind and a fast mouth. "Do I look like some stand-up comedian or what?" "I'm not really sure, but they seem to learn something after I beat them with a stick and make them bleed." "I hang 'em by their toes and flog the comma splices out of them twice a week, don't you?"

In my more ambitious moments, I've often thought I could actually say something about how I teach writing without appearing "uninformed" or "out-of-touch" (terms some of my colleagues use for those of us who aren't particularly blown away by some new brand of "critical theory," theory of the imagination, development, or invention). This book is a product of those more ambitious moments. Although I'm mainly concerned with answering the big question How do *you* teach writing? indirectly, but more importantly, I'd like to answer those who often seem to think that teaching writing is no fun or best done by some hungry graduate student straight out of his/her Keats seminar armed with a fat rhetoric-reader, a few dry bagels, some on-line, computer-assisted grammar drills, and a statement of department goals and purposes.

Before I begin, however, I'd like to make a few disclaimers and qualifications.

First, I would point out that I've built this book around the notion of "thirteen weeks," but I have no particular stake in this period of time. I've taught longer courses up to fifteen and sixteen weeks, and I've taught shorter ones. At least for the sake of my argument, one or two weeks either way probably won't make much difference at all.

Furthermore, although I may make comments about teaching writing in general, I'm mainly concerned with *college-level* teaching. I'm aware that there are differences in the ability levels and experience levels at different institutions, but here, I'm mainly concerned with typical, middle-range, well-meaning, mainstream college students—those with some academic aspirations, some idea of syntax, and often a reasonable amount of untapped intelligence and resources. We've not said much about teaching such students—very little, in fact, about what we do with them in class. Those of you who teach other students will have to filter what I'm saying through your own experience before you pass judgment. That doesn't mean that my advice is completely inappropriate for "nontraditional" students, members of minorities, or "basic writers" in open-admissions universities, but the book is already fat enough as it is, and I'd rather not lose control of what I know something about.

Instead of teaching such students everything, I will focus on teaching "academic writing"—writing that requires students to argue or discuss issues, make assertions, deal with data and other people's ideas—and do what academic people do in academic places. In doing so, I realize that many people will object immediately. Some will say that our task is to teach students to write for all kinds of audiences, in all major styles, in all kinds of weather. Others will suggest that academic writing is somehow too limited and useless—that no one writes academically in the "real" world, or no one takes academic writing seriously except other academics—and the only people who want to teach such stuff are strange, short-sighted beadles who want to turn writing courses into "service" courses. Still others will suggest that I'm attempting the impossible—that academic writing makes sense only if we teach it in *specific contexts,* as in engineering writing or writing in the social sciences or writing in art.[1] Still others will suggest that teaching students academic writing teaches them to conform, limit themselves, and buy into structured, stifling values and rules that prevent them from asserting themselves and challenging the very underpinnings of academia.

In spite of such objections—and in different ways, each makes some sense—I want to teach students academic writing. I hope that my reasons become clear as you read. But for now, I would emphasize that I don't see academic writing as necessarily boring or uninspiring or constricting. I don't see that academic writing inhibits students or keeps them from being politically aware human beings. And I don't see that academic writing leads to some denial of the liberal arts, life, "style," or whatever else it is that makes human beings feel alive or "real." I see academic writing (at least the kind of academic writing I'm concerned with here) as good and valuable—and learning to write it a valuable way for students to *begin* to become intelligent, aware, and healthy members of a world where ideas matter, where we learn from each other, argue with each other, and challenge each other to think more clearly, evaluate more thoughtfully, and in so doing, become more responsible, academic human beings.

I emphasize the word *begin* in that last sentence to underscore the necessity to keep evaluating what we can do and what we can't do and to gain some distance on our aspirations as human beings and earthshakers. I suppose that learning to write is part of the American Dream—Thirteen Weeks to a Sexier, Wartless Body. Thirteen Weeks to a New Vocabulary. Thirteen Weeks to Winning Bridge. Thirteen Weeks to Dale Carnegie. Thirteen Weeks to E. B. White. But students don't always change as much as we'd like in thirteen weeks. Their glands don't dry up. They're still bogged down (and may be bogged down for years) in a system that rewards them for passivity, for thinking like their parents, for reacting against their parents' values, for making do, for relying on blind faith. Sometimes, we're lucky if we can get them to think just a little differently about their writing *even though they may not yet write differently.* And sometimes changes come long *after* we've given up hope—after they've gotten married or gotten a job or found God or found . . . found what? (In my case, I found middle age and that probably helped.)

We are, after all, dealing with young minds and young people—young people who will grow, change, and get smarter over time—many of whom will learn enough and experience enough some day to make us feel inefficient and even envious in our old age. But I'm not so sure that we can ever claim that they will grow and change and get smarter over time or reach their potentials *just because of* our well-meaning exhortations or timely challenges or just because they wrote ten or even fifteen papers for us in English 101.

Some of you will want to criticize me for making assertions that I can't "prove." I can't, for instance, prove that students shouldn't save the best for last in academic writing. I can't prove that students ought to be *conscious learners*—aware of their own limitations and perceptions. I can't prove that we can't teach students much about "finding things to say" if they don't have much to say about a particular topic to begin with. I can't prove that teaching students how to use thesis statements doesn't inhibit them at least somewhat. And I can't prove that my system is any better than anyone else's—even though my students often tell me so, and I believe that what I'm doing makes sense. (The question, of course, is even more complicated because none of us can probably prove much without some direct line to the fabric of the Universe.)[2]

The evidence for my assertions comes mainly from my own teaching and my own attempts to make sense of the collective wisdom of the field. I suppose I am, first of all, a teacher, and I don't pretend to be a researcher or linguist or cognitive psychologist. I have had teaching experience on the high school level (three years, grades seven to twelve) and in large and small college writing programs. I spent five years running a writing center for Idaho State University, a medium-sized, open-admissions university, and now teach at Whitman College, a small, private liberal arts college in Washington state. While at the University of Michigan, I received a Distinguished Teaching Fellow Award; at Idaho State University, I was chosen Distinguished Teacher of the Year in 1981; and at Whitman College, I have received the Burlington-Northern Faculty Achievement Award for outstanding college and university teaching and been chosen as a Paul Garrett Fellow for "high professional qualities" and "a high degree of demonstrated competence in teaching." I have also been elected to the Executive Committee of the Conference on College Composition and Communication. I'm not in the habit of mentioning such things in public and dislike talking about pedigrees, but this is probably the only visible proof I have that what I propose is at least somewhat reasonable and respectable—at least to some people in certain parts of the country.

Over the last twenty years, I've thought about left brains and right brains, developmental models, programmed instruction, collaborative learning models, rewriting, "process vs. product," and writing "across the curriculum." In the late sixties and early seventies, I taught my students about freewriting, notebooks, honesty, and personal commitment; in the seventies, I wrote a Ph.D. dissertation on theories of communication and assignment making, taught students a nine-celled tagmemic model of "invention," designed educational "games," assigned book critiques, and taught sentence combining, controlled composition, speed reading, transformational grammar. I even wrote a whole set of "programmed self-instructional modules" while working at the University of Michigan Reading and Learning Skills Center. In the eighties, I did work on adult learning, cognitive styles, readability, spelling, individual differences, and computer-assisted instruction. Through all this experimentation and exploration, I've come to realize much more clearly than I ever have before that much of what we say and make students do doesn't make any difference at all, that hype is hype, that technology doesn't replace teaching, that the more things we try to do in class, the fewer things we are able to do well.

Ultimately, then, a large part of my task here is to convince you that there are *practical limitations* imposed by this peculiar job we're trying to do and the number of useful things we can do and say in class about writing. Some of you, of course, will want to make things more complicated by adding things that I choose to omit, such as complex, ambitious discussions of "audience," Burke's Pentad, the research paper, invention, prewriting, and writing-as-learning—and that's all right, I suppose, so long as you know what you're doing and understand the dangers of doing more than you can and expecting too much in too little time. I say that in all sincerity because in the end, this book is not about particular "methods" at all or about "doing things in the classroom just like Hashimoto" but about *thinking* about methods and *thinking* about why we want to do things in the classroom in the first place.

I hope that even if you still disagree with my suggestions after you've worked with this book for a while, we will be able to articulate our disagreements in reasonable ways, pinpoint differences in our assumptions, and make practical suggestions for each other with some knowledge of the constraints we all work under and some understanding of the value of articulating limited goals and being reasonably practical.

●●●●●●●

Notes

1. Part of this argument is that we should be teaching students the *differences* rather than the similarities between "discipline-specific variations" of academic writing. See, for instance, Susan Peck MacDonald's "Problem Definition in Academic Writing," *CE* 49 (1987): 315–31. I'm not sure this is the place to argue this, but we have to look very carefully at such attention to differences—especially since there are so many different disciplines out there to begin with, and nobody knows very much about very many of them, and nobody will probably know very much about very many of them

in the near or distant future. Perhaps even more important, looking at differences can make us overlook or simply undervalue the sorts of things that any intellectual—regardless of specialization—has to know about writing to be productive in any specific academic discipline.

2. For a good discussion of some of the limitations of our experimental knowledge, see Part IV—"The Researchers"—in Stephen North's *The Making of Knowledge in Composition: Portrait of an Emerging Field* (Portsmouth, NH: Boynton/Cook, 1987).

one

Plans
and
Assumptions

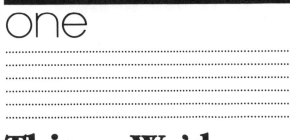

one

Things We'd Like to Do but Can't Always Do

Before looking at my own goals, I'd like to look at some of the more unreasonable goals we sometimes set for ourselves. I expect some people to disagree with some of my conclusions, but I hope such disagreements won't obscure my main intention—to suggest that each of us has to begin to establish a way of thinking about our teaching that includes criteria for judging what we do and why we do it. Without such thinking, we're likely to try to do too much, to expect too much of ourselves and our students—and we're likely to disappoint both ourselves and our students.

Reasonable Things We Can't Teach in Thirteen Weeks

Some notions are probably true—or at least reasonable—but we ought to think twice about taking the time to try to teach them, given the problems we have demystifying, clarifying, or narrowing them down in *teachable* ways.

Taste
While many of us probably have some "good" taste in art, life, and literature, we probably don't know how to *teach* students to have good

taste—especially if they don't already come to us with a history of good taste or "decent" lives. We could give them good literature to read for an entire semester, but reading good literature is no guarantee that they will like good literature. We could invite famous people to class to tell them what to read, and we could extol the virtues of certain famous writers. But many students won't care. We could exhort students to think better, feel more intensely, love life harder, or become one with the poetic wonder of language, but such students might still dislike Ralph Stanley, fail to recognize the aesthetic value of Sonnet 23, dislike the word *eggplant,* find words mysterious, and love Jerry Falwell.

While we might tell students what we like and implore them to try to talk about the "good" and the "bad," I doubt that in thirteen weeks (or sixteen weeks, or sometimes, five or six years), we can convince them to like what we like or enjoy a greater good than they enjoy right now. (Deep inside, I know that there are great teachers of literature, even gurus and saints out there somewhere who command respect and lead students by sheer example to discover the sweet juices of art and language. But there aren't many of them, and I'm not one of them and don't want to become one of them. Because I don't want to and probably can't command such respect and lead anybody to the joys of good taste, I'd downplay "taste" as a short-term goal and go on believing that as long as students read, live, experiment, change, and do whatever else *we* did to acquire our own "taste," they'll do just fine even without classroom intervention.)

Creativity

I believe in creativity, too, even though I can't define it, don't know how to recognize good examples of it, and can't predict when it will appear. All I know is that some of us have it and some of us don't. (Usually the people who have it are my friends and the people I respect.)

Writing teachers often talk about creativity but have the same problems I do. Some even believe in a close link between creativity and synectics, brainstorming, heuristics, metaphor, language play, incubation, issue trees, analogies, diet pills, booze, and exercises of certain sides of the brain, but without clear definitions of creativity and criteria for judging the creative, all such beliefs remain nice to think about but at least for me, unpersuasive.

(Notice that I'm not saying that we can't *stifle* creativity. It's always easier to kill something than to make it live, especially if we don't know what it is. But that still doesn't mean that we blindly assign creativity exercises or encourage students to be "creative" without knowing what we're doing or what we're saying.)

Honesty, Integrity, Rhodes Scholarships, and Boy Scout Oaths
According to Cecil Rhodes, good scholars can be characterized by their "truthfulness, courage, devotion to duty, sympathy for and protection of the weak, kindliness, unselfishness, and fellowship; exhibition of moral force of character and of instincts to lead and to take an interest in one's contemporaries; physical vigor, as shown by fondness for and success in sports." According to the Boy Scouts of America, a good scout is trustworthy, loyal, helpful, friendly, courteous, kind, obedient, cheerful, thrifty, brave, clean, and reverent.

I admire such characteristics and I hope that my students do, too. But I don't know how to make students into Rhodes Scholars or good boy or girl scouts. Richard Nixon, Ted Bundy, Kim Philby, and Billy the Kid probably could never have become Rhodes Scholars or good boy scouts, but I don't think that it would have made much difference even if they had taken a good introductory composition course from a responsible teacher.[1] And it probably wouldn't have mattered if they took two semesters or just one.

Voice, Tone, Flavor, Pizzazz, Electricity
Too often such words as *voice, flavor, excitement, spirit, life, vigor, deadness,* and *imagination* become part of vague exhortations to "Do better!" "Write more like me!" "Write with Style!" "Write more like John Bozarts!" or "Write more like a professional!" Students may not know how to become "better" or write with "style" or "flavor," but it's easy to convince them that whatever they're now doing is bad: dull, humorless, lifeless, dead, spiritless, unvigorous.

In that sense, vague terms lend some authority—even some mystery, magic, and power—to our enterprise. Secret societies and evangelists have always known that the way to improve their status and power is to appear powerful, use language that only the select understand, and offer eternal grace for the damned. Caliban knew what we all should know: that everyone wants to be part of the mystery and take part in the magic of life. And everyone wants to be included in that small circle of the elect who, by carefully licking the shoes of their masters, have found recognition and dragged themselves out of the swamp.

Interdisciplinary Thinking
Students should know that context is important, that different disciplines have different conventions and often require different kinds of thinking. A geologist might tell us that D-alloisoleucine/L-isoleucine (D/L) ratios measured in *Tridacna gigas* calibrated against radiometrically dated coral reef terraces show distinct intervals encompass-

ing a fast epimerization phase at 0.077/ka for the first 8 ka, 60 ka for a transitional interval, and 60–185 ka when D/L are at quasi-equilibrium. And we might recognize the obvious: that this geologist doesn't think like we do.

But what can we do about that in thirteen weeks? How can we help students to think like geologists? mathematicians? biologists? beauticians? lawyers? English majors? chess players? economists?[2] In purely practical terms, how much are we ourselves willing to learn about writing as geologists, mathematicians, biologists, and lawyers? (Probably very little. After all, one reason we teach English is so that we won't have to teach math, biology, or law.)

In thirteen weeks, we can probably help students to begin to make simple assertions, introduce simple ideas, recognize other people's ideas, and do one thing at a time. But we ought to be wary of trying to be all things to all people and trying to hoist the weight of the entire academic world on our backs as we trundle toward Christmas vacation.

Reasonable Beliefs We Struggle to Teach in Thirteen Weeks

Teaching students even the simplest things takes time. We'll take a more careful look at some simple things in later chapters, but before we do that, we ought to look at some more difficult things we often want to teach.

Audience Analysis

Good writers pay attention to their "audience." They try to say things without insulting, looking stupid, revealing too much or too little, or failing to consider their readers' values, rights, beliefs, or predilections. Sometimes, good writers try to "put themselves in their readers' shoes" and understand problems from different perspectives. Good writers often construct audiences, imagine audiences, learn by predicting what audiences might do. If they are lucky enough to get feedback on what they have written, they try to account for that feedback in their further revisions.

But what can we do as teachers to improve students' audience awareness? Probably little besides get them to read each other's papers and exhort them to "know who you're writing for." More than anything else, we exhort students to think about their audience or their "readers," and then we exhort them again, and we comment as if we ourselves know something about imaginary people in imaginary worlds reacting in predictable ways:

"You are absolutely right, James Brown would agree with you that . . ."

"Try babies. Everyone loves babies!"

"I like the 'yo dude' at the beginning, but come on, now, who do you think you're writing for?"

"Sell the sizzle, not the steak! But don't forget that you have something you have to say."

"When in doubt, your best bet is to write for a rational, reasonable audience of your peers. . . . the sort of person we all are . . ."

"Let's take a vote! . . ."

Some of us try to get students to "analyze" audiences by getting them to write letters from two or three points of view; or we get them to write letters to real life Chambers of Commerce or submit fake proposals to fake school boards arguing that some fake school ought to allow the school newspaper to print articles about sex and drugs. We have students make charts of audience characteristics and try to get them to predict how certain audiences will think, feel, or do.[3] (What do executives at Nabisco or Exxon think about plastic Cracker Jack prizes? What do they think about starvation, fear, life in the fast lane, death, destruction, the Super Bowl, the effect of aerosol sprays on the environment?)

But how do we measure or predict the reactions of fake school boards, relatives we've never met before, roommates we've known only by hearsay? How do we measure or recognize student progress in "audiencing"? For that matter, how well do we even know our own students? Do we know how they respond to our own comments? Do we know what their friends do to influence their behaviors in class? Do we even know what they say about us after dark?[4]

When it comes to skills in audiencing, students come to us with what they have; they make do for as long as they can; and maybe, just like the rest of us, way down the road, after they've lived and loved and lost, bought one or two used cars, hired a few bozos who "didn't quite work out," or looked into the eyes of countless fools, predators, and barkers, they begin to find additional wisdom and success and even a touch of cynicism and skepticism about the limits of their intuitions and ability to empathize on command.

Habit Formation of Any Kind

We all develop habits of thinking or of writing. We often habitually begin sentences the same way; we use prepositions and articles and phrases like "sort of" or "a lot of" or "I think" or "ugly things" without thinking. We have our own hobby horses that shape our thoughts and direct our attention to particular problems and solutions. And one of our goals as teachers is to teach students a few of these valuable, "good" habits: the habit of writing well-formed sentences without thinking about those sentences; the habit of recognizing clichés; good study habits, professional habits of mind, spelling habits, and maybe even habits of living.

But many students have spent ten or fifteen years developing their own habits of thinking and living, and even if we exhort them or give them workbook drills and write threats all over their papers, they don't give up those habits without a fight that will last more than thirteen weeks.

One of the arguments in favor of teaching students to do "sentence combining" is that by combining little sentences into big sentences over and over and over again, students build the habit of writing longer sentences. And it may be true that by sheer repetition, we can build such habits as "increased words/T-unit," instinctive punctuation, moderate diction, or style. But such repetition and practice takes *time*. According to some experts, we might be able to increase the size of "T-units," but it might take over twenty hours of class time to do it.[5] Similarly, we might be able to get students to write in notebooks over and over again and by the end of the semester, some of them might even have developed a habit of keeping a notebook. Likewise, we might get students to use a structured "heuristic" over and over again to help them to "think" about their ideas.[6] We might even get them to rewrite over and over again until somehow they get into a "habit" of rewriting.

But nothing is without its cost. The more time we take in class to talk about sentence combining, to read sentence-combining exercises out loud, to talk about notebooks, hype notebooks, write in notebooks, read notebooks, and pass them in and out, the less time we have to do other things—and we've got a lot to do in thirteen weeks.

Prewriting

There's nothing wrong with suggesting that students ought to do something before they begin to write—to "prewrite." Yet even though most of us prewrite in some way or another, we have difficulty formalizing what we do in any recognizable way. We teach students to use charts, algorithms, and spider diagrams; freewrite, outline, research, create "invisible writing"; use five *W*'s; nutshell or shell nuts; make issue trees; use ven diagrams; talk into tape recorders; make lists; talk to friends; make "proposals"; ask Kenneth Burke; ask twenty questions; or make analogies and develop metaphors—but somehow we never teach prewriting. Instead, we teach students that somehow, prewriting is "doing things" or going through certain mechanical procedures that dredge up good stuff out of the depths of our minds, that somehow, prewriting is an activity rather than a vague, possibly spontaneous, uncontrollable experience deeply rooted in time and space, experience, maturity, knowledge, intelligence, culture, personality, beliefs, and predisposition.

More important, even if particular prewriting techniques seem to work with certain problems in certain contexts (they always work in our examples), such techniques may not be helpful for different students and in different contexts—and different problems may require entirely different ways of thinking that we don't have time to teach in thirteen weeks or don't know anything about ourselves.

Popular Forms of Surprise

Good writing often surprises us—sometimes by a turn of phrase; sometimes by a startling observation, a new vision, or a sharp statement that draws blood or makes us want to howl in pain. Some people can even write what the textbook writers call "attention-getting introductions" or "attention-getting hooks" that grab readers and make them want to read on and on and on.[7]

But how do we *teach* students to be surprising?

Students often think that they can layer surprise onto the top of their essays—add small jokes or heartfelt stories, change style (by which they seem to mean add small jokes or heartfelt stories), and make big rhetorical flourishes (by which they usually mean to add small jokes or heartfelt stories). But surprise may have more to do with *ideas and content* than anything else—and how long does it take for any of us to be able to come up with surprising ideas or surprising insights? How many Shakespeare professors get surprised by what undergraduates do with *Hamlet*? (For that matter, how many of us ever wrote anything surprising about *Hamlet*?) When we were undergraduates, how many of us discovered surprising insights into American culture for our sociology classes? How many of us could write anything truly surprising about George Orwell's "Politics and the English Language," James Thurber, inflation, comparisons of X to Y, genetic engineering, throwing a football, or subliminal advertising?

Academic Complexity

I suppose nobody tells students "You will be complex or you will remain your dumb old ignorant selves forever and ever, and your writing will mold and eventually rot," but we tell students to be "complex" in many other ways.[8] For one thing, we hold up models of complex writers and thinkers—E. B. White, Joan Didion, John McPhee, Jonathan Swift, Ernest Hemingway, Alice Walker, Barry Lopez—and we tell them something about our standards and values as we discuss the subtleties of voice, tone, irony, symbol, figurative language, rhythm and sound, antithesis, chiasma, and good heavens, even zeugma.[9] Even if we're not interested in zeugma, we constantly exhort students to write in complex sentences, be less direct and predictable, and more subtle, serious, insightful, or metaphorical in a wonderfully thoughtful way.

But we can't expect students who aren't already academically complex to become academically complex in thirteen weeks. That doesn't mean that such students are too dumb, inept, or disabled to become academically complex, but students who are not already academic often struggle toward academic complexity at an amazingly slow rate. How, for instance, would this student go about doing something more academically complex?

I found Georgie Coogan's statements to be confusing. I used statement "I" to explain the disorganization of the others. The disorganization can be explained by the "ill kept order."

The things he writes about do not make any sense. He puts words together that do not describe his statements in a normal way. For example, in statement "A" he says "pretty feet are nice." When I think of feet I do not think of them being pretty, I think of them being dirty, stinky, and ugly. This makes me regret ever reading them. . . .

How long would it take for him to write or think like E. B. White? or Thomas Jefferson? How soon will it be before he can write something like this:

I do not think I speak only from my prejudices, although in justice I must admit that I approached Riesman's work with animus. Still, even a sympathetic reader could hardly be unaware that his writings wander, his emphases shift, his articles are headed by important titles and introduce important subjects only to dissipate them, until time and again the essay comes to a close after pages of decelerated discussion, almost as if he were a verbose and needy lecturer who has lost his point, glances at his watch, discovers he is half an hour over and will be charged for continuing to use the hall and so comes to an abrupt end by reciting the final dramatic sentences he had memorized before he began . . .[10]

This is more complex than anything we'd get in a beginning writing course—and Norman Mailer probably learned nothing at all about writing by taking a college writing course. He was, after all, a physics major. But even though we might not admit it, I suspect many of us expect students to "loosen up" like Norman Mailer, develop style like Norman Mailer, confidently use words like *animus* and *dissipate,* and come to a point where they, too, can talk about essays that "decelerate" and essayists who recite their final sentences as if they had them memorized. No wonder we sometimes fail miserably as teachers.

And here's Marylynne Robinson:

Say there were two or three inches of hard old snow on the ground, with earth here and there oozing through the broken places, and that there was warmth in the sunlight, when the wind did not blow it all away, and say she stooped breathlessly in her corset to lift up a sodden sheet by its hems, and say that when she had pinned three corners to the lines it began to billow and leap in her hands, to flutter and tremble, and to glare with light, and that the throes of the thing were as gleeful and strong as if a spirit were dancing in its cerements.[11]

I like that word *cerements,* but I wouldn't have the guts to use it myself, and I wouldn't know how to teach my students to use it, either, without sounding like students. I'm still trying to use *inexorable* and *disabuse* in well-formed English sentences. (Come to think of it, I don't know how to teach vocabulary at all, even though I'm apt to exhort my students to try to build one.)[12]

We can probably teach students how to recognize simple sentences, play with simple ideas, recognize simple comma splices and sentence fragments—but in thirteen weeks, few will learn to write like famous authors or feel complex syntax in their blood (and if they do, we shouldn't take credit for teaching them such things).

The Marginally Useful, Sometimes Dangerous

Along with the almost impossible things to teach are all the things that are easier to teach but equally easy to abuse.

The Five-Paragraph Theme

Many people teach students to write the so-called "five-paragraph theme"—one paragraph of introduction, three paragraphs of "body," and one paragraph of conclusion. Those who teach the five-paragraph theme emphasize that the formula is just a teaching device: easy to teach, it provides a structure for students when they find themselves drifting without a plan. According to these advocates, the five-paragraph theme is simply a starting point for beginning writers, who would otherwise suffer without a plan of some kind.

The problem, of course, is that "formulas" are not, necessarily, *strategies,* and beginning points often become ending points. We can tell students that they should be able to plug their ideas into a set number of paragraphs; we can even count their ideas to make sure that they have exactly three of them for the central three paragraphs. But in teaching the formula, we don't always teach students *why* they might use such a formula, where it doesn't work, how ideas themselves often shape their arguments, what paragraphs are for, what to do when they have fifteen ideas or one big idea and a half dozen little strange ones.

Even more important, as we teach students to count ideas and plug them into a set number of paragraphs, we teach them that their ideas are less important than the structures that they build to hold them. Their problems become, then, "what to put into the introduction" and "what to fill up the middle" and "what to put into the conclusion" rather than "what is an introduction good for?" or "what can we do to break down or set up our information or our argument to say and do what we want to do?"

Formulas for Compare/Contrast

I have similar problems with the formulas for so-called compare/contrast papers. There are many ways to use and set up useful comparisons, but most of the time, English teachers set out two basic patterns for compare/contrast—the *a a a a b b b b* pattern (sometimes called a "block" pattern) and the *a b a b a b a b* pattern (the "alternating" pattern). And as with the five-paragraph theme, students who learn to organize their comparisons in one of the two basic patterns often don't understand that these patterns are not ends in themselves, *that writers compare or contrast things for particular reasons.* Only students write comparison/contrast papers simply to put two things side by side. Good writers use comparisons to *clarify* observations and insights, *evaluate* alternatives, and *discover* alternatives by exploring the implications of different models, visions, or perspectives.

The Critique as a Form of Academic Inquiry

It's always good to have students weigh or evaluate what they read—to challenge what people say, to argue about the ways people say things. But we ought to be careful about putting such arguments into a stiff format for critiques before students understand why people write critiques, how they organize arguments, how they carry on intellectual debates.

It's too easy to teach a two-part formula for "thinking" about a text:

Part I: Talk about the book, its thesis, author, organization, format, use of evidence, plot, themes, etc.

Part II: Think about the book, your agreements, disagreements, doubts, praises, insights, criticisms, etc.

It's much more difficult to get students to *think* about that text—to get them to understand that the formula isn't an excuse for building monstrous, boring, two-part papers heavy on the plot and light on thought, that critiques ought to be selective and have a point, that doggedly following a formula is less important than selecting one solid, interesting idea or one important or pivotal issue and pursuing its consequences.

Persuasion

Of the many ways to teach "persuasion," I am most skeptical of those that emphasize "models" of persuasion—especially when those models become formulas for persuasion. Some teachers go back to traditional formulas that include *narratio, explicatio, partitio, confirmatio, refutatio, peroratio.* Or they teach students to recognize major premises and minor premises, and "enthymemes," or maybe learn how to use the components of Toulminian persuasion—claims, evidence, and warrants, rebuttals, concessions/qualifications.[13] Or they get students to distinguish between "ethos," "logos," and "pathos." Or tell them to save their best ideas for last because we always want to leave our readers with something important to remember.

But it's misleading to suggest that formulas or "formats" for persuasion work in general or as a rule or usually—especially in a *writing classroom.* We don't know how to measure the persuasive impact of a persuasive student essay or even what *persuasion* means when we suggest that students can persuade their teachers that they are "right" or that individual student essays have power to change other people's opinions, beliefs, or intentions. Even more certainly, we don't know whether grading students on how well they follow formulas ascribed to Stephen Toulmin, Aristotle, or Carl Rogers will ever help them to sell brassieres by mail, apples without stems, lost causes, dumb ideas, or slimy political candidates without experience or brains.

Indeed, the real problems in persuasion may have nothing to do with format at all. No one persuades anybody of anything without good ideas, good presentations, good luck, and a persuasive *campaign* that involves among other things time, belief, expectation, inclination, benefits, pictures with Ronald Reagan, cost/benefit analysis, relative audience stupidity, gland power, hunger power, thirst, association, bluff, political power, coercion, and/or attention to context. Even then, we probably don't know very much about *teaching* students to weigh, combine, or dredge up such notions. Mostly, we're left exhorting them to "Think about other people's beliefs!" or "Think about what your reader really wants!" or "Try to put yourself in other people's shoes!" or "Make them *want* to do it!"

Logical Fallacies

Trying to teach students to think or write better through analysis of so-called logical fallacies is probably a waste of time, too. We might be able to teach students to recognize cases of post hoc ergo propter hoc, either/or fallacies, rigged questions, equivocations, red herrings, straw men, unsubstantiated claims, arguments ad hominem, band wagons, name calling, appeals to authority, ceremony, tradition, ignorance, and humor. But so what?

One argument is that students who learn to recognize logical fallacies become better readers, and that may or may not be true, I don't know. They learn that logical fallacies have names—but I doubt that recognizing such fallacies and assigning them names will necessarily make students better writers. We teach them not to use logical fallacies because somehow using logical fallacies is morally and ethically *wrong* and only bad people or unfair people should use such methods. But some of the best writers in the country are probably morally corrupt and fully capable of all kinds of underhanded tricks and outright deceptions in the spirit of good thinking and rational argument.

Notecards

I'd like to see people give up on notecards, but I still see sections of textbooks devoted to helping students to put quotations on three-by-five or five-by-eight inch cards and shuffle them up, spread them out on their beds, and somehow put together "research papers" or "reports."

Surely, everybody keeps notes of some kind, and I'm not arguing that writing things down is necessarily bad. But teaching students to use notecards is often wrong-headed, perhaps misinformed, and certainly misleading. People who write research papers don't always use notecards, and notecards may not be the most efficient way to keep notes. People keep notes in many different ways—in notebooks, on computers, in small heaps of Xeroxed pages, on paper napkins. I haven't used a notecard since I was in high school, and I don't know very many colleagues who conscientiously keep their notes on cards[14]—and to suggest that students do what we're not prepared to do ourselves is probably unreasonable, if not hypocritical.[15]

Sentence Variety

We tell students that "sentence variety" is good, that good writers some-how calculate the number of "simple" sentences they use vs. "com-pound" sentences and "compound/complex" sentences, that good writers keep things from becoming boring by shifting around their syn-tax, subordinating and coordinating, using crots and maybe grammar B. And soon, they're aiming at a vague, general notion of sentence variety; they're counting words, worrying about some "Gunning/Fogg Index" for "readability," and trying to begin x percent of their sentences with adverbial clauses, free modifiers, and bojangles.

But no one ever tells students that we don't know much about sen-tence variety—how to measure or judge it, or whether writers with sen-tence variety make more money, or whether sentence variety helps writers to simplify complex ideas or say things they've never said be-fore. We seldom tell students that *content* and *context* and *personality* probably have more to do with variety and interest than a vague notion of sentence salad full of different flavors and different-sized croutons.

Grammar

We'll come back to the problems of grammar later, but certainly there doesn't seem to be much sense in teaching students much grammatical terminology.[16] I've never seen a teacher who taught students to write well simply by having them do grammar drills or exercises on "sentence sense" out of the *Harbrace Handbook*—and I've seen many try. I've never met a good student who found it necessary to think about how to do a passive transformation, how to recognize an auxiliary, how to dis-tinguish a particle from a preposition, or how to distinguish the differ-ence between a clause and a phrase or a compound sentence and a compound/complex sentence.

Other Probably Useless Information

As David Bartholomae points out, we have finally reached the point where scholars in "writing" now write more than any of us can read— "We cannot be kept up with."[17] But it's a telling fact that most of the fa-mous people in "composition studies" are famous not because they are good teachers (although some of them might be), but because they ad-vocate popular or accepted *visions* of the writing "process" or have staked out territories and become "experts" on a respectable aspect of theory or history of rhetoric or descriptive behavioral science or have given us a new term or a new Russian scholar to bolster our criticism or literary worth.

With this tremendous increase in knowledge, this scramble to recognize new and better ideas and theoretical concepts, we sometimes forget that this knowledge ought to make us better *teachers*. How many of us need to teach students to attend to issue trees; speech act theory; brain trust highlighting; tension; Alexander Bain; Fred Newton Scott; tagmemic matrices; the place for "meaning" in generative grammar; tone, mood, inventorying; the differences between simile and metaphor, superordination and subordination, parataxis, hypotaxis, and synpraxis, the left and right sides of the brain; telic modes of meaning; polyptotom, chiasmus, and catachrésis; polysyndeton and asyndeton; connotation, denotation, and detonation; difference and differance; deracination; desedimentation; and chiastic invagination?[18] In fact, how much of this knowledge has made a difference in our own writing? (I suspect not much.)

And a Few Final Words About Textbooks

I suspect it's time to think more carefully about what we expect publishers to do for us. Many of us use textbooks or "rhetorics" or "rhetoric-readers"—mostly because such books are convenient, and often because we're supposed to.[19] But how much can textbooks teach students about reading and understanding difficult ideas? about "thinking"? "organizing"? Despite the "how to" flavor of many of these books, how many of them can teach students "how to write" or how to *want* to write?

How much is useless, time-consuming dead weight? Do we need some author to use up valuable time laying out to students the nine modes of the essay? the two ways to compare/contrast? the proper design of a formal outline? Do we need to assign readings that explain to students that it's good to conform to readers' expectations? that revising takes time and energy? that it's important to have a clear sense of one's goals? that it's important to be active learners? that freewriting is a special procedure designed to loosen people up? that writing is good for getting a job and learning? Do we need to get students to read textbook hype ("James Thurber says . . ." "Ernest Hemingway says . . ." "You can gain the satisfaction of doing a job well done" and "You, too, can learn to write for anyone")?

Do we need textbooks that give us sample student essays, analyzed by mental telepathy and over-reconstruction? ("See how Josie has thought about her topic, gone through her prewriting stage, organized her information using a nutshell tree, and thought about the special quirks of her audience and developed a stunning rendition of tension and personal irony in her revealing self and her own, bravely and painfully realized consciousness about the human condition. . . . Josie herself said in an exit interview shortly after she turned in this final draft, 'Well, it was hard work but the process I went through and the nutshelling made the difference and now that I understand the writing process better, I feel as if I could write a book.'")

Whatever that story is, I doubt it.

In the rest of this book, we'll look at a few things that we can do on our own—without textbooks, without the disappointment that ultimately accompanies their use, after the glitter wears off the newest terminology and our promises fail and we're left out there in the corn field with a pencil and a gradebook and no place to hide.

●●●●●●●

Notes

1. Actually, I suspect that at least Nixon and Bundy did take freshman composition from someone, although I don't know who taught them or whether or not they tried hard enough.

2. I'm not dismissing the importance of the notion of "communities of discourse" and the importance of helping students to recognize that people belong to many different communities of discourse. Nor am I saying that the notion of communities of discourse is an empty issue or that we shouldn't take it seriously when we think about what we do in class. But I don't think we can even begin to understand how to teach students to think in someone else's discipline or do much more than help students to understand that there *are* such things as communities of discourse.

3. I've often thought that such exercises do no more than encourage students to believe in stereotypes, overgeneralizations, right answers, the predictability of human nature, and the efficacy of thought control.

4. For a somewhat similar argument, see my "Bait/Rebait," *EJ* 72 (January 1983): 14–17. For a typical recent discussion of "audience," take a look at Robert G. Roth's "The Evolving Audience: Alternatives to Audience Accommodation," *CCC* 38 (1987): 47–55. Look especially hard for any discussion of how to *teach* audience that goes be-

yond simple exhortation to "think about your audience"—or, in this case, "think in many ways about your audience."

5. See, for instance, discussions in "Using 'Open' Sentence-Combining Exercises in the College Classroom," *Sentence Combining and the Teaching of Writing,* ed. D. Daiker, A. Kerek, and M. Morenberg (Conway: U. of Central Arkansas, 1979) 160–69; George Hillocks, Jr., *Research on Written Composition: New Directions for Thinking* (Urbana, IL: NCTE 1986).

6. See my "Structured Heuristic Procedures: Their Limitations," *CCC* 36 (1985): 55–62.

7. Probably not as many as we'd like, however. See my essay, "The Myth of the Attention-Getting Opener," *Written Communication* 3 (January 1986): 123–31.

8. The term *academically complex* is a little clunky, but I'd like to make a distinction between the kinds of complexity we expect in academia and other sorts of "complexity," particularly the kind of complexity people mean when they suggest that all students are complex by virtue of being sentient beings with complex histories, perspectives, wants, desires, dreams, and expectations.

9. See Fredric Bogel's discussion of prose analysis as essential for revealing "the full range of meaning that written prose commands" ("Teaching Prose," in Fredric Bogel, Patricia Carden, Gerard Cox, Stuart Davis, Diane Freedman, Katherine Gottschalke, Keith Hjortshoj, and Harry Edmund Shaw, *Teaching Prose: A Guide for Writing Instructors* (New York: Norton, 1984).

10. Norman Mailer, "David Riesman Reconsidered," *Advertisements for Myself* (New York: Putnam's-Berkeley Medallion, 1959) 179. While I like this passage, Mailer himself says that the style here is "on the tiresome side" (174).

11. Marilynne Robinson, *Housekeeping* (New York: Farrar, Straus & Giroux, 1981; Bantam Books, 1982) 16.

12. I would also have trouble helping my students to understand why Robinson uses "there were" at the beginning, "there was" in the second line, and "if a spirit were" at the very end, and it might take me even longer to get my students to understand why most of us as readers don't care.

13. See, for instance, the discussion of Toulmin's model in Nancy Huddleston Packer and John Timpane, *Writing Worth Reading: A Practical Guide with Handbook,* 2nd ed. (New York: Bedford, 1989) 122–33.

14. Actually, I know two. One is a bibliographer and the other is a historian.

15. I suspect that many people who teach students to use notecards do so not because notecards help students to write better, but because students who have to spend hours writing things down on three-by-five inch cards to turn in with their research papers are less likely to be able to *plagiarize* those research papers. Certainly, it's easier to check on notecards than it is to check out plagiarism.

16. I want to come back to a few things we can teach in chapter 2. For a nice argument against wasting so much time teaching "grammar," see Patrick Hartwell's "Grammar, Grammars, and the Teaching of Grammar." For a shorter discussion of the issues, see "Appendix 1: The Grammar Questions," *To Compose: Teaching Writing in High School,* ed. Thomas Newkirk (Portsmouth, NH: Heinemann, 1986) 203–08. George Hillocks tells us that his own "meta-analysis" of experimental treatments indicates that grammar instruction "stimulates almost no improvement in composition. In fact, when examined against almost any other systematic effort to improve composition, instruction in grammar results in significantly less improvement" ("The Writer's Knowledge: Theory, Research, and Implications for Research," *The Teaching of Writing: Eighty-fifth Yearbook of the National Society for the Study of Education,* Part II, ed. Anthony R. Petrosky and David Bartholomae [Chicago: U of Chicago P, 1986] 79).

17. David Bartholomae, "Freshman English, Composition, and CCCC," *CCC* 40 (February 1989): 48.

18. For what it's worth, I only messed with a couple of these terms.

19. And some probably because they're lazy.

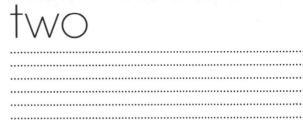

two

Simple Things

• • • • • • • • • • • • • • • • • • • •

I'm aware that teaching simple things is not always so simple in practice or may not be so simple to understand or even *believe in*—but for now, I'd just like to set some simple things on the table to look at, leaving the specifics to later chapters.

Simple Rules

My goals are simple: to teach students a few ways to *deal with other people's ideas,* a few ways to *deal with simple data,* a few ways to *argue* a simple point, and sometime, if they can do that much, to get them to *play* with a few ideas about "style." The practice we do in class ought to apply in practical ways to the writing problems that students face in other classes, but I would emphasize again that I'm trying to help students to *start* writing in academia. I could claim larger goals, but given the amount of time and the difficulty of learning even simple things, larger goals are probably unrealistic for many beginning writers.

Other People's Ideas

Students should learn to recognize and respect other people's ideas—and begin to deal with other people's ideas in direct ways. They should *recognize* that other people have ideas, too; that sometimes they have to

21

sweat to understand those ideas; that they can't blame or attack people for what they don't say; that they can't manufacture their scholarship off the top of their heads.

Students should also understand important conventions and courtesies in an academic community: they should, for instance, learn to introduce other people's ideas, try to summarize whenever they can, and document things in simple ways.

And they should understand a few basic rules:

- Always keep things in a *context* (unless you don't have a context).

- *Explain* things before you criticize them (unless you can get away without explaining things).

- Never let someone else make the important statements that you should be making yourself (unless you think it's a good thing to do).

- Never quote people just to restate your point in other, more famous, people's words (unless those famous people can make you awesomely, incredibly credible).

- Never quote "Webster" (unless Webster is the only one who knows what's going on).[1]

- *Never assume* that anyone reads anything just like you do (unless they do).

- *Never assume anything* about an abstraction or a concreteness (unless everyone thinks about those abstractions and concretenesses just like you do).

- Let people know where your ideas came from—especially if they're not your own (unless those ideas are simpleminded, commonsensical or common knowledge).

Most of these rules are reasonably clear, and I doubt that people would disagree much. Some might suggest that such rules look formulaic, and they probably could if we're not careful. In class, we will emphasize exceptions and ways to think about exceptions, what the rules do and don't do, and questions about the differences between "rules" and "laws"—but such rules give us a place to begin helping students to *think academically*—to begin understanding different academic risks and moves and to begin to weigh and evaluate their own strategies and procedures for themselves.

Data

I'm thinking here of "data" in a broad sense—any material we have to shape, evaluate, sift, understand, simplify, organize, strip, clarify, manipulate, or collect. I'm especially thinking about all those occasions when we have *choices* to make: when we've got several things and we need to decide when or how something is *better* than something else; when we have a mass of things or pile of information or wide range of opinions, and we need to *select* things to talk about, find a focus, do some basic sorting out; when we have too many things to say or too many examples to talk about at one time and have to bluff or establish credibility in a limited amount of space within a limited amount of time.

To do so, we ought to help students to manipulate data in typical academic ways:

- Develop *criteria* to use when they *clump* and *group*.
- *Clump* and *group*.
- *Label* their clumps and groups.
- *Weight the value* of their clumps and groups.
- *Bluff* and *hint* when there's not enough room or not enough time to discuss everything in detail.

I'm less concerned here that students end up with specific "systems" for clumping and grouping, a knowledge of "how to label properly," or faith in a mechanical rule to "always weight things properly." I'm interested instead in bigger concerns—that students recognize that they have to find ways to handle large masses of information. They can't, for instance, choose *not* to deal with something because it doesn't fit nicely into their arguments, or they can't decide to deal with one idea if that idea depends on many different ideas. And they have to begin to realize that it's not enough to sort information or build correct but useless classifications: they have to understand that they have to *do something with their data,* and once they understand that, they will begin to understand how their goals influence the way(s) they break that data down, set it up, weight different aspects, or make omissions.

The Simple Point

To begin to make simple, direct points, students ought to keep in mind a few simple rules:

- Try to do one thing at a time.
- Try not to lead up to your point. (Think about making your point first and backing it up or clarifying it.)

- Expand from the middle, not from the end. (Never expand by tacking new ideas on the end.)
- Don't worry about surprising people with slick tricks and fancy footwork.
- Explain what you found, not how you went about finding it.
- Say it, don't imply it.
- Worry if you have just one example.
- Consider opposing points of view even though only fools would disagree with your logic.

Again, such simple notions are often not simple *to understand.* We're trying to help students to begin to *realize* simplicity—to realize how difficult they make their lives if they try to do two or three things at once, make complex ideas "look" complex, try to make their ideas better than they are, or try to ignore other people's ideas. Once they begin to *think* about simplicity, they can work on being simple, and that will probably take time.

Simple Techniques

If we begin with the simple, academic essay, we need to teach a few simple concepts for achieving simplicity and directness:

- The simple *thesis* statement.
- The simple *introduction* and *conclusion.*
- *First, second, third, fourth . . .*
- *Mainheads* and *subheads.*
- Simple ways to *weight* information or points.

Thesis statements.   We can teach students to begin to use thesis statements to help them set up and predict important organizational constraints and get a feel for the general plan of their essays—and we can do so without saying anything about the number of paragraphs we expect them to write. If we do our jobs, we can teach students to see the difference between clarifying a plan and organization—and plugging things into a constrictive essay "formula."

Introductions.   We can make students *aware* that weak introductions usually come from weak ideas, not from weak or inadequate "attention-getting devices"; that *problems, issues,* and *implications* are at the heart of academic issues—and that somehow, they need to begin addressing those issues if they want to stay in the game.

Conclusions.   Instead of telling students that they need to produce masterful conclusions, we can teach them not to worry so much—that conclusions aren't necessarily the high points of their essays; that some-place along the line, their arguments are important, too; that it's reasonable to think about a simple, ordinary "summary" if they don't know what else to do (or if their ideas happen to be complex, diffuse, or fragmented); and that it's reasonable to think about simple *implications, consequences,* or *results* if they have such things in mind. (And they ought to have such things in mind.)

Cohesion.   Good writers can often get away without making solid introductions and thesis statements because they recognize the value of redundancy. Even though students may understand how to use *signals* and *transitions* and know how to come back every so often to their main points, they often don't value such signals. They seldom use "first," "second," and "moreover," "in addition to,"; they very seldom use bullets or italics or arrows or lists of points set off by white space or diagrams or charts or pictures or mainheads and subheads. They seldom build complex series of parallel constructions.

Mainheads and subheads are particularly important devices for tying ideas together in long or complex papers, but students often seem to be afraid of using them—perhaps because we seldom encourage them to try such devices out.[2]

Weighting.   Students should be able to *weigh* their ideas for us. They should feel comfortable saying things like "The most important idea is this one. . .," "I especially like this one. . .," "These are the only things I have to say but. . .," "Least important is. . . ," "At first glance, this is ridiculous but. . .," or "This one will *especially* grow on you like dead skin." If they can't help us understand what's important and what's not so important, then they might not have a point to begin with, and they might have to find something else to say.

A Simple Style

Mastering a "style" or a "personal style" ought to be a low priority for beginning writers—even though many of us place a high value on style in our evaluations of "literary" writing.[3] We shouldn't begin to worry about teaching style until we think students have the time and confidence to begin to experiment a little without getting into trouble or getting overly concerned with elegance or maturity or grace. While students probably won't become stylists in thirteen weeks, they can begin to think about a few things sometimes and perhaps change a few things when they have time, and if they do that much, they might think about a few more things or change a few more things in the future—perhaps long after they've left us and gone on with their lives. In that sense, students need a few simple things to think about and practice that could change the ways they write *over a period of time and with some conscious effort,* in the privacy of their own homes.

The Simple Sentence.   As a minimum, we can begin to teach students how to:

- Recognize verbs.
- Recognize subjects.
- Recognize modifiers.
- Build mostly subject-verb sentences.
- Recognize how to add things to the end of subject-verb sentences with different kinds of connectors.

We don't need to aim for sophisticated knowledge. Students can, for instance, begin to recognize verbs by using a rough "conjugation" test. ("You can say, 'I eat, you eat, she eats,' but you can't say, 'I even, you even, she evens.' Or 'I fruitcake, you fruitcake, she fruitcakes.'") Students can begin to recognize subjects by finding words that "fit" with verbs, and they can begin to recognize modifiers by testing them with the word *very*—"*very* red," "*very* good," "*very* unhappy." We never have to bog students down in a world of compound, complex, and compound-complex sentences, or adjectives and adverbs, or clauses and phrases, or modal auxiliaries and determiners. Certainly, we never have to bog them down in diagramming sentences, transformations, diagrams of deep structures, and other rock formations.

Tightening up.   With a basic, limited view of sentence building and grammar, students can begin to think about simple ways to keep their syntax under control:

- Keep your sentences medium-sized. (A medium-sized sentence might be a subject-verb sentence with maybe one or two things tacked on the end.)
- Put the point you're emphasizing first and avoid wasteful openings.
- Concentrate on using strong verbs.

- Build sentences with strong subjects.
- Eyeball your prepositions.

Such advice is mostly common sense—or common sense to English teachers—and generally appears in typical books on "style."[4] Strunk and White would tell us, "The proper place in the sentence for the word or group of words that the writer desires to make most prominent is usually the end."[5] But beginning writers should practice writing straightforward subject-verb sentences with their best points first most of the time. Hopefully, we can even convince students that it's *easier* to build long sentences by adding clauses and phrases at the *end,* and that sometimes it takes only a little variety to give readers the *appearance* of variety.

Loosening up. If they do anything, students will probably end up consciously or unconsciously imitating the people they like to read.[6] After all, that's what most of *us* do. Once we grow up, we seldom want to do little workbook exercises or probably even read Joseph Williams's ten lessons on "clarity and grace" when we could be reading Calvin Trillin, Jimmy Cannon, Seymour Krim, or Kinky Friedman.

Students often have more trouble imitating than we do because they don't always know *what* to imitate. So we can help them to begin to recognize typical features that contribute to style:

- Sentence order (especially beginnings).
- Sentence length.
- Punctuation (especially semicolons, colons, dashes, and parentheses).
- Connectors (especially transitions and conjunctions but also typography and white space).
- Metaphors (at least the obvious kinds).
- Free modifiers (especially verb phrases, absolutes, and noun phrases—although we don't necessarily have to call them by those names in class).
- Modifiers.

We shouldn't try to do too much—and this may be too much for many classes. Our goal is to help students to gain a little confidence, a little success, not to bog them down or make them worry about terminology or make them feel bad because somehow, they haven't discovered the "right" style.

Simple Wisdom

Rules and procedures are relatively easy to teach. What's *hard* to teach is the context for and limitations of those rules and procedures—and if we're serious about *teaching,* then we need to keep thinking about what *beliefs* we want students to bring to the content we teach them.

Simplicity

I don't know how to teach students to believe in simplicity. (I could say that about all these beliefs.) But I do know that unless students *value* simplicity, then I can't teach them to simplify. They say, "Oh yeah, yeah," and they do what I tell them, but when I turn my back or when they get out of my course, they're back there glomming things up and twisting and bending things to make them "look better"—and therefore, supposedly, more intelligent or noteworthy.

I keep catching myself saying such things as "Trust me. . . ." and "Trust me. . . ." But ultimately, students begin to trust and believe when they finally realize that what I'm doing myself is simple and that "simple" ideas aren't that "simple" at all—or certainly aren't as easy to learn and apply as they first appear.

I have a certain amount of faith in simple teaching procedures, too. All I want to do is what good teachers generally do: make some assignments, read some papers, and maybe teach a few simple things. I hope my assignments and the comments I make on students' papers will reflect this interest, too.

Game

Most of us have metaphors for writing. Some of us call writing "work"— and talk about how "hard" it is and how students must "put in their time" before they can look for the great "payoff." Students, too, often believe writing is work and complain when they "work sooooo hard" and still get the same grades they got before. Some of us think of writing as a "tool" or a set of "skills" that students can use to "build" large structures that can withstand the winds of fortune or the huffs and puffs of mad, pork-fed wolves. And some of us think of writing as "sharing," "art," "discovery," "exploration," "cooking," "processing," "producing," "visioning," "therapy," or "communication."[7]

There's probably something true about all such metaphors, but for my part, I'd like students to think of writing as "game"—a notion that has important *practical consequences.*[8]

Unlike "building" or "therapy" or "art," games have players, scores, strategies, and rules. Not all games have winners and losers—but some do, and people can *choose* to play different kinds of games, depending on their inclinations and personalities. Not all games require great risks, but some do. Not all games are played on the same-sized playing fields or boards, but most require special "ground rules" and negotiations between players. And perhaps most important, the *best* games require both a certain amount of individual and/or team skill and a certain amount of luck. Luck sometimes overshadows our skill, turns things to our advantage, takes away our advantage, gives us hope, makes us persevere even when we know the odds are against us and the score's already recorded in the book.

If I use game as a model for writing, I can help students to understand that their writing doesn't have to be serious and life transforming (academic writing rarely is), that they can risk making mistakes and trying out ideas they've never been able to explore before. I can teach them to scramble when the ground rules or conventions have changed and change strategies when the other side's got all the red chips or owns three-quarters of the board. And I can encourage them to laugh at their play in particular rounds, negotiate decisions, ask for interpretations of rules, evaluate the consequences of cheating within the ground rules of the particular games they're playing, construct different realities, hope for the best, and try to take into account fate and luck and their own limitations and training.

Patience

People should grow old gracefully, not fitfully. They should learn to set limited goals, to recognize that learning isn't a steady, even, linear, thoughtful progression that leads step-by-step to an earned goal. Learning is often an uneven, unfair affair, where students may learn a great deal all at once but then maybe go through long dry spells where they keep doing the same old things over and over and over again—until suddenly, maybe even without any apparent reason or without any apparent help from us, they may see things differently and become not quite the same people they were just a few minutes before.

Students should understand that learning is often like beating an air bubble out from under a large carpet, that they could get worse when they're learning the most, that it's always much easier to learn what you ought to do than to do it. And because learning to write takes time and patience, they should realize that the things we play with in class always need further development, more exploration, and independent, persistent application in the future where there will be no teachers to goad them on or supply them with small words of advice and encouragement, things to experiment with, and chances to make mistakes.

Distance
Students ought to be free to choose wrong or fail on their own. They should have options—even too many options. They should understand that *everybody's* writing is governed by informed choices, limited knowledge, conscious gambles and risks—as well as trial and error, serendipity, and general futzing around.

While some students might learn better if they are involved or committed to a relevant cause or idea, I'm less interested in involvement, commitment, and relevance than I am in detachment and distance. Students should begin to stand back and look at what they're doing—even be a bit clinical about it. They should begin to recognize that they are responsible for what they see and how they see it. They should begin to understand that writing assignments are not inherently good or bad but *become* good or bad because of the ways they perceive them. In the long run, motivation is not what we do *to* students, but what they choose to do *for themselves*—and they can consciously choose to do things sometimes in spite of us.

Finally, if we want students to choose to do whatever they do, we should make them aware that they are responsible for making conscious decisions about their own strategies, ideas, organizations, bluffs, and gambles. They should begin to think about what they *could do,* not what they have to do. They should begin to understand that no matter what assignments we give them, those assignments are less important than what they themselves choose to do with them, that they should be able to step back, get some distance, analyze problems and their own priorities before jumping in and messing up the water.

Pain
Learning at its best is often painful. That doesn't mean that it has to hurt, make people cry, traumatize them, or leave gaping wounds in their thighs. But some of the most difficult things we learn are not without some pain, boredom, and suffering. Certainly no one who becomes good in any of the performing arts becomes good without paying his or her dues. Musicians practice hours and hours, running through the same scales hundreds and hundreds of times. Tennis players hit hundreds and hundreds of balls in a row to learn how to hit what Vic Braden calls "the same old boring winner." And the pain and suffering may even be greater—although less visible—in the "intellectual" arts like reading and writing, asserting, and theorizing. None of us learns how to write without some struggle and doubt and the pain it takes to break deeply

seated ways of seeing and thinking that inhibit our performance; to see what we've been taught not to see; to accept the value of simplicity when we've lived our whole lives trying to be complex; to accept imperfection; to give up that absolutely incomprehensible belief in instant success and the American Dream that often makes us miserable and spiritless.

In the classroom, students should begin to confront their biases about writing, begin to think about things they've never had to think about before, begin to feel sometimes disoriented, sometimes unsafe and challenged, and ultimately, begin to step back and consciously compare what *they* think about writing and learning to what *we* think about writing and learning and what *others* think about writing and learning.

Again, I know that such a goal is ambitious. I'm as biased as the next person, and I hate to change, accept defeat, or reevaluate my own convictions, values and inclinations. But I don't want to change *all* my students' beliefs, anyway. And I don't want to scramble their minds, corrupt them, persuade them to give up, or change even half of one of those other, larger, more deep-seated beliefs they might have about the nature of humans, the power of evil, the state of the economy, the power of prayer, and the nature of prejudice, herd-like behaviors, gluttony, avarice, and self-love.

All I want them to do is to begin to think about how they think about writing and learning. And that's sweat enough to last for much more than thirteen weeks.

It's worth pointing out now (and again later) that the goals in this chapter are general and related. I don't expect to cover them one at a time, nor do I want to put them all into some necessary sequence. We'll come back to them in different ways and at different times, and where possible, I'll call attention to some of them. But methods shouldn't look too simple or too formulaic. Our task is to plunge students in and try to address many things all at once—and then plunge them in again, over and over again, in different ways. I hope all this will make sense as we get to more concrete discussions later.

•••••••

Notes

1. The issue here, of course, is not "Webster" at all, but whether or not students understand that when they define words or clarify their own use of words, they have to pay close attention to the particular

context in which that word is being used. And part of this issue has something to do with students' faith in authorities like "Webster" to have "answers" that everyone has "agreed on."

2. As far as I can tell, many of us seldom emphasize such devices in class—probably because they look a little too easy or too "journalistic" or even, I suspect, "nonliterary."

3. Trained as we are to judge "good writing" by literary standards, I suspect we often say too much about style too soon and with too much enthusiasm. As a director of a writing center, I see students all the time who tell me they're getting *C*'s and *D*'s because of their "grammar" or their "sentences"—even some who have little notes from their teachers about their "grammar"—but in almost every case, no matter *what* we do with their grammar, no matter how slick or clear we make their sentences, many of them will *still* get *C*'s and *D*'s unless they do something with their organization, thesis, time management, outlook on life, or whatever *first.* At least in my experience, many problems in syntax or style actually go away all by themselves or improve when students get some confidence in what they're trying to say and how they're organizing it.

4. See Richard A. Lanham, *Revising Prose,* 2nd ed. (New York: Macmillan, 1987); Joseph M. Williams, *Style: Ten Lessons in Clarity and Grace,* 2nd ed. (Glenview, IL: Scott, Foresman, 1985); Rudolf Flesch, *The Art of Readable Writing* (New York: Collier, 1962).

5. William Strunk, Jr., and E. B. White, *The Elements of Style,* 3rd ed. (New York: Macmillan, 1979) 32.

6. For a really nice discussion of imitation in this spirit, see Burton Hatlen's "Old Wine in New Bottles: A Dialectical Encounter Between the Old Rhetoric and the New," *Only Connect: Uniting Reading and Writing,* ed. Thomas Newkirk (Portsmouth, NH: Boynton/Cook, 1986) 59–86.

7. See Elizabeth Cowan Neeld's description of building an adobe (*Writing,* 2nd ed. [Glenview, IL: Scott, Foresman, 1986]). See also Peter Elbow's "cooking" (*Writing Without Teachers* [New York: Oxford, 1973]); Roger Garrison's "sculpting" and "cabinetmaking" (*How a Writer Works* [New York: Harper, 1981]); May Sarton's "flower arranging" in the ninth edition of McCrimmon's *Writing with a Purpose* (Boston: Houghton, 1988). Another good source for such metaphors might be the two volumes of *Writers on Writing,* edited by Tom Waldrep (Random House, 1985, 1988). In the first volume, we have French stockpot simmering (Louise Wetherbee Phelps); circus performing and chess (C. H. Knoblauch); a '39 Ford

negotiating hard terrain (Sue Lorch); making pottery and doing karate (Harry Brent); plumbing (Hans Guth); wolves culling carabou herds (Richard M. Coe); and dancing (Richard L. Graves). In the second volume, we have a safari adventure (Lil Brannon); DNA and funnels (Charles W. Bridges); combing out a head of long hair (James Raymond); selling someone out (Susan Miller); making pudding in a futuristic kitchen, casting using the lost wax technique, building, journeying, giving birth, electricity, exploration, climbing, groping, and fighting (Barbara Tomlinson).

8. This notion of "game" is certainly not a new one. See, for instance, Eric Berne, *Games People Play* (New York: Grove, 1964); Clark C. Abt, *Serious Games* (New York: Viking, 1970). The notion is also related to "play" (see, for instance, Johan Huizinga, *Homo Ludens* [Boston: Beacon, 1955]); and "puzzle solving" (see Thomas S. Kuhn, "Normal Science as Puzzle-Solving," *The Structure of Scientific Revolutions,* 2nd ed. [Chicago: University of Chicago, 1962] and Neil Mck. Agnew and Sandra W. Pyke, *The Science Game: An Introduction to Research in the Behavioral Sciences,* 2nd ed. [Englewood Cliffs: Prentice-Hall, 1978]). In the language arts, see Kenneth Davis and John Hollowell, eds., *Inventing and Playing Games in English* (Urbana, IL: NCTE, 1977).

three

Issues in Course Design

●　●　●　●　●　●　●　●　●　●　●　●　●　●　●　●　●　●　●　●

Given the state of the art, it probably doesn't matter whether we all come to the same conclusions about course design and syllabus building. (Knowing what I know about writing teachers, that's hardly realistic, anyway.) But even if we don't agree—possibly can't agree—about specifics, we can have something more to discuss than vague notions such as course content, reading, thinking, and the pursuit of rhetoric as a professional discipline.

General Aims

We can design many different courses, but we ought to deal with the main issues:

Time
As I've already said in many different ways, by far the most important issue here is time—how much time we have, where we have it. Most of us want to spend a considerable amount of class time having students read each other's papers. If we meet three times a week and spend one day having students read each other's papers, that's about a third of the class time—or about four weeks. Out of the nine remaining weeks, suppose we block out one week to introduce the idea of "notebooks" and

one week to do something with "in-class writing"—with practice taking mid-semester and final examinations. And maybe a week and a half or two weeks to deal with the notion of a thesis statement, how to write introductions and conclusions, and how to handle transitions and simple signals for cohesion. And time to review or expand on things that for some reason have given students trouble. And time for class evaluations both at the end of the semester and sometime around week seven.

Suppose we also throw out marginal instructional times such as the first day of class, the days before and after each major vacation, special "preregistration" weeks, fraternity and sorority "Hell" weeks, major all-campus football games, and the days our supervisors or department heads choose to come to class to "observe" us in action. And suppose we set time aside for guest lecturers, discussions of special or difficult readings, library orientations, orientations on word processing software and microcomputers, documentation (both APA and MLA), practice using other people's ideas, freewriting, peer editing, working on style. . . .

I'm not sure how all that adds up here, but no matter how we plan things—even ignoring or discounting those days when we're in bed coughing out our lungs with some spring virus or out of town for some unforeseen emergency, out to lunch, job hunting, giving papers at some professional conference in New Orleans, attending some special meeting with alumni in Spokane or some teacher workshop in Issaquah, or attending to a crisis in the basement after a major rainstorm—we're barely going to get things done even if we simplify, block out our time carefully, never get sick, never fall in love, never have to go to traffic court, and never serve on jury duty.[1]

Course Structure

Whether we choose to begin with structure or nonstructure, we ought to be able to imagine a "flow" or plan for this course. Will it move from "big" issues like organization and thesis to "small" issues like sentences and punctuation? Or will it move from sentences and punctuation and the *Harbrace Handbook* to organization and thesis and (perhaps) the research paper as a capstone to the whole adventure? Will it move from topic to topic without any sense of movement at all—maybe from writing in the social sciences to writing in the sciences to writing in the arts to writing in literature classes. . . ?

I usually begin with "big" issues of plan, design, and the value of ideas; then move to "smaller" issues like transitions and general issues of wordiness; and end with issues that may have no end—like vision, style imitation, and personal writing. I prefer to move from structured ideas and control to less structured ideas with more freedom or sense of freedom, more choice or sense of choice. In my experience, it's much easier to move from structure to less structure than to move from less structure to structure—especially when it's so tempting to let students tell stories for the greater part of the semester or write descriptions of roommates, their home towns, secret places, and pizza parlors. Furthermore, since many students are relatively unstructured people who have had to write only a little academic writing, I'd like to challenge some of their initial values about such writing immediately, to get them to see that writing clear, academic papers isn't as easy as they might think, not always "boring" or like what they "did in high school," that in academia, ideas ought to stand on their own and call attention to themselves, that freedom doesn't always come from less structure but from conscious choice.

Flexibility

What are we going to do during those times in the semester when students freak out or fall apart—when they've got two or three other papers due in other classes, when they're trying to write important mid-semester examinations or trying to recover from walking pneumonia after missing two weeks of class? What are we going to do to keep students from blaming us for all the work we require and for turning them into galley slaves? If we are willing to be flexible, what are the limits to our flexibility? At what point will we have to tell students that we can't allow them to turn in late papers or do rewrites? At what point do students take advantage of our good will and deserve no more good will?

I plan on a reasonable amount of flexibility—students who know they have problems ought to be able to negotiate special changes in deadlines if they see me early in the semester or before crunch time. I also allow students to skip a certain number of papers without penalty during the semester and try to set up a policy for late papers that discourages late papers but doesn't keep students from doing them. If, for instance, I take off 5 points out of 100 for a paper that's one day late and a maximum of 10 for a paper that's more than one day late, many students will still feel it's worthwhile to write those late papers even if they lose points. But if I penalize them too much by taking off too many points or automatically lowering grades too far, students can lose interest in writing those late papers. While I want them to suffer some and know that I'm not happy with their planning and foresight, I don't want them to give up without trying. And while I might let students turn in papers late, I set up deadlines after which I no longer can be flexible about late papers or rewrites.

Classroom Activities

Are we going to base this class around "small group" work? Are students going to write all the time? Are we going to begin each class with ten minutes of free writing? Are we going to spend much time going over workbook exercises? If so, what are we going to do to keep students from becoming bored? How can we keep them interested in doing the same old thing every day in class? How are we going to challenge them to think of new things when we do the same old thing every day? How are we going to "surprise" them or keep them off balance if they can predict what we're going to do and how we're going to do it?

I don't want to build this course around a single class activity like small group work or freewriting or discussion.[2] I'd like to tell students that I plan to keep them slightly off balance, slightly confused. If they can predict what I want them to do, then they won't necessarily learn anything. If they know what I want them to do, all they have to do is ape that knowledge without thinking or evaluating anything. But I want them to be slightly defensive, to make mistakes and discover that it's all right to make mistakes. And they can't make mistakes if they know the game too well, if they don't watch the rules carefully, if they're not interested in the way they play the game. I hope this will all become more clear later in this book.

Assignments

In the next chapter, we'll consider the subject matter for assignments, but before then, we ought to have answers to more general questions:

Number

Can we get students to think about writing all the time if we assign them one paper each week? Can we get students to make mistakes, approach new problems, and experiment with their own strategies and techniques if we spend most of the semester having them write only three, four, or maybe five papers?

Lately, I've been assigning about seventeen one-page papers (one each day for the first four weeks) and seven four-page papers. Students who have to write something for each class period have to think about writing more often—and because they have to start over on new problems each time, they begin to worry less about doing things "right" and "polishing" what they've written. Furthermore, because they have to write so many papers, they get many different chances to experiment, change approaches, and learn from their mistakes.[3] More assignments don't necessarily have to mean more work for the teacher. If we simplify the criteria we use to evaluate papers, we can minimize the work we have to do on each paper—and we don't have to look for everything on each assignment. (We'll come back to such criteria later.) From a purely practical point, I might add that reading a bad one-page paper is considerably less painful than reading a bad four-page paper. Especially early in the semester when the bad student writing often seems to pour in, I'm all for minimizing the amount of pain I have to go through at any time as I try to evaluate whole stacks of student writing without becoming insensitive, unfair, or overly cranky.

Order or Sequence

We sequence assignments any number of ways. Some of us begin with "personal" assignments and move to "impersonal" ones—from "description" and "narration" to "process analysis," "cause and effect," "comparison/contrast," and "argument." Others try to move from "easy" assignments to "more difficult" ones. Still others buy into a textbook sequence and move from chapter to chapter, assigning the questions at the end of each unit.

There may be benefits from such sequences, but whatever we do, we ought to be able to have answers for such questions as these:

- What is the relationship of one assignment to another? (If we choose to begin with personal narratives, do we know that writing from personal experience necessarily gives students practice that will help them to write about other people's ideas? If so, what do we know and how might we defend it?[4]

- How do we move from one assignment to another? Do students have to "succeed" on one assignment to be somehow prepared for the next? If so, what? and why?

- Do we know that one type of assignment is necessarily "harder" to do than another? (Is "narrative" necessarily easier to do or more "simple" than "argument"?)

- Do we *need* a sequence of assignments at all?

We often make too much of the need for a logical sequence of assignments—when most of us know little about how to sequence assignments. In fact, lately, I've become perfectly happy assigning two basic assignments over and over again for the entire semester—an assignment that boils down to "What do you think about so-and-so's ideas?" and one that boils down to "What do you think about all this stuff?" The first requires students to respond to someone else's ideas; the second requires students to manipulate data—clump, group, label their clumps and groups, and *use* what they've found in some way.

All this should become clearer in chapter 5 and also in appendixes 2 and 3. From the beginning, I assign things that are the same level of difficulty as those toward the end. Some assignments might be harder or easier than others for individual students, but that's all right. I often can't predict which students will have trouble with different assignments, anyway. Besides, I'm not trying to push students to reach a profound level of self-discovery or thought. I'm trying to give them opportunities to practice a few skills that will make a difference in their future academic writing.

Even more important, by giving assignments that are "the same but different," I can begin helping students recognize that assignments are not as important as what each of them *does* with those assignments. By doing so, I can begin to shift the burden back onto them to transform my assignments into something different, and if I can do that, then no one will complain that they are bored or unenthused or somehow disappointed in *me* as ringmaster in an academic circus.

Specificity

Do we need to give students detailed assignments? Many people would argue that we need to make assignments perfectly clear—spell out whom students are writing for, what the context is, what the problems are that students need to address, what genre or mode they need to respond in, and what techniques they ought to employ. Regardless of what we do, we ought to be able to explain *why* we choose to do what we do.

Certainly, the more we tell students, the less they have to do for themselves, and the less they do for themselves, the more they become reliant on "experts" like us to tell them what to do. As I see it, they ought to begin as soon as possible to find out how to analyze situations for themselves. They don't have to practice a series of special, separate methods or techniques that may not be useful some day. We don't have to tell students to "use chronological order" if they have to write about a "process" or "procedure." They already know that.

We don't have to tell them to try to define something if they're writing about something that needs a definition. They ought to begin figuring that out for themselves. Similarly, we don't have to tell them that they need to write a comparison if they are working on a problem that needs a comparison. They ought to begin to recognize comparison as a strategy, a way of thinking—not as a format.

Students ought to begin to ask their own questions, look things up for themselves, and begin to recognize for themselves what context they want or need to work in or what strategies are appropriate; they ought to be able to experiment with whatever genre or mode they think will do the trick (not just the genre or mode highlighted on a weekly syllabus).

We don't, then, have to teach them to "follow the rules" if we can get them to recognize that they need to make their own mistakes, make their own decisions, ask their own questions, be aggressive, and begin to interpret their own mistakes.

Openness or Freedom

There are benefits in allowing students to choose what they are going to write about or to choose their own readings to write about.[5] Some students have lived more and seen more than we have; some of them read the *Wall Street Journal* or the *New York Times.* I've had students who have been pimps, professional wrestlers, bricklayers, mothers and fathers, and computer jockeys—and some of them have had plenty of things to write about.

But are students who write for themselves or on topics they really care about ever really free to write for themselves or draw conclusions that are their own?—or do they get better at knowing what we want them to write about? (How can we get students to feel comfortable enough or safe enough to choose to write about their love of bigotry without worrying about the social consequences? to choose to write about their disgust for their writing teacher's mind or the unpopular sexual hangups of their friends? to advocate inhumane causes? to challenge cultural beliefs about fairness, culture, and the American Way?)

For the most part, I'm perfectly willing to give assignments. If I design the problems, I can push students a little, challenge them to negotiate or bend my assignments, write about ideas they might never discover on their own, demand that they deal with other people's ideas, and give them practice working on problems that are hard enough to make them suffer yet easy enough to make them assess their own abilities.

I might add that I do give students "free" writing assignments toward the end of each semester—even though a "free" subject may not make much difference in the quality of their writing. In many ways, all my assignments are free if people look at them carefully. Whether they need to or not, students look forward to some choice, and if we don't give it to them, we can appear to be unfair, unsympathetic, and overstructured. In that sense, it's good public relations to provide a choice in subject matter, even though free assignments may not necessarily be better than more structured ones. Perhaps even more important, students ought to learn that freedom is not necessarily freeing. If anything, freedom is more difficult and challenging and requires much more insight than students often believe—especially after they've learned something about writing.

Reading

My own answers to these questions will show up in the following chapters, but for now, it's worthwhile to ask.

Literature

Some of us like to get students to read good literature and believe that good literature is also good to write about. But if we do, we ought to keep asking ourselves questions like these:

- Are we assigning Emily Dickinson and Ernest Hemingway or that new book of "literary nonfiction" because we don't know what else to assign?

- Do we prefer to teach this book because we would prefer to be teaching a literature course anyway and "they" won't let us?

- Do we think that forcing students to read good books will help them to write good papers? (If so, what evidence do we have that is so?)

- Are we assigning good reading to teach students how to read? (If so, what do we mean by that? and do we have any training in teaching reading?)

- With so much else to do, can we afford to spend several hours each week helping students to read and interpret literary texts?

- In what ways does reading *King Lear* or *The Great Gatsby* or some other literary text help students to write *academically*? (Or are we teaching students to write about literature?)

- How do we plan to get students to read big doses of good literature without reinforcing what students already believe: that English teachers like us are nitpicking folk with "right answers" and nothing else to do but bring culture and taste to the masses?

There are good reasons to inspire students with models of good writing and to teach them "how to read." And certain literary texts can supply subject matter for assignments. But teaching literature is tough work and takes time, especially if we assign much of it and try to be very good at it. And the more time we spend going over "meaning" and "interpretation," "tone," "literary devices," "point of view," and "art," the less time we have to deal with students' writing problems, and the trade-off is not always worth it.

Research

How much time do we have to spend taking students to the library to do their "research"? Research is often difficult and time consuming—even when students have a subject to research and have enough familiarity with that subject to narrow it down in informed ways. But it's even harder for those students who, almost without effort, waste hours and even days out of their lives on fruitless rambles in the stacks looking for checked-out books, obscure or missing journals (have you noticed that all the important periodicals are always "at the binder's"?), ten-pound bibliographies, illegible micro-fiche indexes, and lucky surprises in the card catalog.

Other Forms of Writing

According to the Commission on Composition of the National Council of Teachers of English, students should write on a wide range of assignments, including those that require expressive writing, writing across the curriculum, and writing that takes place in "the world beyond school."[6] In California, they're evidently busy talking about different "domains" of writing—the sensory/descriptive domain, the imaginative/narrative domain, the practical/informative domain, and the analytical/expository domain.[7] And there are people who suggest that we need to give students a chance to keep notebooks, freewrite, write in class, write letters, write as lawyers, botanists and geologists, and write for themselves. But before students practice all kinds of writing, we ought to decide what we can and can't do in thirteen weeks.

Different Domains

How much time do we have to spend on "different domains"—and when do we have to limit what we expect students to do? Can we ever successfully isolate different domains? Do we believe that an analytical/

expository paper has nothing to do with the practical/informative domain? the imaginative/narrative domain? (In fact, aren't all such categories vague descriptive conveniences that look good on paper but have no theoretical substance?)

Rewriting

What are our goals for rewriting? Do we, for instance, think that students will get better at writing through rewriting? (Or get better at fixing what we think was wrong with their last drafts?) Will we use rewriting just to get students to pay attention to our comments? How will we encourage students to rewrite on their own?

How will we use rewrites in class? Do rewrites become "punishment" for mistakes? Will we allow rewriting as a form of "extra credit"? Will we "average" students' grades on rewrites? accept only "final" drafts after all the rewriting has been done? Will we make promises ("If you rewrite conscientiously, you will get better")? Will we try to sell used cars ("Every good writer rewrites!")?

The more I think about rewriting and the limited amount of time I have to get students to practice their writing, the more I use rewriting as a way to give back points to students who've lost too many on their initial drafts. In that sense, the rewrites I invite are largely "public relations." Students who do them may do better, and I'd encourage anything that gets students to write more often and reconsider their mistakes. But I wouldn't want to place too much pedagogical burden on rewriting papers, and I wouldn't want rewriting to replace or somehow overshadow more important things like solving problems on one's own or experimenting with new ideas in new contexts.

In-Class Writing

Again, what are our goals? Do we expect practice on in-class writing to have any effect on students' out-of-class writing? If so, what effect? Do we expect to teach students how to take examinations by giving them practice in English class? (If so, what do we teach them? And when do we teach it to them?) And how do we expect to use in-class writing? Will we collect it and "grade" it? Will we try to give feedback on everything students do in class?

For the most part, we ought to keep our goals minimal. I like to have students practice taking "tests"—because most of my students are freshmen, and I can help them quickly to do two things well: read directions and manage their time. If I can get them to do those two things well, and if they've done their work and memorized the right things, then they will do reasonably well. And I'll get credit for helping them with practical things and addressing their immediate needs as students. (Students need to believe that we *are* helpful—and that our help extends beyond the English classroom.)

Mostly, though, we should use in-class writing as throwaway writing: something to do right on the spot, without much thinking and without great expectations. If we can get students to do things, respond to things, experiment with what they're trying to say, and put their ideas and skills on the line, then we're not out there in front of them trying to cajole them into thinking or entertaining them with fancy hats and juggling acts. In fact, the more we can get students to do, the less likely they will be to blame us for being "dull" or "poor lecturers" responsible for giving them the Monday-morning blues or death in the afternoon.

Notebooks (Journals)
What should students learn from keeping notebooks? How much time should we spend teaching them to keep notebooks? (And experimenting with notebooks does take a considerable amount of class time.) What will we do with all those notebooks students write? (Do we intend to read them? If so, what do we look for? How do we give students feedback on their notebook keeping?) How will we ensure that students don't write five or six "different" notebook entries (using two or three different pens) the hour before they turn them in? In that sense, how do we keep notebooks from being busywork for those students who just don't want to bother with them?

Teachers who use notebooks are often true believers. They use them to get ideas for individual students' assignments. They read them for pleasure. I'd rather not put so much weight on notebook keeping. Some people like them and benefit from them; others (like me) don't benefit much and probably shouldn't keep them. You might (as I do) assign notebooks as "extra credit" late in the semester—something students can try out if they have the time and the inclination.

Freewriting
Here's another kind of writing that many of us have strong feelings about. I've known people who write brilliantly and swear that their success is largely because of their practice of freewriting—dumping their ideas nonstop on paper for ten or fifteen or twenty minutes. Many of these people are positive that freewriting will help just about everyone to free up, find good ideas, and possibly even get in touch with "honesty" and their true selves.

But I would ask the same question about freewriting that I'd ask about notebooks: How can we teach all students to enjoy and profit by freewriting when many of us (like me, for instance, and many academics I know in other disciplines) never freewrite and don't see much sense in pouring ideas on paper nonstop without thinking much about them?

Grading

In chapter 6, we'll consider the problems we encounter by not separating grading from evaluation. Here, I'm much more concerned with practical problems:

Record Keeping

Most of us probably keep our records in the form of letter grades, but letter grades have drawbacks. It's harder to average out the grades. Does one *A* and one *B* equal a *B+* or an *A–*? If we give letter grades, how do we add in extra credit? Do we give letter grades for extra credit? If so, does this mean that extra credit should be weighted the same as individual papers? If we assign papers of different length, how do we average the grades? (One of my least favorite grades is *"A/B"*—a grade that means absolutely nothing but keeps students worried for the whole semester.)

We could keep "scores" rather than grades. Scores are a bit more flexible. If you give a student a 79 and an 86, you can average them together and get an 82.5—and that seems more accurate than averaging something like a *B–* and a *B+* and coming out with a *B* for an average. (Depending on the scale, an 82.5 could be a *B* or a *B–*.)

Numbers are also easier to combine. Short papers can be worth a certain number of points and long ones more points. Extra-credit and mid-semester exams can vary in value depending on what we think they're worth. More important, students who keep their own scores can know immediately what their grades are at any particular time in the course. They won't have to guess or juggle letter grades and hope for something positive without knowing for sure. And the more we can give students a sense of certainty about their grades, the better off we will all be.

Grades and Peer Evaluation

Are we going to let students grade each other's papers? If so, how much weight are we going to give those peer grades in our grading scheme?

Student Progress

We can penalize some students by not taking their progress into consideration—especially hard workers whose poor scores on early work keep their grades from reflecting their improvement. How can we take such progress into consideration without making progress dependent upon our state of mind on the last day of school or our feelings about different students? How will students know that they don't have to brownnose us or wheedle and whine about how hard they've worked during the semester to get us to give them the benefit of the doubt?

One way to do this is to throw out their lowest scores. Another way is to weight the papers toward the end of the semester. (I do both and double the value of the last two four-page papers of the semester.)

Record Keeping

Record keeping is such a time-consuming task that some of us avoid keeping detailed records. Part of the problem is that we often see record keeping as a way to keep track of students' grades even though record keeping is also part of *our own accountability.* If, for instance, a student comes up to us at the end of the semester and says something like "You never paid any attention to me, and I never knew what you wanted me to do!" what kind of proof will we have that we did pay attention to that student? How will we prove that the problems here are not our problems but problems we've tried to address for an entire semester?

Ideally, we ought to make sure that students keep track of their own papers and grades, but we ought to keep a fair number of records—even if they seem like busywork and we seem like high school teachers or bureaucrats.

Although we can't keep every scrap of evidence about every problem every student has, we ought to keep track of those students who have the potential to make us miserable, cause us bureaucratic problems, or create other uncomfortable hassles with review boards or parents or department heads—those who don't give us any credit for knowing anything; those who don't turn papers in or try to get us to accept phoney alibis; those who tend to blame circumstances beyond their control; those who get other people to write their papers; those who "lose" their papers or "forget their assignments" or "mail" them to us or claim we "never gave them back."

In special cases, we ought to keep records of our conversations, of our comments on particular papers; we ought to keep track of attendance; and we ought to lay down a paper trail so that if anything happens by the end of the semester, the problem, if there is a problem, will not be ours.

Final Plans

There's no final solution to any of these questions. We change plans from semester to semester. We modify goals as we learn more about our discipline. I've included in appendix 1 a sample organization for a typical English 110 class of my own. At one time, I might have put that sample plan at the end of this chapter, but I've decided to try to resist giving answers too quickly. As I've said, the questions and thinking are more important than any syllabus or game plan you can get from me. I'd like it much better if we all tried to solve problems for ourselves before we ran off to plug our ideas into someone else's prefabricated solution to our own problems.

●●●●●●●

Notes

1. To see how I would block out time in my own syllabus, see the sample calendar in Appendix 1.

2. Different levels of classes, of course, demand different kinds of activities. In an advanced writing class, for instance, I see nothing wrong with doing the "same old thing": have students read each other's papers every day in class. As students get better, as they understand the questions and problems that they're each trying to face, they themselves have to become much more responsible for the questions they ask and the issues they think are important. But until that time, while we ourselves are responsible for directing our students' attention, even for convincing them that academic writing is not necessarily easy to do, that being smart and well spoken may not be enough to survive in academia—we need to plan our activities carefully and take advantage of classroom dynamics and the resources we have as teachers to give students feedback on what they think and how they *think* they think.

3. Some experimental work suggests that neither the number of writing assignments nor intense marking automatically leads to improvements in writing. See, for instance, George Hillocks, Jr.,

Research on Composition: New Directions for Teaching (Urbana, IL: NCTE, 1986). But such conclusions may not fit with what I'm trying to do. For one thing, people who design such experiments rarely can take into consideration the kinds of "feedback" I'm talking about or put such feedback into a large enough and complex enough environment.

4. This is one of the more traditional approaches to assignment sequencing. It's possible to defend such an approach, but it may be more difficult than many of us think. Simply saying that personal writing is more personal is not enough. Nor is it enough to link personal writing to some developmental model or to suggest that personal writing is good because all of us are storytelling creatures or that practice with personal writing will make academic writing more "honest" or enjoyable to read.

5. This is a major way to deal with (or not to deal with) assignment making. For typical discussions, see Donald M. Murray, "What, No Assignments?" *Learning by Teaching* (Portsmouth, NH: Boynton/Cook, 1982) 129–34; Donald H. Graves, *Writing: Teachers and Children at Work* (Portsmouth, NH: Heinemann, 1983) and "Break the Welfare Cycle: Let Writers Choose Their Topics," *FForum* 3 (Winter 1982): 75–77. See also, Lou Kelly, "Toward Competence and Creativity in an Open Class," *CE* 34 (1973): 644–60; Stephen Judy, "The Search for Structures in the Teaching of Composition, *EJ* 59 (February 1970): 213–26.

6. See "Teaching Composition: A Position Statement" (Pamphlet. Urbana, IL: NCTE, 1983).

7. See Nancy McHugh, "Teaching the Domains of Writing," *Practical Ideas for Teaching Writing as Process,* ed. Carol Booth Olson (Sacramento: California State Dept. of Education, 1986): 71–77.

two

Assignments
and
Evaluation

four

....
....
....
....
....
....

Assignment Making

• •

I have no magic wand or mainline spiritual connection that helps me design assignments that work for everybody, and I'm not convinced that everybody can or should do as I do. All I can say is that the assignments here seem to work for me the way they are; that is, they help my students do what I want them to do—write a little bit, experiment a little bit, and begin to question what they are doing. Whether you're ready or willing to try out some of the materials I use in class, I believe that the kind of thinking I'm doing here is reasonable and can lead you to view assignments in a practical, educationally sound way. With these reservations in mind, I would like to offer some general advice for assignment making, emphasizing the *thinking behind the assignment making*. In the next chapter, I'll try to put assignments in a larger framework that includes grading and evaluation, but for now, we'll look at general problems in finding things for students to write about.

....

Rules of Thumb

Try Not to Invite Simpleminded Solutions or "Explications"
Most of us emphasize more things than simple interpretation and explication of great pieces of literature—but as English teachers, we probably spend more time than anybody else on campus helping students to

read, explicate texts, show how carefully they can draw out symbolic, metaphorical, interpretational, or intentional/unintentional/imagined meaning, and make sense (often chronological sense) out of *Lord Jim,* "The Death of Ivan Ilich," "Heart of Darkness," or "The Wasteland." Sometimes, even without knowing it, we invite students to make simple, often chronological explications of images or symbols when we invite them to trace a character's development or explain how someone changes or tell what's going on.

While we may want students to read better and defend their interpretations of complex texts, we ought to emphasize ways they can *use* their interpretations, *criticize, weigh, evaluate, apply* what they read, *explore* implications, *risk* choosing sides, *debate* abstractions, or *try* to put things into practical contexts. If they don't formulate their own questions and do something with what they read—if they just tell us what they've read or what someone else has said about what they've read—then they aren't doing enough.

Suppose, for instance, we want students to write on the following passage from William Carlos Williams's *Kora in Hell*:

The trick is never to touch the world anywhere. Leave yourself at the door, walk in, admire the pictures, talk a few words with the master of the house, question his wife a little, rejoin yourself at the door—and go off arm in arm listening to last week's symphony played by angel hornsmen from the benches of a turned cloud. Or if dogs rub too close and the poor are too much out let your friend answer them.[1]

We can invite explication by asking students to talk about or explain meaning: What is this "trick" that Williams is talking about? Where is this door? How can one "rejoin" himself or herself? And what about those dogs? Are they real? imaginary? metaphorical?

But even if we don't explicitly invite explication, many students have gotten so good at expecting questions of explication that they explicate even when we don't want them to. They can write entire essays on what William Carlos Williams thinks about dogs or whether William Carlos Williams is confusing. If they are confused or can't get "into" William Carlos Williams, they can profess ignorance or boredom or tell us what happened when they began reading the passage and how they discovered that William Carlos Williams was talking about "life" after all.

The problem isn't that explication is bad, but that it's not enough for students to explain what they've "found out"—to show that they've read the work, answered the questions, looked up new words, or gotten the "message." In academia, they have to *do something* with what they've "found out." So what? Is Williams right? wrong? helpful? dangerous?

If we want to nudge students past easy explication, we have to design problems with constraints that require them to stretch out, risk, or take a stand:

Just how far out to lunch is William Carlos Williams in the following passage?

Based only on this one passage, would you feel good about inviting William Carlos Williams to lunch?

In what ways is William Carlos Williams's explanation simply an old shoe on the wrong foot?

What's wrong with William Carlos Williams?

To answer such questions, students will have to "explicate" the text, but they will also have to do more: explain what "out to lunch" means and explore the implications of being "out to lunch"; explain what they mean by "feeling good" and put "feeling good" into a context; be able to evaluate the metaphor of "old shoes" on the wrong feet.

Some students expect to explicate everything they read—especially if texts are hard or make them "think" or if the ideas are complex or have many different parts:

Here Are Opinions of Mr. Dooley:

1. If ye put a begger on horseback, ye'll walk ye'ersilf.[2]
2. If Rooshia wud shave we'd not be afraid iv her.
3. A woman's sinse iv humor is in her husband's name.
4. Most women ought niver to look back if they want a following.
5. If ye dhrink befure siven ye'll cry befure iliven.
6. Miditation is a gift con-fined to unknown philosophes an' cows.
7. To most people a savage nation is wan that doesn't wear oncomf'rtable clothes.
8. Play actors, orators an' women ar-re a class be thimselves.
9. No man was iver so low as to have rayspict f'r his brother-in-law.
10. Most vigitaryans I iver see looked enough like their food to be classed as cannybals.
11. An Englishman appears resarved because he can't talk.
12. What China needs is a Chinese exclusion act.
13. A mean man is wan that has th' courage not to be gin'rous.
14. Thrust ivrybody—but cut th' ca-ards.

The easiest way to talk about these quotations is to "classify" them, and in this context, classification becomes a simple form of explication: "There are three kinds of quotations here"; "Mister Dooley is concerned with three ideas"; "This is what I found out about the meaning of this list of quotations"; or "This classification will help you to understand how to classify these quotations by Mr. Dooley."

Many other equally easy solutions depend in one way or another on oversimplifying "what's there": "Only one of these quotations means anything to me"; "Mr. Dooley is confusing to read"; "Mr. Dooley has common sense"; or "I think at least three of these quotations are about foreigners."

But instead of inviting simple explication, we can make students worry a little more and work a little harder by shaping our assignments around different kinds of problems:

- Do you like Mr. Dooley?
- What is the most important thing Mr. Dooley stands for?
- Which of these quotations is (are) the best?
- Which of these quotations is (are) the worst?
- Is Mr. Dooley a better thinker than Elbert Hubbard?
- Is Mr. Dooley a better thinker than Josiah McIntosh?[3]

The simplest way to answer such questions is to categorize Mr. Dooley's quotations. If they write on "Which of these quotations is (are) the best?" students could also cop out and try to do something simple: select the one quotation that seems best and argue that it is best. "I believe that quotation number fourteen is the best because . . ." Categorization also allows them to simplify the problem and allows them to talk about aspects of a *group* of quotations. In this case, talking about groups or categories suggests that students have done something more than choose by whim. In fact, choosing by whim is almost always a cop-out.

But these problems ask students to do more than categorize. Students who explain which of these quotations is the "best" or "worst" or tell us that Mr. Dooley is a better thinker than Josiah McIntosh have to deal in some way with the quotations they have rejected. In other words, even though we may not explicitly tell them to "make a comparison" or "consider the opposition," the problem itself (at least when given in an academic setting) requires a comparison with alternatives.

Any time we can complicate things, make success dependent upon recognition of underlying issues and unstated constraints, we can get students to think a little, begin to make decisions on their own, and do more than react in predictable ways.

Figure 4-1

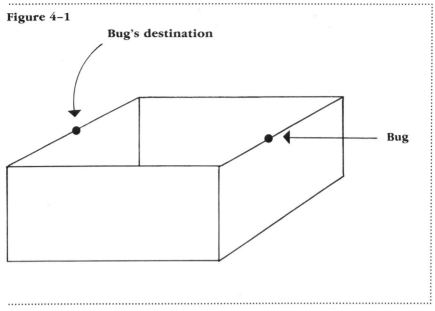

Keep Assignments Reasonably Open Ended

A long time ago, I remember seeing a puzzle about a box and bug. This bug is on the top edge of a cardboard box, and it has to walk to the opposite edge (see Figure 4–1). The question is, how do you measure the shortest distance that bug will have to walk?

The solution is simple: you lay the box out flat and draw a straight line between the point where the bug is now to the point where it will end up. Then you use geometry (see Figure 4–2).

I've always considered most of the assignments we give students to be box-and-bug problems. We give them a poem by Wallace Stevens, a short story by William Faulkner, or an essay by Steven Jay Gould, and we ask them to tell us what they think or whether Stevens is good or bad or whether Faulkner has something important to say. We encourage them to use their imaginations, to find "new angles" and be "audacious." But in their eyes, no matter what we say or how we invite dissension, the problem is still pure box-and-bug: all students have to do is find out how to fold things down the right way, and they can solve the whole thing with geometry.

I don't think we can overcome students' perception of our assignments as box-and-bug problems if we give them assignments that close

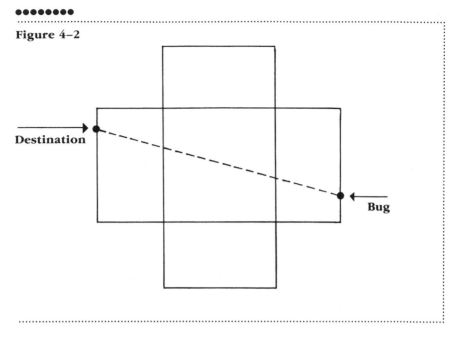

Figure 4–2

things down, narrow their options, and suggest that there are single, "correct answers" or "desired outcomes." That's what's often wrong with the readings in textbooks or "rhetoric-readers": bland, polite, nice readings in Sociology for Composition Students or Psychology for the Home or Office or Joan Didion or E. B. White or James Thurber or Charles Schultz that invite polite, nice reactions and acceptance.

Even though we tell students how open minded we are, and no matter how we emphasize that there are no right answers, and even though we suggest that some of our best friends are prone to strange, twisted thinking—deep inside, students know that when we coax them to admit their strange feelings about William Faulkner or to make light of James Baldwin or Virginia Woolf, we're coaxing them into a literary form of parent bashing. In fact, they know deep in their hearts that certain issues like the greatness of great literature, the greatness of literature, the importance of Stanley Milgram, war, sex, race, free speech, AIDS, nukes, Mothers Against Drunk Driving, George Orwell, the Ku Klux Klan, Al Capone, Richard Nixon, "A Modest Proposal," and child porn have right answers, correct readings, proper angles, and reasonable, acceptable points of view *no matter how strange or immature or conservative or liberated or carnivorous their own private views about such topics are.*

Certainly, we can get some students—usually our best students—to commit themselves to their own interpretations and risk their own opinions about the great "models" of great literature or classical literature or even prize-winning student writing.[4] But we might do much better if we gave students something to write about that they don't know so much about or have an intellectual stake in—or, better still, that *we* don't know much about or have any intellectual stake in. Here, for instance, is Elbert Hubbard on dentists:

A dentist to be successful must be a surgeon, an artist, a sculptor and a mechanic. He must have the same mental grasp of the laws of physics, chemistry and biology as is needed by the physician. He must have the manipulative skill that is required by the surgeon in his most delicate work. He must be able to take advantage of the finest requirements of the mechanic, and must have the ability to carry out those mechanical operations on living tissue in such manner as to cause no irritation thereto. His workshop is a hole in the face about two inches in diameter; in that hole he has to perform all of his operations and the patient takes the work away with him. In nine-tenths of the work done by the physician or surgeon, Nature is expected to complete what he leaves. The dentist has to do his work. His failures stand out where he can always see them. The doctor buries his.[5]

How many of us know anything about Elbert Hubbard? Better still, how many of us *care* to know very much about Hubbard? Most of us probably don't care if students praise him, make fun of him, or compare his words with their friends or parents—but even as they praise him or make fun of him, we can ask them to be fair to him, to read carefully (or read as carefully as we might read), and deal with what he says, not what students want him to say.

Here's an important poem by Wanda Wiggins Willies:

> Choice
> Along the bank beside the rushing brook
> Sits little Willie smiling in the stream.
> She stirs the current with a silver fork
> And edges in the greeny seaweed flame.
> Oh how she loves to sit up on the bank—
> In rolled up hair with bonnet bright.
> She has no cares. The city's sank
> Behind the hill—and so, behind the sight
> She's pleased as punch to stir the water with
> Her little fork.
>   No dogs she hears; no peeps
> From Toms. There are no runts that come along
> With magazines to sell or porno-flicks.
> No exposes of bodies barely hid.
> No samples of delusions brightly seen
> Come on t.v. from places far away

And congressmen we've never seen except
For pictures brightly cast on barroom walls
And telephone poles and placards stamped in yards
With faces fat and smiles wide with naught
Between their ears but dust and dreary peat.

Why go back? She thinks upon that scene.
She does not know. She thinks some more. She smiles
Because she knows she must. To fight for rights
To smile plainly in the face of those who'd steal
Her light and plant destruction in her place.
For when one backs away by choice and leaves
To those she grimly snears, she leaves it fair
To them to interfere—who reek
Upon the land—upon the land so weak.

Who should care whether Wanda Wiggins Willies is real or not or whether her poem is good or bad?[6] Who should care if a student says that Wanda Wiggins Willies is "greater than Shakespeare" or "no better than grandpa"? Certainly, no one ought to take Wanda Wiggins Willies as a threat to Shakespeare's reputation. And because they risk less, students ought to be willing (or at least more willing) to play—to risk saying things they might not say about "real" literature, or literature that carries with it the intellectual baggage of their elders and our own mentors.

We don't have to ask students to write ordinary, boring, predictable "freshman English papers":

- "Write a comparison paper on two items of your choice."
- Do you suppose Stanley Milgram's insights can be applied to the community where you live?"
- What are the arguments Orwell uses to support his points? Are they, as he suggests, good ones? Or is he, as he suggests, also prone to making the same mistakes he criticizes in others?"
- Take a look at Virginia Woolf's style. Why do you think she takes so much time talking about that moth? What does she wish to convey to us about her own sensibility?"

We can ask students to do unexpected things:

- What makes Wanda Wiggins Willies's writing so salutary?
- What would Wanda Wiggins Willies say about turtles?
- Was Wanda Wiggins Willies a better poet than Julia A. Moore, the "Sweet Singer of Michigan"?[7]
- Can you yourself write better poetry than Wanda Wiggins Willies?

And we can, if we want, make the problem even more difficult or longer by giving them a few more poems:

At least two of the following poems were also written by Wanda Wiggins Willies:

(I)

A snowflake is a fragile thing
Six arms of ice, a look unique
Their praises my neighbor likes to sing—
Too bad her mouth looks like a beak.

My neighbor sings some lofty tunes:
Praises snow that looks so white
Applauds with glee her own snow dunes
As her dog gives mine a yellow blight.

Let's fight with might the snow that's yellow.
Fight the blight with city ordinances:
Keep Fido's owners on their toes
Keep yellow snow outside our fences.

(II)

Willie had a purple monkey climbing on a yellow stick,
And when he sucked the paint all off it made him deathly sick;
And in his latest hours he clasped that monkey in his hand,
And bade good-bye to earth and went into a better land.

Oh! no more he'll shoot his sister with his little wooden gun;
And no more he'll twist the pussy's tail and make her yowl for fun.
The pussy's tail now stands out straight; the gun is laid aside;
The monkey doesn't jump around since little Willie died.

(III) SONG!!

A cry of great alarm went out
On the corner of Fifth and Stout
When two gray kitties made a fuss
As they tried to dodge a Greyhound bus.

The cry went out when kitty bones
Were lost beneath two Firestones:
Crushed and Smooshed into the ground
Until their little throats made not a sound.

And then a second cry went out
On the corner of Fifth and Stout:
The cry was for a rubber mop
To clean the kitties' bodies up.

A simple assignment might be, "Which of these four poems is better?" (Comparisons of three or more items are never simple.) Another assignment might be, "Which of these three poems was not written by Wanda Wiggins Willies?"[8]

Students can ruin such assignments, too. They could believe that people think that Wanda Wiggins Willies's writing is salutary in the same humorless way they might treat a Petrarchan sonnet. They could spend half their papers defining *salutary* by quoting "Webster's Dictionary." They could explain the etymology of *salutary*. ("The word *salutary* comes from the Latin word meaning . . .") They could disappoint us with dull, boring thinking or miss the fun. Worse, they could tell us that we're full of baloney—that writing about imaginary people and their imaginary poems isn't real enough, doesn't allow them the practice they need with "real world" problems or issues—and we'd have to negotiate with them and let them write on alternative assignments.[9]

But no matter what they do, students aren't forced into predictable, safe angles with predictable quotations to support their predictable arguments. If they choose to write from safe angles and defend themselves with safe, predictable, boring arguments, then that's *their* choice, not ours—especially if we can encourage them to risk something, experiment, write parodies of academic discourse, say audacious things about turtles, make Wanda Wiggins Willies into a hitherto unknown guru of the West, and step out of predictable, oversimplified visions of the "good" and "thoughtful."

Don't Spell Everything Out

Sometimes we think that a clear assignment is a complete assignment that tells students exactly what they are supposed to do. So we provide them with information on audience; we require them to use particular techniques such as narration, description, persuasion, process analysis; we explain too much about tasks and provide too much biographical information ("Wallace Stevens was a great poet. . . ." "Shakespeare wrote some of the most important plays ever written in the English language. . . ."); we explain the particular "tone" they should attempt ("Try to explain without alienating. Try to keep your tone simple and pleasant. Remember that no one wants to read something written by a sourpuss. . . ."); and we often try to suggest structures and approaches ("Spend at least three paragraphs summarizing and three paragraphs criticizing. . . ." Don't forget to begin with a definition of the word "good." "Try to end your narration with an explanation of your point of view and a clear discussion of what you have learned from your experience.")

Yet in one-page assignments, we don't need such completeness.[10] Take a look at the following assignment, for example:

In one page, explain which of the following understands a rock.

1. A white-faced hornet eating the entrails of a dead locust on a sycamore tree.

2. A large conch grazing in the Atlantic Ocean off the Florida coast.

3. Ronald Reagan.

4. A woman named Henrietta tying signs onto bumpers in the parking lot of the "Trees of Mystery" in Northern California.

5. A 110 lb. man named Frederick Pillsbury contemplating the koi that swim in a large horse trough next to the San Bernadino Freeway.

6. A sixty-year-old woman setting a No-Fuss-No-Muss gopher trap in her front yard underneath a rose bush.

7. A lady named Sally collecting wild poppies in her apron in Blue Dome, Idaho.

8. A man named Joe collecting wild poppies in his apron near Bald Peak.

We *could* tell students that this is a difficult assignment, that they might want to approach it "metaphorically," and that at some point they might need to explain the evaluative nature of "understanding a rock." We could also tell them that they ought to think about "comparison" and say something to convince us that only certain items in that list could "understand a rock." But we don't have to.

Here's a more complicated example:

Steve Martin says in his book *Cruel Shoes*:

I, for one, am going to know what to say when the ducks show up. I've made a list of phrases, and although I don't know which one to use yet, they are all good enough in case they showed up tomorrow. Many people won't know what to say when the ducks show up, but I will. Maybe I'll say, "Oh ducks, oh ducks, oh ducks," or just "ducks wonderful ducks!" I practice these sayings every day, and even though the ducks haven't come yet, when they do, I'll know what to say.[11]

In one page, can you explain whether Steve Martin is right? Will he know what to say? Some commentators don't think so and suggest that Martin should consider some of the following things to say:

1. Hey, Dude! How they hangin'?
2. Don't take it personally, but your beak's on upside down.
3. You look like my Aunt Martha in boxer shorts.
4. Do you mind getting your foot off my dog?
5. Well stay as long as you want—but don't splash and don't do disgusting things in front of the kids.

What do you think?

After practice on other assignments, students will begin to recognize for themselves that this problem has several parts, that in an academic game, they ought to *summarize* or clarify what Martin says before they decide whether he is right or wrong, and that they ought to say something about the different parts to the assignment in their introductions—unless they want their papers to fall into two halves. We don't have to tell them to think metaphorically. We don't have to give them special hints and warn them to consider a certain number of issues or require them to summarize here before criticizing. In fact, by the end of the semester, they should be able to handle extremely vague assignments:

- Discuss Charlie Poole.
- React to the following quotation by Elbert Hubbard.
- What do you think about "A Message to Garcia"?
- Do something intelligent with the following material. . . .
- Here it is. What do you think?
- Well?

There's no reason to simplify problems if we want students to begin asking their *own* questions, recognizing their own problems, and understanding that there are often unstated assumptions in academia—that criteria are important, explanations are important, and certain explanations require comparisons.

Until we get students to ask questions actively, to begin to recognize problems and important issues on their own, they remain under our control, trapped in their own passivity. And no matter what we do to encourage them to think or be creative, we remain the givers of knowledge, the gatekeepers of excellence and fine taste that we have always been, and students go away believing what they've always believed—that the only way to write "academically" is to follow directions and do things the way we tell them to do them.

Keep Assignments Reasonably Self-contained

Here's a typical assignment on Alan Fobbs:

Here are the most important things Alan Fobbs ever said. What's most regrettable about them?

1. "No one walks a straight line."
2. "On a bus, it's better to know where you're going than where you've been unless you've been there before."
3. "Every year, more and more people grow old."
4. "You should try to live a happy life unless you have no choice."
5. "Some things float."
6. "If you look at a bird, it may not see you."

7. "You can tell a lot by what you think."
8. "You seldom see inside a tree."
9. "Everyone walks on the right side of the road."
10. "You should open a dinner roll before eating it."
11. "Most people cannot talk in a vacuum."
12. "You can learn a lot by watching the watermelons grow."
13. "You always start somewhere."
14. "Beware of tornadoes that come from disturbances of the air."[12]

Such an assignment is limited. Students don't have to know, for instance, that Alan Fobbs said other important things like "If I saw you and you saw me, it was probably by accident"; "Never wonder what's on the bottom of your shoe"; and "No one needs a tree with imagination." And they couldn't do more research even if they wanted to.

The value of such an assignment is that it frees students from worrying about some expert at Johns Hopkins whose knowledge and special expertise on Alan Fobbs could ruin their credibility and make them feel small and inadequate. They don't have to worry about knowing any *more* about the public's value of Alan Fobbs or his position in the academic community. For that matter, they don't have to worry much about knowing more about Alan Fobbs than we do. In fact, everyone starts off with the same amount of information; no one gets rewarded for prior knowledge—and, hence, no one needs to feel "unprepared" or overexcited by their old ideas, "high school learning," or some special "prep school training" or "graduate school" that gives people an edge in understanding or a premature sense of intellectual security.

Because no one knows what Alan Fobbs means or what angle is most appropriate when approaching his sayings, students can more readily accept the limited, game-like nature of the problems they're playing with. They can't be wrong if there is no clear-cut "wrong." And we can emphasize the rules of the game they are playing. Since they are playing an academic game, they have to understand general academic rules: simplicity, directness, support for assertions, and clarity of expression.

Encourage Parody
Forms of parody have a way of making fun of themselves, and if it hasn't been obvious, I would emphasize that I appreciate the *distance* we can get when we can laugh at ourselves and see that we're deflating something we could take too solemnly.

There is, of course, a danger in such humor and parody: students can begin to devalue the entire academic enterprise. But I see no simple correspondence between studying "serious" topics, committing ourselves to humankind, writing solemn papers, and learning to write well. Certainly, we can learn as well by relaxing, playing, and gambling a little in a world that doesn't threaten academic extinction for thinking strangely or incorrectly.

Build in Room for Negotiation

We ought to build room for negotiation into our assignments. We can either include something in every assignment ("Feel free to negotiate any assignment in this class. . . .") or we can include something at the beginning of the semester to make it clear that regardless of how we think about our assignments and the fine materials we've used to build them, they are, after all, *opportunities to write,* not prescribed events that automatically lead to mastery learning in a foolproof sequence.

Students who negotiate with us, ask for options and explanations, or decide that we are full of baloney sometimes cause us problems but don't disappoint us. If they are convinced that they have better things to write on, then they probably do have better things to write on. Certainly, they are making decisions on their own and making a commitment to their own ideas about learning, and we ought to respect that commitment and encourage it, even though we may not know where it will lead.

Design Experiments, Not Tests of Right Thinking

We've also touched on this point already: too often, we give students writing assignments simply for accountability, to find out if they've been keeping up with the reading or listening to us give them answers in class. But the more students have to prove or "show," the less they are apt to challenge our ideas, experiment, play, or make mistakes.

Longer Assignments

We should have *good reasons* for assigning longer papers. If, for instance, we want to teach skills such as writing "thesis statements" or making assertions, we might be able to do better by asking students to write three short papers or introductory parts to three longer papers— each with a solid thesis statement—than to write one long paper during the same amount of time. Similarly, if we want to give students practice writing or want to give students an abundance of feedback on their writing, we could probably do that better with shorter papers, too. Certainly, shorter papers are easier for us to comment on and less painful for students—especially those who run into trouble setting up their longer papers and often end up slogging their way through muddy bogwater because they "have to have something to turn in."

On the other hand, longer paper assignments provide opportunities to control more data, develop larger ideas, and set up more complex arguments. In doing so, students get important practice clumping and grouping; highlighting important features or points; signaling different levels of argument; expanding ideas with longer explanations, examples, and quotations, and controlling the drift with mainheads and subheads, bullets, or white space. Longer assignments also require better time management, better planning, and better ideas. It's one thing to whip out a weak one-page paper; it's another to draw out a weak argument and then have to keep drawing it out until you see it crumbling around your feet.

Special Considerations

Many of the rules for one-page assignments also apply to longer assignments—but it's worth keeping in mind special considerations in setting up longer assignments[13]:

Spell Things Out a Little More Than You Would in One-Page Papers
Students who begin working on an unproductive angle for a four-page paper may be stuck with that angle for a long time—and sometimes, if they get stuck or have an unreasonable amount of trouble with content or direction, they may even give up or do unfortunate things like ignore assignments, give detailed plot summaries, compile random lists of quotations, plagiarize, claim uncontrollable boredom, or oversimplify. When students begin to resort to such survival tactics—and that's what they are, ways to avoid disaster and "have something to turn in"—they learn little about writing, and most of the time, we waste our time trying to give them useful feedback on what they've done.

I often give students more advice and even hints when they start doing longer papers:

Four-Page Paper #1
Rough draft due: Monday
Final draft due: Wednesday

Here are several wooden nickels. They were manufactured in San Antonio, Texas, by Norman Brock. Do something with them. (You may want to clump and group to get an idea of what you've got, but DON'T SIMPLY TELL ME WHAT

CLUMPS OR GROUPS YOU FOUND WHEN YOU CLUMPED AND GROUPED. Don't, for instance, tell me "These wooden nickels fall into three types," or "I found out that wooden nickels fall into three types," or "I found out that wooden nickels are about three things," or "There are four kinds of people who would like these wooden nickels.")

And don't deal with just one or two of these nickels. Try to deal with more of them—try to find an angle, make a point about them or many of them (or about Norman Brock) (or about whatever). You also may need to say more than "Norman Brock is a conservative."

Do not simply tell a story about Norman Brock. Try not to organize chronologically. Concentrate instead on examples, illustrations, explanations. Concentrate on logic, clarity, and vision. And be fair to Norman Brock.

In this case, I'm willing to give hints about the dangers of writing about categories and hints about organization ("Don't organize chronologically. . . . Don't tell a simple story"). When students make up simple categories and enumerate those categories, they don't have to work on their transitions, their logical movement from point to point. And the minute they slip into a chronological treatment of events, they no longer have to work to set up solid arguments. If they don't work on solid arguments, they might as well not even bother to write all four pages.

Here's another assignment, this time for a more or less "free" assignment:

Four-Page Paper #5
Rough draft due: Tuesday
Final draft due: Thursday

Write four pages on something important that you have read. Your restrictions are these:

- Don't simply tell a story. (In fact, don't organize your paper chronologically.)
- Don't write about Plato, Socrates, Greek philosophers, or Herodotus.
- Don't write on a novel or a fat book of any kind. You might write on a very small *part* of one, though.
- Don't simply report what you've read.
- Don't write a "how-to" paper.
- [IMPORTANT] Put a box around twelve (12) consecutive lines someplace in your text and tighten those lines up. (I'll take off points for wordiness in those twelve lines.)
- [IMPORTANT] Use at least three (3) cumulative sentences at least two lines long each. Mark these with ** in the margin.

This is not a simple assignment. Your main problem, however, will be to find something to write about. You can respond to editorials in magazines or newspapers (even the *Pio* [the student newspaper]). You can pick a topic and look up something about it in the library. I am particularly interested in black walnuts, rats, hubbard squash, carp, carpenter ants, roaches, and weevils of all types. You can choose to write about something you yourself have a special interest in—a hobby or a recreation or whatever. (If you look up something in the library, try to stay away from dull or overworked topics like abortion, women's liberation, marijuana, friendship, love, true love, unrequited love, misunderstood love, gun control, euthanasia, child porno, child abuse, self confessions. . . .) Of course, if you *really want to,* you can write on one of those topics—but be careful. It's easy to be simpleminded and write predictable things about such topics.

Use standard format. Don't use forms of you or we unless you have to. Don't simply tell a story. Back up everything you say with facts, evidence, proof, explanation, or bluff. Clarify, clarify, clarify. Introduce all quotations except those you don't have to; explain all quotations that need explaining. And DOCUMENT your sources.

This assignment is more or less free—if I'm working on getting students to experiment with cumulative sentences and documentation, I don't want them to write something completely free. It's easy, for instance, to write cumulative sentences in personal narratives, but it's harder to find out how to make them work in more *academic* writing.

I'll also try to keep students from writing anything in chronological order because I don't want to read how-to papers detailing step-by-step the way I can change the oil in my car. I don't want to read about grandma or what happened last weekend. Such topics are fine, but for my purposes they don't require discussion of other people's ideas and texts—essential academic tasks.

Finally, I want to use the idea of a free assignment as part of a lesson in academic thinking. "Free" in academia doesn't mean "off the top of one's head" or "right out of my parents' brains," and I want students to worry a bit about the intellectual value of the topics they choose. I want them to work to figure out something that's not vague, general, or that comes to them as a vision. I want them to begin to realize that despite what they *want* to write about, certain ideas have more academic "worth" or currency than others.

Try to Avoid Issues That Look More Open Than They Are

Over the years, I've collected information on "Bigfoot"—the manlike monster who's supposed to live in forests of the Pacific Northwest. So far, I've got nine paperbacks of sightings and lore, pictures of footprints, and letters to local newspapers. I've got newspaper articles from the *Walla Walla Union Bulletin* and even a piece written in an airline magazine. But I've never been able to find anything to do with this material in class.

Issues like Bigfoot often look better than they are. There's usually plenty of information from many sources—but the more we read, the less we learn. Students could tell us that yes, Bigfoot exists because who knows? maybe he exists. Or they could tell us that Bigfoot doesn't exist because there's "no scientific proof" that he exists. Or they could compare sightings of Bigfoot with sightings of Abominable Snowmen and Loch Ness monsters. If they're good, they could talk about the strange people who claim to have sighted Bigfoot.

But none of these approaches is complex or likely to lead to more than predictable insights that rehash obvious concerns and conclusions. Do students have to wrestle with the information? (Well, maybe not.) Do they have to worry about definition or comparison? (Well, maybe not.) Do they have to worry about categorization or labeling categories? (As far as I can tell, there aren't many categories besides "believers" and "nonbelievers.") Do they have to weigh or evaluate sources? (Well, maybe not. The sources all cite the same type of vague, inconclusive anecdotal evidence; the photographs are always smudgy; and the drawings people make are ridiculous.)

Unfortunately, there are many other issues like Bigfoot—the history of the NAACP, "flying saucers," "life after death," "the value of a liberal education," "the dangers of television," "the value of the Greek system," "astrology and life," "the effect of smog on Los Angeles," "the value of intercollegiate athletics," "the relevance of Jesus Christ." Even complex, controversial issues can become Bigfoot issues in the classroom: abortion, sex education, legalizing marijuana, bilingual education, the disintegration of the American family, nuclear war, acid rain, and saving the whales.

Such issues are often complex—and often more important than Bigfoot—but in writing classes, they generate limited options, predictable outcomes, and easy generalizations.[14] Flying saucers probably exist unless they don't exist no matter how much students read about them. Marijuana should be legalized because it's no worse than alcohol unless we see it as different from alcohol and not addictive, unless, of course, we believe those who think it's just bad for you. Everyone is either for or against the Greek system except those who see it as both good and bad. Everyone is for a liberal education. Sex exists and we ought to do something about it. And everything ever written about abortion leads to the general conclusion that abortion is a debatable issue hinging on women's rights and the rights of the fetus and the ability to just say no. (The fact that such topics generate obvious angles and recycled discussions is bad enough, but we can't even make fun of the most interesting of them without alienating somebody or looking stupid, unsympathetic, insensitive, or uninvolved. Just listing them here, I risk making somebody mad at me about something.)

For more examples of assignments, take a look at appendixes 2 and 3. While assignment content is important, more important is the way we use assignments in a teaching context. In the next chapter, we'll take a closer look at that context and try to pull a few loose strands together. At that time we can try to clarify the relationship between assignment making and larger issues of feedback and evaluation.

•••••••

Notes

1. William Carlos Williams, *Kora in Hell: Improvisations* (San Francisco: City Lights Books, 1967. Original copyright 1920, 1957) 39–40.

2. For more information about Mr. Dooley and Finley Peter Dunne, his creator, see *The World of Mr. Dooley,* ed. Louis Filler (New York: Collier, 1962).

3. I have no idea who Josiah McIntosh is. I made him up.

4. Actually one of the best collections—that is, one of the most *usable* collections—of student writing could be Leonora Woodman and C. Beth Burch's *Students Write: A Collection of Essays* (Glenview, IL: Scott, Foresman, 1986). It's the only one I know that's full of the sort of student writing that students like mine write.

5. Elbert Hubbard, *The Notebook of Elbert Hubbard: Mottoes, Epigrams, Short Essays, Passages, Orphic Sayings and Preachments* (New York: William H. Wise, 1927) 173.

6. She's not real, although she's modeled after one of my mother's next-door neighbors in Denver, Colorado.

7. If you're interested in Julia A. Moore, the "Sweet Singer of Michigan," check out *The Sweet Singer of Michigan* (Chicago: Pascal Covici, 1928). In the introduction to her last book, Moore wrote, "All of you which peruse my work will find a great many things in this book to please you, especially the words I have took the time to say to the public. If all books could be read as I am sure you love to read this one, there might be less ignorance and crime in the world, and I would be well paid for the valuable time I have spent in doing good to mankind" (xxvii).

8. The second was written by Julia A. Moore, the Sweet Singer of Michigan (1928, xxii).

9. As I emphasize later on, this is, of course, not all bad. But I always worry about arguments about "relevance"—especially if they lead toward "nonacademic" thinking or doing things that are more "fun."

10. If we give longer assignments, we may need to direct students more. See the discussion at the end of this chapter on longer assignments.

11. Steve Martin, *Cruel Shoes* (New York: Putnam's Sons, 1979) 103.

12. I made Fobbs up myself.

13. I've included some examples of longer assignments in appendix 3.

14. I'm not suggesting that any of these issues are unimportant or simple. I am, however, suggesting that in students' minds, such topics often suggest very limited, even frozen, lines of argument, and the real problems become unfortunately simpleminded and academically trivialized.

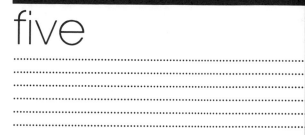

five

Assignments, Grades, and Evaluations

• • • • • • • • • • • • • • • • • • •

This chapter is about the relationship between what we ask for, what we think we ask for, what students think we ask for, what students write, what we think students write, how we know what students think about what they write, how they know what we think about what they think about what they write, how we "grade" what students write, and how we evaluate what they write. Even more important, this chapter is about trying to help students distinguish the relationship between structure and freedom: How we can structure our assignments and feedback to get what we want yet help students to understand that what we want has something to do with thinking and awareness—not right answers or formulas; how we can help students to understand that structure and control can give the freedom to say and do things that they might not be able to say or do if they were totally free to say or do whatever they wanted in whatever way they wanted.

General Observations

More Assignments Can Lead to Better Evaluation
In saying that, I don't assume that everyone is going to assign as many papers as I assign, but we should constantly be aware that beginning writers need to practice—probably much more than they usually get in a typical writing class. Assignments are opportunities for them to see

what they can do—occasions to try out their learning on new contents and new problems—and get feedback on how well they experiment with new techniques or designs; how well they approach new ideas, new subjects, new problems; or how well they manage their time, organize their lives, study, cope, rationalize, procrastinate, or try to make do.

Even more important, students who are not particularly good writers sometimes take a long time to begin to do simple things well and to think about writing as more than a set of procedures to do things correctly. I know many teachers, for instance, who think the idea of a thesis statement is simple, but I've had students who have written sixteen or seventeen one-page papers before they've finally understood that a thesis statement is more than a mechanical tool that teachers look for at the beginning of a paper—and I've known some who have taken four more years to become even somewhat proficient at formulating thesis statements that they could develop in four or five pages.

I might also add that the more assignments we can give, the less any one effort counts, and the less any one effort counts, the more likely students will feel free to experiment and make mistakes without risking bad grades or failure. Learning to think like a writer takes such freedom—especially when we're trying to teach students to risk giving up things they've learned before.

If We Intend to "Grade" Students, We Should Do So Using Clearly Articulated Criteria

We should do everything we can to take the mystery out of grading. Students should know what we are looking for, how we will "score" what we are looking for, and what they should be able to negotiate.

Certainly, we should always type our directions and hand them out to students so that they know what we want them to do. But we should also make sure that students understand the criteria we'll use to grade their efforts:

Warm-Up Paper #1
Due: Thursday
Write a one-page paper in which you say something intelligent about the following quotation by Bill Nye:

> I am convinced that there is great economy in keeping hens if we have sufficient room for them and a thorough knowledge of how to manage the fowl property [*sic*]. But to the professional man, who is not familiar with the habits of the hen, and whose mind does not naturally and instinctively turn henward, I would say, Shun her as you would the deadly upas tree of Piscataquis county, Me.

Do not assume that I understand the ideas here or read them just like you do. Format: For this paper (and all other one-page papers) type or neatly print your name, the date, your section number, and your paper number in the lower right-hand corner of the BACK side of your paper. Do not use a coversheet. Use a title. (Don't handwrite that title in at the last minute before you turn it in.) Double space. Set up one-inch margins.

Criteria

- You will lose points (out of 25) only as follows:
- −7 for each typo/spelling error.
- −5 for each error in following directions.
- −5 for each unclear or fuzzy sentence (unless you mark it with * and explain your fears). (If you have real worries, see me after class or during office hours.)
- +3 for a magnificent infelicity (if you mark it with a + in the margin and explain why you think it is so magnificent.)

By listing such criteria at the end of this assignment, we can assure students that we will be reasonable and fair. Here, we can't take off points for weak thesis statements, poor cohesion, unacceptable ideas, or imperfectly executed plans. We can, of course, give students feedback on their thesis statements, poor cohesion, and weak designs, but according to these criteria, *we can't penalize them for such things*. And this is crucial: by specifying what we will take off points for, students know how much freedom they have. (They also know how much room they have to experiment with their ideas, their strategies, and their language.)

Stating our criteria, of course, doesn't ensure that students will understand them. We can do our best to clarify such criteria in class, but we can also make clear to students that they themselves are responsible for understanding the criteria that we use and holding us to them. If they don't know what a "magnificent infelicity" or a "fuzzy sentence" is (and they probably don't), they ought to raise their hands in class and question whether we can recognize a "magnificent infelicity" from a "fuzzy sentence." (I doubt it.) I am not always sure I can tell the difference—and I'm perfectly willing to admit that such decisions are *always negotiable*. In fact, by building into our criteria occasions for students to challenge and negotiate, we begin to teach students to ask questions and look out for themselves. Grading, after all, has to be more than a matter of faith in our fine taste and good will—it has to be part of an agreement between students and their teachers, and agreement requires mutual understanding and consent.

I might point out that some teachers are skeptical of using grading systems that require teachers to tally up numbers like accountants and enter them into spreadsheets. Some even suggest that there is something wrong with negative systems where you take off points rather than give points, and that you can quickly end up with negative scores, depending on how ruthless you want to be. These are legitimate worries, but every system has its trade-offs. In my own experience, it doesn't matter if we take points off or give points back to students—what's important is whether we're consistent and fair.[1] Furthermore, even though we list these criteria, we don't have to be overzealous in applying them. We can find ways to flunk students if we want to. There's no end to the ways we can be unfair. But the way we apply our criteria will say something to students about the way we will treat them as learners and students. We don't have to give negative scores or take off spelling points for ticky-tacky spelling problems or words that don't appear in typical computer spelling checkers. We don't have to take off points each time a student makes the same error. We don't have to take off points for poorly formed sentences that only English teachers find poorly formed. And we don't need to penalize students who have major perceptual handicaps that already inhibit their efforts and make them look more inefficient and less conscientious than they are. And we can *always* give back points if students ask questions or try to negotiate with us.[2]

Later assignments might look similar, but we can modify our criteria from assignment to assignment to fit our instructional goals. Criteria for the third paper of the semester might look like this:

Criteria

- −5 for each spello/typo.
- −5 for not following directions.
- −5 for unclear sentences (unless you mark them and say something about them).
- −5 for an unclear or strangely incoherent THESIS STATEMENT.
- −10 for simply telling a story.

Students who have trouble dealing with difficult assignments often fall back on storytelling when everything else fails: instead of explaining the information that I give them to work with, and formulating arguments using that information, they want to tell me a "story" about the information and imply their arguments. Sometimes, they even insert imaginary characters or make up imaginary circumstances. We'll discuss problems in class and by the third assignment, I'll begin to discourage such strategies and encourage students to explore their options.[3]

By the ninth paper, the criteria might look like this:

Criteria

- −5 for not following directions.
- −5 for an unclear or strangely incoherent thesis statement.
- −5 for overblown or cosmic introduction.
- −3 for a weak or nonexistent topic sentence where a strong one is needed.
- −3 for each unclear sentence (unless you mark it and say something about it).
- −3 for each typo/spello.
- −2 for missing apostrophes.
- −1 for a weak title.
- −5 for failure to show that you understand what Bill Nye says.

By the thirteenth and fourteenth papers, the directions and criteria might look like this:

As you write your paper, try to *imitate* at least two sentences from the following passage by Joan Didion. I don't care if the sentences fit well and I don't care if you even use some of her own words. I just want you to see what happens. Mark these with * in the margin.

Criteria

- −5 for not following directions.
- −5 for an unclear or strangely incoherent thesis statement.
- −5 for an overblown or cosmic introduction.
- −2 for a weak or nonexistent topic sentence where a strong one is needed.
- −2 for each unclear sentence (unless you mark it and say something about it).
- −2 for each typo/spello.
- −2 for missing apostrophes.
- −1 for a weak title.

As students get better and as the semester continues, we can assign longer papers with increasingly complex criteria:

Four-Page Paper #2

Rough Draft Due: Tuesday
Final Draft Due: Thursday
Here are two passages from John Ruskin's introduction to *The Harbours of England* (in Volume XIII of *The Works of John Ruskin,* edited by E. T. Cooks

and A. Wedderburn [New York: Longmans, 1907], pages 13–16, 24–25). Read through this material and see if you can explain why a person like Wilmar Shufflestone could read this same material and decide to enter the shipping business, become a salvage operator, and ultimately become a major entrepreneur and swindler of insurance companies on the Great Lakes.

From here on out, start putting your names in the upper right-hand corner of your papers with dates, etc. (Type these in—don't handwrite them.) For this assignment, don't use forms of *you*. Don't simply tell a story. Back everything you say with facts, evidence, proof, explanation, and logic that cut to the heart of things. Never assume that I read anything the same way you do. Don't let your quotations float. Don't quote unless you can't get out of it. (Paraphrase but let me know you're paraphrasing with in-text documentation.)

Criteria .

Out of 100 points, you'll lose points as follows:

- −5 for not bringing in a rough draft on Tuesday.
- −10 for a missing or unclear thesis statement.
- −10 for not following directions.
- −5 for a weak introduction or conclusion.
- −5 for not using clear, relevant examples, illustrations.
- −5 for each case of lazy reading.
- −3 for pronoun problems, problems of agreement, apostrophes, spelling, unclear sentences.
- −2 for a weak or useless title.
- −5 for each case of poor documentation.
- −15 for simply telling a story.
- −965 for telling a simply awful story.
  [Note: I will give you 5 extra points for a joke, if you can work it in smoothly and efficiently. Mark this joke with $$ in the margin.]

Students know I won't take off 965 points for telling a "simply awful story," but they also know that I don't like to read awful stories and that's worth reminding them.

Grading and Evaluation

Setting up clear grading criteria in our assignments also gives us a way to make clear the distinction between grading and evaluation. Grades should indicate student accomplishment, effort, participation, and success in meeting course goals. Ideally, grades measure final outcomes—students succeed or fail to meet course objectives; they succeed or fail to meet criteria on assignments. We put grades on students' papers based on criteria for student progress or learning; we record those grades in our grade books; eventually, we fiddle with those grades and put something on a final grade sheet at the end of the semester.

On the other hand, we evaluate students' papers by giving students feedback on their strengths, weaknesses, and *progress*—feedback that will help students to evaluate for themselves what they are doing, set their own goals, and negotiate with us if they don't understand us or don't think we are right or reasonable. Pedagogically, it doesn't matter whether students write "perfect" papers or not—or even whether they consistently earn all the points on a given assignment; what matters is whether students understand and accept suggestions for changing or modifying their writing strategies.

While grading and evaluation are both important (grading considerably less so than evaluation), we ought to separate them. If we don't, our feedback almost automatically becomes muddled and counterproductive. We praise students for their understanding, creativity, and inventiveness, and we encourage them to continue learning, trying things out in the future, and setting up simple, achievable goals—but we give them *C*'s because their experiments fail, they haven't found a good idea yet, or haven't apparently thought enough about the mysteries of life or discovered writing strategies that aren't boring and obvious. We ask students to feel good about how much they are learning and how well they've done so far, and then we grade them on an absolute scale of goodness that may or may not have anything to do with what they've just learned.

On the other hand, if we separate grading from evaluation, we can write all over students' papers and up and down the margins. We can use red ink or green ink or blue-green ink. We can even say such things as these if we want to:

- You're awfully careful, aren't you? (Looks like you're afraid to be wrong, huh?)
- Your idea is full of baloney, and you don't pull it off yet—but I like the risk you took.
- Why not begin with your main point? Why make me wait around and drink water?
- OK, but not very risky.
- Where'd you get that idea? From TV?

- This is good, and I can give you bonus points for your imagination. But if you quote "Webster" one more time, I think I'll throw up.
- How come you don't try for those bonus points? We'll get to thesis statements by next week, but for right now, think about that conclusion you got—why not move it up to the first paragraph?
- How come you never asked me in class what a "upas" tree is?
- Hey, did someone teach you to live and die in five paragraphs? (Sure looks stiff, doesn't it?)

If we stick to our criteria and our criteria say nothing about taste, creativity, pizzazz, good ideas, or fun, students won't start worrying about having taste, right answers, pizzazz, good ideas, "right" approaches, or vision. We can comment on anything that strikes us as interesting, funny, helpful, disappointing, or regrettable, and students won't have to worry about whether such comments will affect their "grades." They won't start going to the library to find good secondary sources to make points they should be making themselves or points they think we want them to make. They won't worry so much about trying new ideas out, being wrongheaded, or being different.

Ultimately, students will risk more, ask us more questions, demand more explanations, seek us out and argue with us, and we ourselves will begin to think about our students and assignments differently. Instead of viewing assignments as occasions where students must show direct mastery, where they must do more things right than wrong, and where we grade them by weighing all their mistakes against all their successes on an absolute scale, we begin to view assignments as *experiments* and occasions for students to make mistakes, to try things out as they *gradually* learn some things about writing over a period of time, perhaps even semesters or years. And we begin to recognize good students as those who progress, change, learn from their mistakes, question our every move, challenge our conclusions, see things they've never seen before—and do many things right, even while they may continue to do many things wrong.

Evaluation

Even though we can separate grading and evaluation, we ought to keep in mind that evaluation itself requires separate considerations:

Some People Appear to Get Worse Before They Get Better

One reason English teachers sometimes hate to look at student "academic" writing and call it "Engfish" or "Black Rot" may be because they see in it all the badness; the stiff, thoughtless sentences; the cramped writing; the mediocre ideas—but they may not see all the successes, all the possibilities that the badness sometimes overshadows and camouflages.

Mistakes aren't necessarily signs of weakness or failure to learn. We can work on organization and thesis statements, semicolons, and comma splices, and students will seem to figure those out, but their writing may become progressively stiffer, less free, more controlled, and suddenly, they may be using semicolons where they never used them before; and shouldn't ever; again! And they're making sentence fragments. Where they used to only make comma splices.

As learners, we all go through periods where we lurch forward in ungraceful ways before we smooth things out and polish up our acts (if we ever polish up our acts). Anyone who has tried to learn anything has experienced the hesitations of the untrained—the overcompensations and overgeneralizations our bodies and minds make as we try to place our feet out there where everyone can see them while we move our knees, and smile and bow and do things we've never tried to do in public before, all the time worrying whether we've "smashed our rabbits," sucked water up our noses, guttered the ball, ridden the clutch, or made fools out of ourselves and looked like beginners, even though, of course, we looked like beginners.

We should accept learning for what it is: a messy, sloppy, sometimes uncontrollable process where people do things wrong in all the ways people can do things wrong even while they start doing things right.

Students Learn to Do Best Those Things We Can Demonstrate

We may like to talk about vague things like "feel," "timing," or "creativity." We may like to emphasize "goodness" and "diction" and "cliché" and "the boring." But we ought to be careful. We can probably *talk* about such things, but we'll have a hard time getting students to improve them and to change their own behaviors—at least in thirteen weeks.

We can, for instance, tell students that "one fell swoop" is a cliché, or we can point out errors in diction or word choice. (It's wrong to say "If I was" if you mean "If I *were*.") But even though we supply students with long lists of clichés or lists of taboo sentence openers or trite phrases, such feedback is small compared to the task involved. I doubt many of us know how we learned that "one fell swoop" wasn't a top-drawer phrase. And learning that "one fell swoop" is a tired phrase doesn't help students to learn that they ought to be careful using "one day at a time," "honesty is the best policy," and "awesome" instead of "good." Likewise, we can point out the problems students face when they use too much jargon, but we probably have no simple way to help them to recognize jargon in general.

The More We Expect, the More We Have to Set Priorities

Some people will tell us not to comment on everything and not to make students' papers "bleed." But the problem may not be bloody papers. I use red ink all the time, and I write all over my students' papers—even between the lines and often on the back. But if we want to write all over students' papers, we have to give them a way to sort through our comments—to weigh and evaluate them.

Someplace—perhaps on a cover sheet or in a clean space at the end—we need to consolidate our explanations, to weigh and evaluate them, and to tell students what to work on first:

- This is OK, but before you begin to fiddle with everything, think about working on that thesis statement. (If you do, some of the small problems might just go away.)
- Hey. Your spelling is a bore, but you can fix most of that by using your spelling checker. But at this stage, you ought to begin to worry about . . .
- This looks like a lot to work on—but concentrate on:

  1. Nailing down your introduction. (What's your point, anyway?)
  2. Thinking about one idea. (Here, you want to do too much—maybe because you're too ambitious?)

  Don't worry about the rest for right now. We haven't covered some of those things in class yet, anyway. (Just keep them in the back of your mind for a couple of weeks.)

If you want, you can give students a description of your own priorities:

How to Interpret the Comments I Make on Your Papers

I will always write many things on your papers. Sometimes you will have trouble sorting through them. (If you do, come see me.) As a general rule, however, think about solving your problems in the following order:

1. Always work on organization, thesis statement, and setting up your problem. (No matter what you do, no matter how bad your sentences are, and no matter how hard you work on your grammar and spelling and style, you will still get *C*'s and lower from other teachers on campus if you don't set things up clearly and directly with clear thesis state- ments and clear main points.) (Sometimes you will luck out, but I'm not interested in luck.)
2. Concentrate on your transitions. The more you practice setting up clear signals when you move from one point to another, the better your papers get. The more clearly you highlight your main points, the better your points have to be.
3. Think about the quality of your evidence and amount of your evidence.
4. Deal with matters of style, syntax, spelling, etc. Never labor over one sentence to get everything "exactly right." Sentence errors may be the most highly visible and create the most exasperating problems, but they are also the hardest to fix—and, in the long run, they will probably matter only after you begin to get success in getting your readers to think about what you want to say.

Many Students Don't Learn Anything Difficult the First (or Second) Time Around

We should never assume that students see things the same way we ourselves do. If people learned things quickly, if they always listened to their teachers, we would all be out of jobs. Teaching is often full of repetition. We keep reminding. We keep restating things differently. We keep on giving examples. We keep writing priorities in the margins of students' papers. Sooner or later, students begin to see the patterns in our repetitions, the sense of urgency in our restatements. They learn that we don't see things the same ways they do, that sometimes the most obvious things are not obvious, that it's always easier to understand something if you already understand it.

Evaluation and Rewriting

Students don't always revise or rewrite like we do. Or like professional writers do. Or like their parents would do if they had a chance to become undergraduates again. Many students don't have much time to revise. I know some who are trying to work on their writing while taking sixteen hours of math, science, history, and sociology and working part-time, rehearsing for a campus drama production, going through fraternity or sorority rush, trying out for the school soccer team, and playing intramural flag football. Some are even getting drunk on weekends and doing other things I'd rather not know about. And marginal students— the ones who need the most time—usually have even less time than others because they're often studying harder in all their courses, always trying to catch up, meeting with tutors, talking to teachers, doing their reading, or sleeping off their frustrations.

Many students don't revise because their ideas aren't good or they *think* their ideas aren't good. Many have never been empowered to speak with "authority" and therefore see their writing as a way to keep their teachers off their backs, to "get by," to make as few waves as possible and hope they don't get in too much trouble for not cowering enough within the margins.

But they often cower. And while they cower, they relinquish all claim to good ideas and often feel bad about themselves and their helplessness. When we tell them they ought to rewrite something, they apologize or scramble for excuses, saying things like "I know it isn't very good, but . . . but I just couldn't get the hang of it" or "I feel sick and I don't know when I'll recover or if I'll just die" or "I don't know if I'll have access to my roommate's computer tonight . . . she's studying with her boyfriend" or "I was up all last night talking to my friend about his parents' divorce" or "Oh, you know, I have to be in the right mood" or "I hate that paper so much I don't even want to see it under my neighbor's duck."

I still have papers of my own from my freshman year—a year full of frustrations and experiences—including painfully regrettable experiences revising. One paper on April 9, 1964, says in large print, "REVISE!" The next week, I find "REVISIONS N.G." written across the top of the next paper. By Thursday, May 21, my teacher was still saying "REVISIONS N.G." And hell, I didn't want to revise that paper on *King Lear*—and I'm not sure I ever did. (At least I didn't save the revision.) I suppose during that year, I didn't revise or fix anything well. I don't suppose I learned anything about revision, either, until I got older and had more time to find good ideas to revise and had more time to take my own revising, expertise, and play seriously.

This last point is worth exploring more. Students often revise because their teachers say to revise—and they often have no clear idea what their revisions should accomplish. If we think students ought to revise something, then we ought to be able to show them (1) that their revisions are *possible* given the amount of information they have or the knowledge they possess, (2) that their revisions will be worth making, and (3) that they will *learn* something about writing by revising. If, for instance, a student writes something like the following, we ought to be able to show him or her how it might look revised:

Reaction

The poem "Swineherds" serves as a reminder to me that it's important to read poetry more than once to fully understand it. On one of the first readings, the poem is usually interpreted and the reader reacts to the poem. Upon further readings, both the interpretation and the reaction may change. In this poem, or me, the interpretation stayed the same but my reactions differed upon further readings.

My interpretation of the poem is fairly simple and straightforward. It is that not everyone can be a leader; some have to be followers, "We can't all be swine-herds, some have to be swine" and that people are given a station in life and one must accept their position and not complain about it. "There's noises to make and we shouldn't just pine/when the task we must do is so clear."

Now, that I understand the poem, I was able to react to it. On the first reading of the poem, I felt outraged that someone almost demanded that people stay in their "place" and never try to achieve more, "If you can't be an ox-herd, then just be the ox." Once people stop trying to better themselves, they stop learning which to me is equivalent to dying. A world in which everyone is dead is not too appealing.

On my second reading and as I thought about the poem more, I came across another reaction or thought, one of almost acceptance. Without some conformity and acceptance of place, the world would be a chaotic mess with everyone trying to get ahead of the other. This vision of the world seemed only a little better than that in which everyone has stopped trying.

As I continued to think about the poem, I began to realize that there was no real "pat" way to act. People themselves are different, some content in their position and others dying to change.

This student is writing an initial "warm-up" paper on the following short poem by Danny Reynolds:

> We can't all be swineherds, some have to be swine
> There's something for all of us here.
> There's noises to make and we shouldn't just pine
> When the task we must do is so clear.
>
> If you can't be an Ox-herd, then just be an ox,
> If you can't be a board, be a splinter;
> It isn't by size that you win your new sox,
> Be the best for what you're inter.

And there are obvious problems here. The student doesn't deal well with the negative notion that people ought to be beasts of burden or even nonhuman (splinters). Furthermore, he tells us that the author of the poem (who is never named) says that we should "never try to achieve more"—which is probably a misreading. (Reynolds never says anything about "achieving.")

These are problems of interpretation, and we could focus on them in some detail, yet the main problem here is probably organizational: the student tells a little story of discovery. This is a common student strategy—one that often begins, "When I first read . . ." and ends, "but when I looked again . . ." It's related to plot summary and the all-purpose chronological "discovery" approach to any text that's hard to understand: "How I read whatever I read and what I learned along the way."

Even though we often tell students not to tell stories, they often don't understand the difference between what they've done and what they might have done. Here, they may understand what we're saying but not agree, and we may need to give them even more direct feedback by rewriting things ourselves:

Rewrite of "Reaction"

"Swineherds" is straightforward: not everyone can be a leader; some have to be followers. Reynolds says, "We can't all be swineherds, some have to be swine" and suggests that people have to accept their stations in life. ("There's noises to make and we shouldn't just pine/when the task we must do is so clear.") To any moderately liberal reader, this view, of course, appears simpleminded. The view is, however, difficult to attack. To attack it, we need some reasonable alternatives; without alternatives, all we can expect is some compromise.

Most ambitious people are outraged that someone can suggest that people ought to stay in their places and never try to achieve more—that it is somehow good enough just being "the ox." [EXPAND WITH EXAMPLES.] Once people stop trying to better themselves, they stop learning and begin to die.

Yet while we might be outraged, what are the alternatives? Without some conformity and acceptance of place, the world would be a chaotic mess with everyone trying to get ahead of the other. [EXPAND WITH EXAMPLES.] This vision of the world seems only a little better than a dead world of swine.

Somewhere, then, we may need to accept a compromise—part swine, part swineherd. For even though we must have the spirit and energy to reach our potential, we must also accept those restraints that come from being part of a herd.

Such a revision isn't fair and was never meant to be. I've changed the vocabulary and even changed the focus of the conclusion. I haven't even tried to address the student's misreading—something we can talk about in class. Instead, I've concentrated on showing that there are powerful ways other than chronological to organize papers. In this case, I want to illustrate that a logical structure can make it easy to include examples and illustrations and explanations; in contrast, chronological arguments are harder to keep simple and direct and lend themselves to less efficient, implied, or indirect arguments.

In doing this rewrite, I can give students feedback about their writing strategies and on rewriting in general: we rewrite to shape arguments better, to make our cases stronger; we don't rewrite just because we're supposed to rewrite. Furthermore, I can show by example that rewriting isn't a chore that we use to force students to do more work. I take every opportunity I can to convince students that some teachers like me write even when they're not contractually obligated to do so.

Here's another student example in response to the following quotation by Martha Wolfenstein:

A recent development in American culture is the emergence of what we may call "fun morality." Here fun, from having been suspect if not taboo, has tended to become obligatory. Instead of feeling guilty for having too much fun, one is inclined to feel ashamed if one does not have enough. Boundaries formerly maintained between play and work break down. Amusements infiltrate into the sphere of work, while in play self-estimates of achievement become prominent. This development appears to be at marked variance with an older, puritan ethic, although as we shall see the two are related.

Fun: Something that Provides Amusement or Enjoyment

Wolfenstein's observation is that American perceptions of fun are changing. Previously considered unvirtuous, "fun has tended to become obligatory." Rather than causing post-party embarrassment, a lamp shade is now a mark of true achievement. This new perception of fun has a certain irony: if we go to great pains to have fun, then doesn't that take the fun out of fun? The implications of such an irony are that work and play become one and the same. We strive to incorporate fun into our work, and we work to have fun when we play. The reason such a merge is bad is because it takes the spontaneity out of "real fun."

The idea of working for fun is totally uninspiring. Fun should be inspiring, it should also be relatively easy. It should be, well, fun. Take family vacations as an example. I, for one, never *really* enjoy them. The reason is that they are too planned out—not to mention the endless stops to see roadside monuments of pioneers and missionaries. Cocktail parties aren't terribly fun, either. So much frustration over hors d'oeuvres just so a bunch of nicely dressed people can stand around and make "small talk." Boring. Some people think exercise is fun. Sorry, but sweating and flailing one's arms around in order to reach one's desired heart rate is not my idea of fun.

Working hard for fun is a contradiction in terms. Fun should be . . . fun (i.e., it shouldn't require too much effort.) Lying on the beach is fun. A hike in the woods is fun. A good meal out is fun. Wolfenstein makes an excellent observation about the confusion between work and play. If we work too hard to play, then we aren't playing.

This student does many good things. I like the way she plays with style, and I'm happy with her obvious attempt to add examples. Still, her examples are generic and safe, and I would push her to be more specific—even unsafe. Since I can't get in her head and rummage around for examples I know she would use, I can't rewrite things the way she would—but I can rewrite using my own unsafe examples:

Rewrite of "Fun: Something that Provides Amusement and Enjoyment"

Wolfenstein observes that American perceptions of fun are changing. She says that "fun" has become "obligatory." If Wolfenstein is right, this new perception of fun has a certain irony: if we go to great pains to have fun, then maybe we don't have fun after all.

Imagine how much Fun we're supposed to have driving across the country on a fun family outing! Maybe down the turnpike to . . . to . . . PHUNNNN Salt Lake City with maybe a small fun stop at fun Pocatello for a late lunch on Yellowstone Avenue in the fun afternoon heat if we don't take too long eating our fun cold sandwiches out of the fun cooler someplace overlooking the fun Snake River. And when we get off our funnnn schedule, we can take a lot of phuhhn pictures real fun fast—and maybe compare fun notes when we get home about what we saw when we drove past fun Mountain Home. And Twin Falls.

(Looky way off down there . . . see? You can just make out those itty bitty falls with his magnifying glass. . . . Wasn't that FUN? Didn't we enjoy that ride when the cooler leaked all over the backseat and we lost the dog out in that desert?)

And if we don't have all that much FUNN with our funn families, then we ought to go to our fffunnn family therapist who'll help us straighten out the ugly wrinkles in our morbid, depressed, and burnt-out psyches. And maybe he'll help us find ourselves on the job, too—maybe working for some funnn Factory building fun American products like grease guns or hubcaps or insulated copper wire for fun-loving folk in fun Waco, Texas, or in Winnemucca, Nevada, or Gary, Indiana. Imagine the FUN we should have sweating away with no idea in Hell how much FuNNN they SHOULD HAVE if they maybe jogged more in some fun New Balance sneakers or wore fun paper hats at work or joined a fun bridge group or learned how to collect stamps or went to Cocktail parties!

It helps to know about Fun hors d'oeuvres and the joy in little sandwiches cut out like little clovers.

But it probably helps most if we can kill the obligation—and maybe buy out of that part of our culture that has bought into fun as a fast fix for frustration.

Sure, this rewrite isn't completely successful. For one thing, I get tired of all that play on the word *fun*—it was phfun while I was doing it, but the overkill doesn't stay fresh enough. I'm also not sure what the repeated changes in spelling are supposed to do. And I haven't completely succeeded in making things better by concentrating on making things more concrete. Certainly some of it seems better—especially the beginning and the end—but the rewrite of the middle paragraph in the student's original draft probably isn't an improvement.

But we can talk about my failures. Sometimes rewrites are not better than the original, and we should all keep reminding ourselves that. Even more important, my failures are *different* from my student's failures. While she fails because she picks safe examples, I fail because I try to risk more—and if nothing else, I can suggest by example that it's all right to risk more, to stretch things too far and see what happens.

Few of us try such overwriting in front of students, conditioned as we are to be expert academics and masters of careful, thoughtful prose, but I'm going to do it all the time. Here's another example, this paragraph full of nice, one-line generalizations:

Consider, that every day the population is increasing and with this population increase there is a directly proportional garbage increase. This means that when the population reaches a point where the whole world is covered by people, it will at the same time be covered with garbage. This could be where Katie Kelly got her idea that the world will someday be lost under an immense pile of garbage.

This is not too good, not too bad. The first sentence is a safe observation in the same spirit as "The more trees there are, the more leaves there are" or "The more times Reggie Jackson goes to bat, the more times he strikes out." The second sentence is a restatement of the first in a more dramatic fashion. (I like the second sentence—especially the slight difference between the two uses of the word *covered.*) The final sentence sets up an obvious cause-and-effect relationship: If Katie Kelly thought about all the people covering the world in garbage, she could have gotten alarmed and gotten an idea for her book about all the people covering the world in garbage.

But what annoys me most is that this student doesn't get into the spirit of things. Here's Katie Kelly gleefully covering the world in garbage and asking, "If today we are still searching for the mythic civilization of Atlantis, will future generations seek fruitlessly for twentieth-century America?" and a student who asks, "I wonder where Katie Kelly came up with that idea?"

So what do we do when we get students who insist on asking simple questions, who try to ignore the fun Katie Kelly must have had sinking America under mountains and mountains of trash? We can try to jump right in and look at some of that garbage and maybe have some fun, too:

Rewrite

Every day, the population grows—new little fat babies bawling their demands, soiling millions of Johnson and Johnson disposable diapers, drinking milk from disposable plastic milk bottles with disposable rubber tits, eating disposable food from disposable paper cartons (microwave safe) safety-sealed with disposable aluminum-coated paper, drooling disposable drool (mopped up by disposable Handiwipes and thrown into disposable plastic garbage bags with disposable twist ties. Arggggghhhhhh. When this population of new little fat babies reaches adulthood, when its numbers cover the whole world armpit to armpit to armpit, these now little fat adults will cover the world in new, humongous piles of garbage, their back yards and front yards now paved in more disposable diapers than we can even imagine (now for their own new little fat babies), their own nonreturn plastic bags from K-Mart, McDonald's burger boxes and disposable twin-bladed, Teflon-coated Bic razors and five-pound turds from disposable Irish wolfhounds and disposable Christmas trees for disposable Christmases (complete with the usual tasteless gifts wrapped in their disposable metallic wrapping paper, disposable bows from disposable yellow plastic bow-makers once packed in disposable shrinkwrapped, easy-peel packages).

And by then, cursing our children who now think we, too, are ugly and disposable, buried up to our crotches in the rubble of life, we won't have to worry where Katie Kelly got *her* idea.

Buried somewhat unrecognizably under a large heap of its own garbage, this piece also fails as an example of excellent rewriting. But as a *teaching device,* it can be more useful than a more controlled, safer rewrite. As a matter of fact, I wrote this one with a considerable amount of pleasure and zeal, and although there's too much here and it's too messy, I like some of the ideas—especially the idea of disposable pets and people. I worked too hard and played around too much—but such failure is worth talking about, especially with students who don't like to risk much.

Evaluation and Our Own Writing

It's not enough to bring in an occasional essay we've written on an academic topic. We have to show students what we'd do on the same subjects they themselves are writing on. If we are serious that writing is discovery and that our assignments are valuable in any way, then we should discover something by writing our own assignments and be able to talk about our own efforts in class.

This doesn't mean that we have to do every assignment we give students, but we should be able to show them what goals we would set for ourselves and how we would go about accomplishing them. Without such feedback, students can't judge what we expect from them or what we value in our own writing. Furthermore, we should continue to show them that we can take criticism and encourage criticism, that we can learn something about our own writing when other people—including students—read it and comment on it. Writing papers ourselves doesn't mean we have to slave away and turn in masterpieces of professorial prose. We ought to be content to turn in half-finished, sometimes rough, first drafts. To make it more fair we can limit ourselves to about an hour for one-page assignments and a couple of hours for four-page assignments. We can crank them out on our computers, spell-check them, and dump them out. Sometimes we can talk about these pieces in class; or we can just pass them out when students pass in their own papers or read them out loud in class right along with everybody else.

Here, for instance, is an assignment on smell:

One-Page Paper #9

Here are some facts taken from chapter 9 of Ruth Winter's *The Smell Book: Scents, Sex and Society* (Philadelphia: J. B. Lippincott, 1976):

1. Japanese perfume things they use in daily life; they even play smell games with friends.
2. Orientals enjoy heavy, spicy, animal fragrances.
3. Mediterraneans like sophisticated, floral fragrances.
4. Ten-year-olds like the smell of chlorophyll.
5. Men in their prime like the smells of musk and orange.
6. Girls between eight and fourteen like naphthalene.
7. Children don't like flower smells as much as adults do.
8. Smart children like the same smells that adults do.
9. Adults don't like to smell strawberry essence.
10. Men like the smell of wild roses more than women do.
11. Men like musk ambrette more than women do.
12. Before they are five, most children think nothing smells.
13. Introverts don't like flowery smells.
14. Women like to smell bay leaf more than men do.
15. Orientals like the root extract valerian; Europeans don't.
16. Introverted Americans like to smell camphor.
17. Northern Europeans like heavy fragrances.
18. Camphor keeps away worms that eat bamboo.
19. Before they are eight, boys and girls like strawberry essence.
20. Boys like vanilla before they are eight years old.
21. Fifteen- to nineteen-year-old men like to smell lavender.
22. Women in their prime enjoy almond and lavender.
23. Men, more than women, like fruity smells.
24. Women like to smell alcohol more than men do.
25. Men like to smell mock orange more than women do.
26. Girls like almond essence (if they are under eight).
27. Boys between eight and fourteen like musk lactone, which has sexual associations.
28. Fifteen- to nineteen-year-old women like to smell naphthalene.
29. Men like lemon grass more than women do.
30. Women like onion more than men do.
31. Extroverts often like the same smells children do.
32. Women like almond essence more than men do.

In a one-page, solid, organized paper, make the most of this information. Don't write a story. Don't use "you."

Criteria

- −5 for a weak or nonexistent thesis statement, weak introduction or conclusion.
- −5 for not following directions.
- −3 for each weak point—one that needs better examples, support, or explanation.
- −3 for each spello/typo.
- −3 for each error in agreement, pronoun reference.
- −3 for each apostrophe problem.
- −3 for each unclear, grammatically questionable sentence. (Unless you mark it and comment on it.)
- −1 for a weak title.

This assignment is a typical one that requires students to clump and group information—perhaps even use labels for categories. Students recognize this as an exercise in clumping and grouping—but they often do no more than explain what Winter says. ("Winter believes that people enjoy different smells at different ages. . . ." "There are differences in the ways people relate to smells. . . .")

Here's my response:

Smell in Winter: An Exercise in Cross-Classification

Although Ruth Winter's information is interesting, it is not enlightening because her categories only lead to confusion.

On the surface, Winter presents information that can lead to many interesting questions: Do introverts, as Winter suggests, dislike flowery smells? Do extroverts like the fragrances that children like? Why do women like the smell of chemical substances like alcohol and naphthalene? Are there cultural reasons that women like smells associated with food and men like smells associated with sex, citrus, and perfume?

The problem is, however, that any such questioning is a waste of time because of the confusing categories Winter uses. First, she describes preferences by sex. But she also describes preferences by age, culture, and tendency toward introversion/extroversion. And the four categories she uses overlap. One cannot describe sexual differences without relating them to cultural differences. Likewise, one cannot describe introversion/extroversion without describing such tendencies as they relate to sex role cultural context.

Because her categories overlap, Winter is unable to make any meaningful generalities about her categories. For instance, she wants to say that men like orange, musk, and lemon grass. But what if a man is an extrovert? Then he won't like such fragrances; instead, he will like the fragrances children like: strawberry essence, chlorophyll, etc. . . . unless that man is a male, extrovert *oriental* who likes (according to Winter) hot, spicy, animal fragrances. The children's preferences lead to equally messy problems. Girls, according to Winter, like naphthalene, strawberry essence, and almond essence. But Winter points out that *Mediterranean* girls must like sophisticated floral smells. If Mediterranean girls like floral smells, Winter cannot say (as she does) that children *don't* like flower smells—unless we agree that all Mediterranean girls are *intelligent*—because, according to Winter, intelligent children like *adult* smells. But Lord help Mediterranean girls who are smart and extroverted. In such cases, they must both like flowery smells and hate them.

With each combination of categories, Winter's problems become more complicated. Her system breaks down and, ultimately, leads to good, brainless cocktail conversation but little if any intellectual significance.

Many students believe categorization is an aim in itself, and unless we challenge that notion, we'll end up with people who think that organizing their information is just like writing—or just as good as having a good idea or arguing a point. And we probably have enough committed taxonomists in the world to last us till the end of the century.

Peer Evaluation

We ought to get students to read each other's papers as often as we can. Students can give each other advice that is insightful, helpful, and thoughtful.[4] But we shouldn't expect peer feedback to replace other types of feedback. Peer feedback is peer feedback: sometimes hasty, sometimes brilliant, sometimes kind and generous, sometimes spiteful and selfish, sometimes consistent, inconsistent, solid, shaky, uninformed, informed, misinformed, and stupid. And sometimes even dangerous.

Consequently, if we choose to use peer feedback, we ought to use it with specific goals in mind and with much care:

1. To give students a chance to see what other people write.

2. To give students practice reading their own work out loud and hearing their own voices.

3. To give students feedback on specific questions or problems.

4. To give students a chance to judge the quality of their teacher's feedback.

Of these reasons, I'm particularly interested in the first: to give students an opportunity just to see what other people do. When students read one another's papers or listen to people read papers out loud— particularly if everyone has written on the same subject—they get one of those rare opportunities to see for themselves how their writing stacks up against their peers'. They also get to judge for themselves which approaches seem to be the best—or which papers stand out from the rest.

I'm also concerned with helping students to get enough feedback to be able to judge or evaluate my own methods and insights. By passing around and sharing papers on a regular basis, we can all get good feedback on how well the assignment itself worked. Were there many good papers? Were there many students who seemed to misinterpret the assignment in the same way? Sometimes, in good classes, I'll Xerox each student's paper and attach that clean Xeroxed copy to the paper I've made my comments on. Then, when we pass the papers around the room, students can read the clean Xeroxed copy first, flip it over, and read my comments on the original. In that way, students get feedback on how they read things differently than I do and how well they think I read. They even get feedback on how fair and consistent I am from paper to paper—and that's essential feedback.

Even though we ought to encourage students to read one another's papers, we ought to be aware that peer feedback can only supplement our own, and the way we use peer feedback in class can send a wide range of negative messages to students. Good students who are required to help other students as their "peers" often learn that peer feedback is only good for others—especially the weakest students in class. Weak students sometimes learn that their advice may not be very useful to better students. And if we use peer feedback as the major feedback in class or if we don't structure the ways students read one another's papers with specific questions, evaluation forms, or checklists, we risk suggesting to students that we're lazy, unprepared, impractical, out of touch with adolescent minds—or worse, that we don't want to or possibly aren't prepared to "teach" them anything beyond the basic exhortations to "listen to others," "look busy," "act concerned," "be kind and supportive," and "fend for yourself."

Evaluation and Time Management

We often tell students that writing takes time and that they should plan ahead, but sometimes they don't know what that means. When they come to college, many don't even own calendars and have never learned much about study skills, taking tests, or reading. Some have never had so many things to do in so little time or been under the pressure of so many deadlines and responsibilities for their own well-being. And even though we often admit that students are under tremendous pressures, most of the time we ignore their problems ("students will be students"). But if we're serious about teaching students—especially beginning college students—we need to give them feedback and advice on how to control their commitments and how to negotiate for breathing space.

Without experience in academia, students may have no way to judge whether their problems are our fault for making them do too much work or ambushing them with our unclear plan for their lives, or their own fault for overcommitting, underplanning, or mismanaging their lives. So, early in the semester, students should have a way to recognize our organization and fairness and their own systems for managing their commitments.

In introductory writing classes, we should hand out a calendar that includes the dates for all our writing assignments with space for students to add the assignments they have in their other classes, their "vacations," their field trips or road trips, their mid-semester examinations, and important social events. Students should know early in the semester when they will be under the most stress and be able to negotiate for changes in deadlines when they know they'll run out of time. (And we need to stress that those are their problems to solve, not ours.)

On our end, we need to let students know early that we are willing to be flexible and responsive to their time problems. This doesn't mean that we should accept all excuses ("My typewriter ribbon ran out") or bend over backward to make sure that everyone is happy with our schedule. But we should plan for problems: allow students to skip one or two papers each semester, allow for make-up papers, or give extra papers that students can do to replace papers they've had to skip, and let them know what to expect if they have to miss deadlines or plead for more time or good will.

We can also pass out a weekly calendar the first week of class and have students fill in their schedules, the times they have when they can study, the times when they have classes, meals, meetings, sports practice, play practice, breakfast, lunch, and dinner. Then we can get them to block out the hours they need to write their papers. Many students don't realize how little time they have or where their free time is—or worse, think that they have more time than they have. And many don't realize that we expect them to think about writing *all week* and not just an hour or two before their papers are due.

There are other forms of feedback than those we've looked at here—individual conferencing, mid-semester class evaluations, special incentives, and so forth. Our personalities control to a certain extent the feedback we feel most comfortable with. One of the best high school teachers I ever met taught in Pocatello, Idaho, and gave her students small stars that they would paste on their noses in class.

But even if we can't take into account all feedback, even if some of it may be vague and uncontrollable—even if we can't surgically remove the mole right below our nose that everyone seems to focus on while we talk—we can at least control some things we say to students and pay attention to some of the more obvious problems we all encounter when we begin to slip into easy ways of talking and evaluating, when we begin relying on simple techniques or methods that suddenly blossom into THE Technique or Method that everyone should use all the time, even in the rain.

Even when we have the best of motives and the best of theories to back our best motives, it's far too easy to give students wrong or conflicting messages. And the more confusion we generate, the less teaching we do.

●●●●●●●

Notes

1. I might point out that over the last fifteen years, I've never had a student challenge my fairness or my grades or complain that my policies were too vague and unpredictable.

2. As a rule, I always give students back points when they question my decisions or try to negotiate with me. My ultimate goal is not to hurt them or keep them in line, but to encourage their thinking, get them to pay attention to plans and constraints, and make sure that I reward them for their courage and self-righteousness.

3. There is a legitimate difference between storytelling and using narratives or anecdotes to support an argument. After students turn in this assignment, we might talk about that difference—especially since it will probably inhibit a few students.

4. For typical mainstream views of peer feedback, see Kenneth Bruffee's "Writing and Reading as Collaborative or Social Acts," *The Writer's Mind,* ed. Janice Hays, et al. (Urbana, IL: NCTE, 1983) 159–69; Mary Beaven's, "Individualized Goal Setting, Self-Evaluation, and Peer Evaluation," *Evaluating Writing,* eds. Charles R. Cooper and Lee Odell (Urbana, IL: NCTE, 1977) 135–53; Anne Ruggles Gere's *Writing Groups: History, Theory and Implications* (Carbondale, IL: Southern Illinois UP, 1987).

three

Essentials

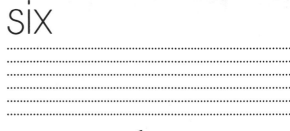

six

A Sample Lesson Plan

. . . .

An Introduction to Classroom Workshops

Understanding this book depends on understanding something about using a workshop approach in the classroom—one that involves student participation, involvement, and experimentation through small five- to ten-minute in-class experiments designed to keep students under a little pressure to think about what they're doing, work quickly, make small commitments to small ideas, and risk making mistakes.

In this sample workshop, our goal will be to teach one idea in fifty minutes—in this case, the notion that we can make things "look alike." While the subject of this workshop is "parallel constructions," I'm not suggesting that parallel constructions enjoy a higher priority in the classroom than other concerns or that people ought to begin writing courses with notions of parallelism. Instead, at least for right now, I would emphasize the *method,* not the subject matter, and hope that priorities will become more clear by the end of the book.

A Workshop on Parallel Constructions

Simple Assessment

We'll begin this workshop with a simple experiment to try to get students to see what they know and how they know it. In this case, we'll begin with something that looks like a typical grammar drill:

99

Parallel Constructions 1

Directions: Correct the following sentences.

1. The lady at the front desk knew that we had not paid our bill and we were going to punch the manager in the nose when we saw him.

2. Several of the dancers were injured when the roof fell in but not being seriously hurt.

3. To climb a high mountain is more pleasant than swimming in bog-colored rain water.

4. The school principal spoke with apparent openness and in a humorous manner.

5. Certain things are not actually taught in the classroom. They are learning how to get along with others, how to depend on oneself, and managing one's own affairs.

   ** *Can you explain why you made the particular corrections you made?*

The most difficult item is probably the first—mainly because there may be some confusion about what the sentence is supposed to say, but it's all standard exercise material, reasonably simple and generally sentence-based.

Many students have had at least some experience with such "textbookish" exercises—exercises that reinforce "doing things right" or "doing things so you don't get in trouble" or "doing things so you get a perfect score on some dumb test at the end of the unit." In fact, I'm always amazed at the number of students who want me to go over the answers to such exercises so that they will know if they've done everything exactly right.

But the final question here isn't what is right, but *why* is it right? And students often don't know how to answer that question. Do they learn to "do" parallel constructions just to be "right"? because they're "supposed to"? or do they have control over such things? (If so, what kind of control? If they don't know why they're following rules and trying to do things right, then they're hardly under control at all—and we want to talk about that.) In particular, we want to emphasize that parallel constructions give clues to readers—signals that certain items look enough alike that they can be grouped or related together. As we go through this workshop, we'll look at simple parallel constructions but also at repetitions, too. There's a difference between parallel constructions and exact repetitions, but at least for our purposes we don't need to keep the distinction clear.

Expansion of Simple Ideas

When students learn about parallel constructions in school or in hand-books, they seldom learn to apply the principles behind parallel constructions beyond sentence boundaries. To do so, we need to apply simple notions of parallelism and repetition to larger (and more important) contexts—paragraphs (and eventually whole themes). We can do so with a second experiment like this:

Parallel Constructions 2

Directions: Here are two sets of sentences. Can you make the sentences parallel?

1. In several eastern states last year, late frosts and freezing rains killed most of the fruit crops.
2. Young corn fields along the central Mississippi valley were flattened by hail storms.
3. Floods in Arkansas and Louisiana took their toll of new crops, which washed away in the waters.
4. Last year's difficulties in many southern states were compounded because Hurricane Adelle punished coastal areas, uprooting trees and burying farm equipment in mud and debris.

1. Some men seek thrills and excitement in big-game hunting and because they like competition and want to assert themselves.
2. Dangerous mountains and unclimbed cliffs are challenged by others out of egocentricity.
3. Others are loners who instead like individual challenges like bear wrestling or survival training.
4. In other cases, caves are explored in search of fame and glory and money.

Students don't always know what we want them to do here. Many have never thought about making whole sentences "look alike" or have the same structure, and we may need to do a few examples on the board after they begin:

John went to the store.
Sally went to the movies with her dog.
To jail went Bill.
Randall stayed home.

(Which of these sentences is not like the others?)
or

Never run red lights.
Never put your head out of the window while you're stepping on the gas.
While driving a stick shift, never eat popcorn.

(How would you make these sentences "look alike"?)

After a few minutes of work—before they have a chance to make things "perfect" or start looking around for something else to do—we can stop and have students read some of their attempts out loud. When students have to read out loud what they've written, they have to put their ideas on the line, commit themselves in public, and try to articulate their motives—and this is a particularly important part of any workshop. They have to know that everybody reads and nobody hides. (Whenever I have students read out loud, I try to emphasize that I'm not trying to set anybody up for ridicule. People make mistakes all the time, and I'm as interested in the ways they do things wrong as in the ways they do things right. In fact, if I make them do things quickly and stop before they're done, they know they don't have to do things well and can get by with a little sloppiness or indecision—*so long as they have an idea of what they're trying to do.*)

In this experiment, we'll look for students who put things together mechanically, who don't recognize the *value* of tying complete ideas together with parallel constructions. Occasionally, for instance, we'll get students who mechanically put things together like this:

Most of the fruit crops in several eastern states were killed by late frosts last year.

Young corn fields along the central Mississippi valley were flattened by hail storms.

New crops were washed away by floods in Arkansas and Louisiana.

Coastal areas, trees, and farm equipment were punished by Hurricane Adelle, and problems were compounded in coastal areas.

Those who solve the problem this way may not understand the value of parallel constructions as *signals,* as they look for ways to make everything look alike. If they think about the relative importance of their ideas and try to set them up *rhetorically,* they could begin the first sentence here with "last year," because the time signal sets up the context for the rest of the points. Since *place* is particularly important in these sentences, students might also try to begin with those small prepositional phrases of place to help readers to move around the country more easily:

Last year, in several eastern states . . .
Along the central Mississippi valley . . .
In Arkansas and Louisiana . . .

Such a notion is obvious, but obvious only to those who can control their parallel constructions, and we want to emphasize that we don't make parallel constructions without knowing what we're trying to do with them.

The second half of this experiment is slightly different. After we've talked a bit and shared some, I might offer a quick and dirty solution that uses *labels* to solve the problem:

Killers bag bambis.
Egocentrics climb mountains.
Loners tame lions and beat up on crocs.
But fools spelunk.

Some students will think that such a solution is unfair, and when they complain about it, we can talk about what experiments or exercises are good for if we can't bend or change them to suit our purposes. I might add here that using labels isn't a stated part of the experiment, but we should take every opportunity we can to keep reinforcing previous lessons.

Imitation

As a general rule, imitations are nice for "halfway" experiments—experiments that get students to practice while they're still learning about the benefits and limitations of certain techniques. Here's a typical third experiment:

Parallel Constructions 3

Pick one of the following passages and imitate it. Keep the sentence patterns (especially the parallel sentences) but change the subject matter.

1. We are underexercised as a nation. We look, instead of play. We ride, instead of walk. Our existence deprives us of the minimum of physical activity essential for healthy living. And the remedy, in my judgment, lies in one direction; that is, in developing programs for broad participation in exercise by all of our young men and women—all of our boys and girls. (John F. Kennedy)[1]
2. It is perfectly true that our young men should not go to college merely to get their bodies trained, but it is also true that they should not go there merely to get their intellects trained. Far above bodily strength, far above mere learning comes character. No soundness of body and limb, no excellence of mental training—admirable though each of these is—can atone for the lack of what in old fashioned phrase would be called the virtues; for the lack of courage, of honesty, of self control, of temperance, of steadfast resolution, of readiness to stand up for one's rights, and carefulness not to infringe on the rights of others. (Theodore Roosevelt)[2]
3. Speaking as a participant of a "contact" sport, I found when I tackled a man that there was *more* than the hit. To say it was satisfaction is true. To say it was a feeling of security is true. To say it was a cathartic experience might well be true. But it was more. It is more. To say I understood it, or under-

stand now, would be to admit the absurd is accessible through reason. (Howard S. Slusher)[3]

Here's the same experiment, this time with less serious material:

Parallel Constructions 3b

Directions: Imitate one of the following passages. You can (and probably should) change words and choose a different subject. But you should keep the same rhythms.

1. This generation has grown up in a world of baloney sandwiches, where nitrates are valued more than good taste—where texture and flavor are devalued, ignored in favor of extruded meat slicks slapped between two slices of Wonder Bread.[4]
2. Something that simpleminded can't just sit there in its own plain brown wrapper, and so we beef it up, analyze it, beautify it, frost it, redesign it, and fluff it up; we make up theories about its real worth as opposed to its apparent worth; we imagine it in better surroundings and talk about its latent meanings and obvious honesty and inherent spiritual solvency; and if all else fails we string vague praises together and hope someone else will understand our deeply felt, inexpressible vibrations.[5]
3. When gingerbread brownies with whipped cream lead us toward overindulgence, our mirror tries to remind us of our limitations. When chocolate fudge sheet cakes with sour cream frosting beckon, our doctor tries to remind us about our slowly clogging arteries and the minute, floating globules of fat floating freely in our veins. When will-power erodes, when our foreheads swim in sweat as we spy heavy loads of cream cheese and doughnuts and blintzes and Greek pastries oozing honey, our guilt swims up through the dark waters of our mind and thwacks us feebly across the back of our neck.[6]

And here's one more variation, this time a spiritual imitation:

Parallel Constructions 3c

Here are five sentences. Can you reconstruct them so they sound like Martin Luther King, Jr.?

1. This is our hope.
2. It is the faith with which I go back to the south.
3. We will be able, with this faith, to hew out the mountain of despair a stone of hope.
4. We can transform the jangling discords of our nation into a beautiful symphony of brotherhood.
5. We will be able to work together, praying, struggling, go to jail together, stand up for freedom, knowing that we will be free one day.[7]

Application

One of the problems with any notion we try to teach is that students may not make the link between their practice and play and their own writing. To make that link, we can try out simple experiments like this one:

Parallel Constructions 4

Directions: Here is a paragraph from a paper turned in on Monday. See if you can improve it by concentrating on *parallel constructions.*

> Zilch seems to have an inclination towards the ugly fantasies and realities of man's existence in his poetry. In "Charlotte" H. Z. relates the concept of love to a heart attack. Zilch gives not necessarily nice descriptions of women in his poetry, describing one as having a pock-marked crag for a face in "Half Cooked." Not exactly a compliment, Zilch gives one woman credit for stating the unpleasant idea she had that bats throw up on people's heads in "Romance." Bird excrement on the eaves in "Ogre on the Moon" and stale French fries and stomach aches in "Romance" are some of the other grim realities H. Z. writes of in his poetry. While unpleasant, these topics are very real occurrences and therefore relevant.

Again, students can—and do—make formulaic responses in such experiments:

1. In "Charlotte," Zilch relates the concept of love to a heart attack.
2. In "Half-Cooked," he gives not necessarily nice descriptions of women, describing one as having a pock-marked crag for a face.
3. In "Romance," Zilch gives not exactly a compliment . . .

Such an answer would be fine if the writer were just trying to move readers from one poem to another. In fact, students may recall a previous exercise where such a response was appropriate ("In several eastern states . . . Along the central Mississippi valley . . ."). But this paragraph is not about different poems. It's about different "ugly fantasies and realities." In other words, the problem involves a different *focus,* and good writers may want to set up parallel constructions that emphasize that focus:

Love becomes a heart attack in "Charlotte." Charlotte has a pock-marked crag for a face in "Half-Cooked." Bats throw up on people's heads, and people eat stale French fries in "Romance." Bird excrement even coats the eaves of H. Z.'s house in "Ogre on the Moon."

Here, the emphasis is on the particular "ugly fantasies and realities" in Zilch's poems, not on the poems themselves. Furthermore—and this is important—by focusing on parallel constructions, we also begin to solve other, related problems. Here, for instance, just by focusing on parallel constructions, we begin to eliminate *be* verbs and almost automatically begin to prune out excess prepositional phrases and nominalizations.

Play

Finally, no matter what we do to make students conscious of the benefits of using parallel constructions, they will go on doing what they've always done unless we underscore the importance of practice and play. So we can end with a couple of small experiments like these:

Parallel Constructions 6a
Write five related sentences, each beginning with "When the _____ in . . ."

or:

Parallel Constructions 6b
Write one sentence that begins with three or four phrases that begin "When the _____ in . . ."

And we can our read sentences along with everybody else:

When the moon turns green in broad daylight, when the rocks melt in the gutters in Albertson's parking lot, when the white dogs crouch in the doorway of Zillah's treehouse, when the dingbats cruise elephants in alleys behind my house, I'll still love you.

And in subsequent class meetings, we might continue the play:

Parallel Constructions 7
Write a noisy paragraph beginning with three sentences, each beginning with "If _____ . . ." End the paragraph with a sentence that doesn't look like the others.

(Here, we can begin to introduce the effect we can create by breaking the rhythms at the end of a series of parallel sentences.)

....

General Advice

Throughout the rest of this book, we'll explore different things we might do in class—activities, experiments, topics for discussion. But before we go on to deal with specific topics, I'd like to list a few rules of thumb that will underlie discussions of in-class work that follow. Such rules should help to keep the discussions that follow in a classroom context where we end up having to think about practical classroom problems like managing our time, focusing attention, eliciting student responses, combatting laziness and sleepiness, encouraging experimentation and self-assessment, and clarifying our limited goals.

Plan Classroom Activities in Ten-minute Blocks of Time
This seems rather mechanical, and it probably is. But the worst thing that can happen is to run out of ammunition after the first fifteen minutes. In this sample lesson plan on parallel constructions, I've included here more material that anyone could use in fifty minutes. But if I have plenty of things to do, I can go to class knowing that I can dump experiments that don't seem to be moving in the right direction or that seem to get too difficult too soon—and I have things to fall back on when I find myself talking too much.

In any case, we ought to have at least four or five different things to do. (I usually have a couple more, just in case something really bombs out.) Such activities don't have to be all paper-and-pencil experiments like the ones set up here. We can read six or seven lines from several students' papers, read the introduction of an editorial from the newspaper, read old freshman papers we wrote ourselves.

Furthermore, if some experiments work really well, and if the class wants to continue talking about certain things for more than ten minutes, obviously we can ditch some parts of our lesson and make room for longer discussions, but we ought to plan to move on before things slow down.

Plan an Objective Beforehand
We ought to have an end point to move toward—a single point we want to get to by the end of class—a point we can wrap up, repeat, and come back to in following classes. There's no benefit in having "fun" in class without a direction or a special idea we want to set up, clarify, magnify, and play with. Furthermore, these activities ought to be related, and they ought to move from simple assessment problems to more complex problems of application. (There's a difference between getting students to recognize ideas and concepts and getting them to produce things for themselves based on their understandings.)

Simplify
Some teachers—often the smartest, most observant, and most conscientious teachers—try to squeeze out every last observation and fine point from their lessons. If they talk about parallel constructions, they want to move right into long discussions of tone, rhythm, expectation, timing, and sonority. Instead, I'd aim at simple observations—crude rhythms, heavy timings, loud thumpings. The main ideas are more important than refinements. We should always quit before we find ourselves deep in analysis of style and Greek names for tropes. We should always quit be-

fore we find ourselves lecturing while our students draw on the backs of their hands with ballpoint pens or bite their thumbs to keep awake.

Do One Thing at a Time

Sometimes, we have all sorts of things to say. We may want to discuss parallelism, organization, theme, voice, and paragraphing all at once. We may want to convince students to read good literature and be aware of literary nuances and stances and, as an aside, we may want to point to nice examples of parallel structures. But at least in workshops, we should never try to teach more than one thing in fifty minutes— especially if it's something important and demands a change in the way students view their writing.

Do All Experiments Along with Students

Sometimes, we can plan answers beforehand, but we should try to write out our answers with students during class. They like to see what we can do—and we should be able to show them that we can do our own experiments.

Walk Around

Once we finish our own answers, we should walk around and peer over students' shoulders—put them under a little pressure and get them used to having us make instant judgments of what they're doing. We can talk to them and joke with them. (When we walk around, we should make some mental notes of students who have good solutions or novel approaches so we can call on them to read their solutions out loud. We should never assume that our best writers will have the best answers, and we should never expect students to volunteer, even when they know they've got nice solutions.)

Keep Lectures to a Minimum

I've alluded to this before, but we don't have to talk very much. We can make our points, encourage, exhort, praise, demand—but we don't have to make students listen very long. (Even if we talk a lot and the sweat of our intensity dribbles down our cheeks, chances are they're not listening very hard, anyway.)

Keep Students Working

No one should be able to loaf or study biology notes or count the holes in the ceiling tiles during class. If someone gets done early, we should check what they've done and offer suggestions, ways to change what they've done or challenges to look at the problem a little more carefully. (Often, the students who get done earliest are the ones who have over-simplified the problems, who don't sense the importance of what we're trying to get them to see.)

Make Sure Everyone Reads and No One Apologizes

Everyone needs to read something they've written, no matter how half-baked, half-digested they think it is. Students often preface what they write with apologies like "This isn't very good" or "This is totally off the subject but . . ." and I'll stop them and tell them that they should never apologize in class—they have nothing to feel bad about, and if what they're saying is really bad, they ought to say it a little louder than usual.

Plan Follow-ups

We should never assume that just because we've covered things in class, students will automatically do things better. Sometimes, they do things worse, and sometimes that's fine, as long as they know what they're *trying* to do. If we're dealing with parallel constructions, we ought to plan to come back to them when we talk about thesis statements, conclusions, cohesion. We ought to read particularly nice attempts at parallelism in students' papers whenever they appear. And when we write our own assignments, we ought to try to incorporate parallel structures in highly visible ways.

•••••••

Notes

1. John F. Kennedy, "The Importance of Participation," in *The Sporting Spirit: Athletes in Literature and Life,* ed. Robert J. Higgs and Neil D. Isaacs (New York: Harcourt, 1977) 216.
2. Theodore Roosevelt, "Value of an Athletic Training," in Higgs and Isaacs, 145–46.
3. Howard S. Slusher, "Sport as a Human Absurdity," in Higgs and Isaacs, 276.
4. I made this up.
5. I made this up.
6. I made this up.
7. King's original passage goes like this:

This is our hope. This is the faith that I go back to the South with. With this faith we will be able to hew out of the mountain of despair a stone of hope. With this faith we will be able to transform the jangling discords of our nation into a beautiful symphony of brotherhood. With this faith we will be able to work together, to pray together, to struggle together, to go to jail together, to stand up for freedom together, knowing that we will be free one day.

seven

Labeling, Sorting, and Displaying Information

In this chapter, we'll take a quick look at ways to think about and organize "data." These ideas aren't part of a package of invention or prewriting designed to give students something to say. They're just what they are: principles for simplifying information. Organizing, simplifying, and sorting through data aren't enough to guarantee excellent writing or excellent thoughts. But without organizing, simplifying, and sorting through data, there may be no hope at all.

Labels

Good writers recognize the value of clear categories and labels and use them—probably most often unconsciously—to isolate points and clarify their ideas. Lesser writers think life is one big ill-formed catalog of mysterious, unrelated events. Give weak writers ten things to talk about, and they end up trying to talk about all ten things one after another. Or they end up selecting one thing and hoping that no one else will notice that they haven't talked about the other nine.

A student writes:

Euthanasia is a way of dying. Euthanasia comes from the Greek. The word means a good or peaceful death. Euthanasia is a hard word to define. Is it a suicide? Suicide is something we do to ourselves. Is it murder? Murder is something we do to each other. Is it a mass murder? Mass murder is killing those who

111

are a burdon on society. Euthanasia is none of these. Euthanasia is to be able to die with dignity when there is no hope for a human life.

Is euthanasia a "way of dying"? a "death"? an ability ("to be able to die")? Is suicide a "something we do"? Is murder a "something we do"? The student apparently wishes to use euthanasia, suicide, and murder as labels for particular acts or methods of causing death, yet he apparently cannot describe the features of the categories he wishes to label.

Another student writes:

Education is a special process. There is nothing else like it; no other experience could exist without education. Because education is "essential-special," teaching should never be a static system of leftover, year-to-year programs. People change; times change; the learning process must also change or it will become unaffective.

By calling education a "special process," an "experience," a "system of . . . programs," and a "learning process," this student apparently expects his clarity to rise from a flood of approximation.

Bad writing, of course, isn't limited to students. We ourselves regularly cross-categorize and even build towering structures on soft foundations. Many of us, for instance, still like to categorize writing into traditional modes like "process," "compare-contrast," "description," "analysis," "cause-and-effect," and so forth—even though we know that these are not true categories but scruffy curricular conveniences.[1] An analysis may resemble a process; a cause-and-effect may resemble a description; a description may involve large doses of compare-contrast, process, analysis, narration, and cause-and-effect.

What is exposition as opposed to narration? What is creativity? And what does writing across-the-curriculum mean?

What is voice? honesty? communication? purpose? text?

What is an "A" paper?

What do we mean when we label certain teaching problems developmental or basic?

What is mature writing?

Good writers ought to able to categorize and label, be able to recognize the *limitations* of certain categories, and understand that the act of categorization is *value-laden* in important ways.

Often, students don't even think about their labels. They don't see the benefits of good labels or the drawbacks of bad ones. A student who muddies the distinction between education as a "process," an "experience," and a "system" may not even be *aware* that each label designates something that is a little bit different from the others. He may not even recognize that such different labels *separate* aspects of education from one another.

In class, students can practice giving names to things, clumping and grouping, and labeling those clumps and groups.

Labels Experiment #1

Directions: Group the following terms into at least three groups. Give a name to each group. Be able to explain your grouping system.

1. People who eat watermelons.
2. Salamanders.
3. Tree stumps.
4. Unicorns.
5. Great white sharks.
6. Hubbard squash.
7. Rubber chickens.
8. Old baseball players.
9. Dried hamburger.
10. Green tree toads.
11. People who sing bluegrass songs.
12. Cuckoo clocks.
13. Angle worm castings.
14. Road apples.
15. People who make lists.
16. Carpenter ants.
17. Army eggs.
18. Disfigured bowling trophies.
19. Dead flies.
20. Protein bars.

We don't care what students group together here, but whatever they group together, they ought to be able to set up *separate* categories. It may not work, for instance, to label categories "animals," "people," and "junk" because "people" are "animals," but it may be legal to label categories "leftovers," "main dishes," and "desserts" if someone is willing to think metaphorically.

Students also need to practice separating out information and labeling it for particular purposes:

Labeling Experiment #2

Directions: Below are fifteen quotations. Some of them are worth more than others to a bleeding heart. Which ones are those? (Who might value the others?)

1. "Wind hurts. It hurts. It hurts." (John Barlowe)
2. "Tumbleweeds lose." (Randolph Grinker)
3. "Everyday people should worry about what others think." (Sarah Sanders)
4. "When the grass of the world cries, the mowers will stop." (Constance Barlowe)
5. "You, too, should fear seagull feet." (Andrew Melon)

6. "If trees learn, it's because something leans on them." (John Slugge)
7. "Pretty feet are more than an illusion. They are what's left after the shoes are taken off." (Sarah Sanders)
8. "The most disquieting plant is the fiddlehead fern. I don't even like to watch it grow." (Waldo Barlowe)
9. "Those who gripe should be shot." (Randolph Grinker)
10. "A good shin is an asset." (Sarah Sanders)
11. "Boredom is, in fact, a viral infection." (Robert Sachs)
12. "Aggression is what is left one after the smiles, the coos, the politeness, the fumbled plays in the end zone." (Lassie)
13. "Even pine trees sob." (Anthony Barlowe)
14. "When is a plant dead? Can you measure dead from the cut of a knife?" (Anthony Barlowe)
15. "The world is run on looks alone." (Robert Sachs)

The task here is purposely vague. What is a "bleeding heart"? What are its (his/her?) characteristics? And what do people do with the rest of these quotations? Do they think in terms of one big category for all the rest? Or are they willing to separate people into groups and give each group labels? Students are often *afraid* to label things. After all, when they give things names, they solidify a particular vision and attitude toward their data.

Here's another more complex problem:

Labeling Experiment #3

Below is a list of information about the damage to the environment around Clifton Springs, Ohio. Group the information and label your groups.

1. Clifton Springs is the dead dog capital of the world. Old stray dogs come from throughout southern Ohio and somehow find their way to Clifton Springs to die. According to city health officials, eighteen to twenty dead dogs turn up on the town streets every two or three days.
2. Six months ago, yellow-bellied marmots were discovered in the fields and woods around Clifton Springs—six million, by last estimate. (They have undermined the fields and made life miserable for local horseback riders.)
3. Buzzards—a flock of sixty-six—live on Herb Muller's barn south of town. So far, they have polluted Herb's well and scared his chickens so much they no longer produce eggs.
4. Residents, using chlordane, strychnine, and other residual poisons, have laced their fields with bait to kill the yellow-bellied marmots.
5. Dead marmots are stinking up the town water supply, a small reservoir just south of town.
6. So far, only two dead buzzards have been found.
7. A local bean silo went out of business because contaminated mice were found in the beans. The contents of the silo were dumped on the town golf course in protest by the silo's owner, who claimed that the city could have done more to prevent rodent pollution.

8. Six weeks ago, fertilizers were found in a routine check of the town's water supply. Town officials blame excessive fertilization of local fields as farmers attempted to outgrow the appetites of rock chucks.
9. Town officials are quick to blame their problems on acid rain from Pittsburgh steel mills.
10. Recently, a family of black bears attacked a resident at the town's open-pit land fill south of town. The resident fell into the trash and disappeared.
11. Carl Cribbs, mayor of Clifton Springs, claims the town's major problem has been caused by Oak Junction, a town three miles north of Clifton Springs. Cribbs claims that Oak Junction's two-year campaign against pigeons has not only chased the pigeons to Clifton Springs, but also has forced old dogs and rock chucks to leave their old stomping grounds.
12. In November, 1978, a cloud of pigeons settled on the Clifton Springs Town Hall and has never left.
13. Noise makers installed on the Town Hall in January 1979 to chase pigeons away have been recently blamed for two miscarriages.[2]

By the time students finish such an experiment, they should have a set of reasonable labels for the problems faced by Clifton Springs. One student might point out that all Clifton Springs' problems (land, water, noise, and brain pollution) stem from two sources: natural disaster and manmade disaster. Another might point out that the town's problems can be labeled as simple stupidity, tunnel vision, and pass-the-buck decision making. Still another might label the town's problems as lack of imagination, lack of foresight, and lack of hindsight.

Students make labels, but the labels themselves often *create* categories and visions of categories that allow us to call to mind complex ideas. When students say that one kind of pollution is "pass-the-buck" pollution, they are slanting and shaping their categorization in important ways. Later, students should learn to *weight* their categories (which is worse? pass-the-buck decision making or stupidity?), and I will return to labeling as a way to tighten up thesis statements and manipulate data. But initially, we can begin by exposing students to the problems of data and the problems they create for themselves if they don't learn to manipulate their data.

Sorting and Displaying Information

As a director of a college writing center, I often see students who come to college with only marginal skills in organizing information. Most often, they know how to order events chronologically. Many also know how to use simple categories to sort modest amounts of information. The best have learned techniques to help them sort and display information that cannot be clearly categorized and labeled or developed chronologically.

In class, I don't have time to help students deal in depth with such problems.[3] But I'm constantly amazed at how few strategies students use to sort out information and how reluctant they are to spread things out, draw lines around items, and use arrows. For instance, we can give students a list of names like this and ask them to put them in alphabetical order as quickly as they can:

John Paul Jones	Ralph Ribbs
Hosaiah Collingsworth	Sarah Sophia Slenkenthorpe
Uriah Ribbsey	Connie Collingsworth
John McBain	Prentiss Rollingsworth
Bonnie Jean Senderwiden	Donald Macbonker
Hortense Johnson	Frank John Heaper
Hubert Renner	John McBanner
Tom Josephson	Francis Macdonald
Becky (Rebecca) Sonderson	Mac Heath
Macbeth	

Students who are bound into a restrictive mindset that keeps them from spreading out, taking up space, and making a mess often go through this list alphabetically. They begin by trying to find all the names that begin with the letter *A,* and then they try to find the first name that begins with the letter *A,* and then they move to the letter *B,* and so on until they work through the names one at a time. On the other hand, students who are less bound by a slow mental search might take the first name on the list and write it down right in the middle of a sheet of paper:

Jones

Then they might take the next name and write it down where it fits:

Jones
Ribbs

And then the next:

Collingsworth
Jones
Ribbs

By the end, their sheet might be messy, but their system will be quick (see Figure 7–1).

●●●●●●●●

Figure 7–1

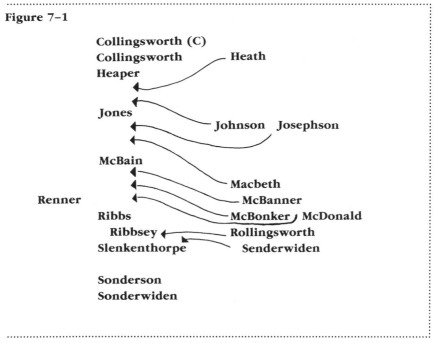

The problem is that some students don't always recognize short-cuts. They may not use charts or graphs. They may not like to draw pictures. Sometimes their English teachers discourage them from drawing pictures in their papers even though pictures sometimes make things more simple and direct. And they may not value white space.

Sometimes, they don't recognize the dangers of oversimple categorization and the need for alternative displays. Here, for instance, is a small experiment in classification:

What is the difference between a sport, a recreation, and a hobby? How would you categorize the following?

golf	playing chess
archery	beer drinking
bowling	running
smelt dipping	chicken stealing
bowling	video games

billiards	dog fighting
target shooting	trout fishing
slot-car racing	baseball
volleyball	boxing
tennis	fiddling
auto racing	bird hunting
pie eating	cockroach racing
salamander hunting	carp fishing
stamp collecting	bird watching
wood carving	bread baking

We teach students to categorize, but in this problem, there is no simple way to categorize this information. Depending on the definitions, golf might be a sport, a recreation, or a hobby. Smelt dipping might be a sport or a recreation. Salamander hunting might be a recreation or a hobby or nothing at all. A simple chart might look like this:

golf (1, 2, 3)	1 = sport
bowling (1, 2)	2 = recreation
baseball (1, 2)	3 = hobby
auto racing (1, 2, 3)	
salamander hunting (2)	
(etc.)	

Yet such a chart doesn't make the relationship between sports, recreations, and hobbies clear. Nor does it help to make clear distinctions between playing and watching. Playing baseball might be a sport; watching baseball might be a recreation. In such a case, where there are overlapping categories, students might have to resort to other displays than simple charts. One such display is a diagram like the one shown in Figure 7–2. This diagram depends on certain definitions that I have not given, but the *method* of displaying relationships in the diagram should be clear—and more important, it should be clear that certain issues need more than simple solutions. Simple categorizations may not be enough; pictures sometimes help; visual layouts sometimes simplify things.

Figure 7–2

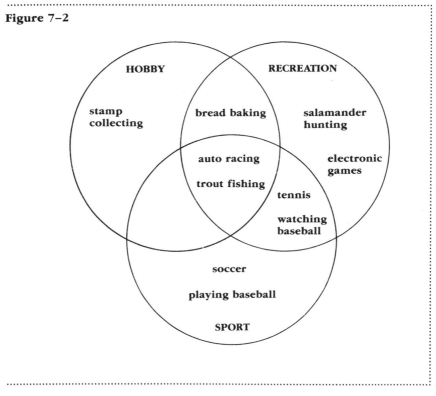

Here's another problem:

Organize the following punishments:

burning at the stake

life in prison

execution by hanging

punishment by mangling the
right hand

execution by stoning

ten years at hard labor
castration

$5,000 fine and a week in jail

five years in minimum security
prison

sixty-nine years in minimum
security prison

$100,000 fine and two years in jail

spanking

execution by poison

execution by firing squad

death by water torture

five years in solitary confinement   starvation

ten years in solitary confinement   flogging

thirty years in solitary   public humiliation
confinement

It is possible to categorize these punishments:

Humane   Inhumane

spanking   flogging
minimum security prison   burning at the stake
fining
etc.

But categorization quickly breaks down. Is execution by poison humane if it kills a person in a couple of seconds? Is execution itself humane? Is ten years in solitary confinement humane compared with mangling the right hand? Stoning? What is worse—thirty years in solitary confinement or life in prison?

In a more complex system of categorization, students can develop an outline:

Type of Punishment

I. Physical

   A. Pain

      1. spanking
      2. mangling
      3. flogging

   B. Confinement

      1. solitary
      2. minimum security

   C. Death

II. Mental

   A. Slow torture

   B. Public humiliation

III. Economic
   A. Fines
   B. Humiliation

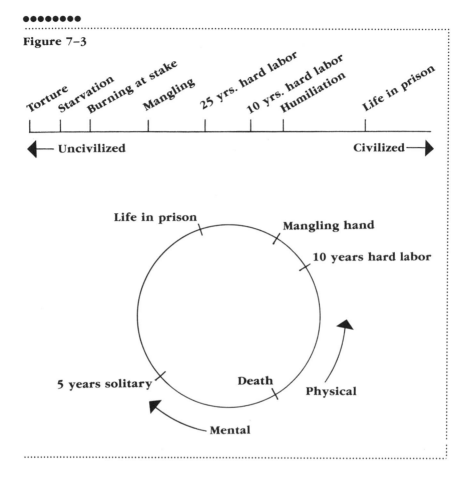

Figure 7-3

But even this organization doesn't allow for shades of difference. How can we separate physical pain from mental pain? Does someone who is executed suffer more mentally or physically?

A different kind of organization may be needed, one that can take into account some of these shades of difference. One such organization might be along continua (see Figure 7–3).

Such continua might lead to discussions of the relative wrongness of certain punishments. They could also lead to discussions of the effects of punishments. In the circular continuum above, the separation of extreme mental punishment and extreme physical punishment might be described as only a point along the line: death.

As I say, we don't have much time to spend on ways to display information, and giving students individual exercises on such things won't make much difference without some practice playing with many different kinds of data. But again, I'm not interested in supplying students with formulas or techniques that they can apply to all data. I'm interested in simply emphasizing that the ways we choose to categorize things, give them names, and display information can themselves dictate what we see and how we analyze what we see. Freedom and understanding don't come from an unrealistic belief that we can learn all there is to know about structure and organization and data. Such freedom and understanding come from a strong grounding in a few basic notions and a way of thinking that gives us confidence and some *control* over the vagueness that often substitutes for "rules," "structure," and "order."

•••••••

Notes

1. See Robert Connors, "The Rise and Fall of the Modes of Discourse," *CCC* 32 (1981): 444–63.

2. I made this information up.

3. See my "Helping Students to Sort and Display their Information," *CE* 45 (1983): 277–87; and "Teaching Students to Categorize and Label," *The Leaflet* 82 (Winter 1983): 30–35. See also Herbert Kohl's *Mathematical Puzzlements: Play and Invention with Mathematics* (New York: Schocken, 1987) for more ideas about sorting information using charts.

eight

Thesis Statements

• • • • • • • • • • • • • • • • • • •

At least while they're learning, I don't want students to imply their ideas, hint at them, save them for their conclusions, or apologize for them. Take for instance, this piece of student writing from the beginning of a semester:

To Do Your Best

In the passage written by Bill Nye, Nye provides the reader with the meaning that people should rely on the skills with which they are most comfortable in order to obtain maximum success.

Nye says; "there is great economy in keeping hens if we have sufficient room for them and a thorough knowledge of how to manage the fowl property." This part of the quotation uses "hens" or the "fowl property" as the trade or skill with which the narrator is most successful. It is symbolic of how people should rely on what they know even if it is a simple or general knowledge. Nye later says; "To the professional man, who is not familiar with the hen . . . and whose mind does not turn henward . . . shun her as you would the deadly upos tree of Piscataquis county, me." This last part of the quotation tells the reader that he should not try and be someone whom he's not. He should rely on what he knows best to be successful.

Nye uses the word "professional" when referring to someone who's best skills are not those of poultry but probably those of a business executive. The "professional" would be of no help to the "hen economy" because he knows very little about hens. The comparison of "the tree of Piscataquis county" to the narrator shows how the narrator would be unsuccessful in the "professional" business.

The passage written by Bill Nye is very informative to the reader by telling him to do what he does best in life because nobody can do it better than one's self.

There are many small problems here—the student doesn't know how to use semicolons and misspells "who's" and "upos" tree—and the style is lumpy and wordy. But the biggest problem here is that the student doesn't want to make a commitment, doesn't want to risk an idea. Is Bill Nye right or wrong? Is he full of baloney? Is any *part* of Nye's ideas particularly good or bad? Can we apply Bill Nye's ideas to anything? Do we care about Bill Nye? If not, why not? Do we sense that Bill Nye is saying anything other than what he is saying? Is that something important at all? How does Bill Nye address bigger things? What are the limitations of what Bill Nye says? Are those limitations important?

This student's introduction suggests that simply telling us what Bill Nye says will be enough, and many students think that plot summary or regurgitation is enough. But it's not. Who cares what students have read unless they've thought about what they've read? If they're simply going to tell me what Bill Nye says, I might as well read Nye myself. They have to do more than a simple explication: they have to show me why they need to clear up that confusion in the first place.

In academia, and any other place where ideas matter and insights are important, writers have to tell us what they *think,* too. They have to weigh and evaluate, argue for or against something worth arguing about, clarify or demystify something worth clarifying or demystifying. They have to take stands, make decisions, risk opinions.

So I want students to write thesis statements—not just to tell me what they're going to say, but to begin to make those commitments, to risk their ideas and opinions. I don't care how awkward or simple their thesis statements look, but I want them to say something about something:

Bill Nye is full of baloney because . . .
Bill Nye is ignorant of . . .
I like Bill Nye's simple idea because . . .

In the beginning, I don't care if students start with simple, perhaps "mechanical-looking" models for thesis statements like these:

- There are . . .: *A, B,* . . . (There are X main problems with Bill Nye's comment. . . .)
- *A, B* . . . are . . .
- . . . because . . .
- In this paper I am going to . . . by . . .
- Although . . . X is . . . I think X is . . . because . . .
- People say that . . . but I think . . .

Sometimes we underestimate the difficulties many students face when they begin to think in structured ways, organize, sort their ideas, and nail even one of them down. Once they get started and understand the argument they want to make, they can *rewrite* such simple thesis statements to make them *look* more graceful or sophisticated. If they are good at it, they can even learn to pare down thesis statements or imply them later. But I'd rather have students start off trying to be direct rather than vague, even if they think they ought to learn how to rewrite those thesis statements to hide them, imply them, or make them less stiff and "mechanical."

Some students tell me that making thesis statements so direct and unambiguous makes their writing too predictable and, hence, boring. Instead, they want to *imply* their ideas; they want to lead their readers on and on and on until their ideas hit their readers right in the face or their point comes together for readers in a blinding flash of intuition or vision. These are the students who read mystery novels and watch reruns of Perry Mason and call essays "stories":

Zilch's State of Depression

I can see by reading the quote that Zilch has many deep thoughts about life. For instance, there is the question of how life's outer beauty can be preserved but its inner soul lost. I will analyze why Zilch feels and thinks as he does on this particular day.

Zilch must work in a museum of some sort where life like animals are on display. On this day, Zilch feels depressed. He sees all of the animals that look beautiful and full of life, on the outside. He knows, in reality, that these same animals have been killed and their insides have been removed. The organs that made these animals and life in general feel, think and exist. He feels bad because he is living and can feel life's good and bad things and knows that the animals can no longer feel anything. He is also feeling sorry for himself, at this time, because he is forced to put up with the miseries of life that the animals no longer have to deal with. He has basically become jealous.

He is becoming old so he believes that he is looking ugly. He is jealous that the animal's outer beauty has been preserved and his hasn't. What he doesn't understand is that looking ugly on the outside doesn't necessarily mean being ugly on the inside. Then again, that is probably why he is saddened today because he has realized that the poor animals can not feel the beauty of life's ugliness.

This student is "responding" to a passage by H. Z. Zilch in which Zilch goes to a museum and discovers "life caught at an angle, souls hobbled."[1] Zilch discovers "The stuffed, overstuffed world with its claim to bodies preserves the outward, but with hobbled hearts." While this student recognizes an important question ("There is the question of how life's outer beauty can be preserved but its inner soul lost"), she chooses, instead, to tell a small story about Zilch's life: he must work in a museum; at this time, he feels depressed; he feels bad; he feels sorry for himself because he is "forced to put up with the miseries of life. . . ." And while such a story may help her to "analyze why Zilch feels and thinks as he does on this particular day," she responds in the *simplest* way: by imagining H. Z. Zilch "on this particular day—and thereby *avoiding* any confrontation or argument with H. Z.'s mind. *Ideas* are more interesting than stories, and students should try to deal with ideas. Many, in fact, often don't realize how exciting and compelling good ideas are. They've never sat behind a desk and watched the baloney roll in—long, fat rolls of pretension, cholesterol-choked assertions and visions.

Part of the problem may be that students don't like to argue with others or make sharp, clear, no-nonsense assertions that they have to back up or clarify or further develop. They often seem to *like* to be vague, let their ideas unfold organically, imply their points and let their readers come to a gentle shock of recognition. But they should be blunt and assertive. They should do more than simply tell what they have read or tell stories about people's lives. Their ideas should sit out there naked and vulnerable. The more naked and vulnerable they are, the harder they will have to work to protect them, support them, and otherwise keep them from sounding foolish, incomplete, or wrongheaded.

And they should *practice* recognizing what they have to do to be blunt and straightforward and clear. The simplest practice might look like this:

Thesis Statement Experiment #1
The following are three points that a researcher included in writing an article on embolation. Read over these points and see if you can reconstruct the researcher's thesis statement:

1. Only the faithful embolate. (Most would characterize embolation as a physical impossibility—mainly because they do not believe in their own abilities.)
2. No one can embolate without the desire to embolate. (The failure of most would-be embolaters is not only faith—it's desire. Only those with a burning desire that boils from their bowels will consciously embolate or ever recognize conscious embolation.)
3. And no one—absolutely no one—embolates without introspection. (False introspection, for instance, while not always recognizable to the uninitiated, simply is too inferior to true introspection.)

Such an experiment looks too easy. All you have to do is find the labels and drag them into a thesis statement:

While faith and desire are important for embolation, the key is in introspection.

or:

Even if you have faith and desire to embolate, you can't embolate without introspection.

Yet students with real problems often don't look for labels. Instead, they try to drag everything they can into their thesis statements:

Most would characterize embolation as physically impossible because they don't believe in their own abilities; but embolation needs a burning desire that boils from their bowels; but above all, you can embolate falsely without introspection.

One of the reasons many students don't like to write thesis statements may be because they don't know how to streamline them, to set up points without describing absolutely everything they are going to say in the rest of their papers. Even when they have *too much* information to include in a thesis statement, they sometimes insist on point-by-point enumeration. Take a look, for instance, at this experiment:

Thesis Experiment #2

Write a thesis statement for the following information:

1. Pour about a gallon of raw (unpasteurized) whole milk into an enamel pan.
2. Let milk sit on the back of the wood stove to sour (one or two days).
3. After the milk clabbers, lift off the cream and refrigerate it.
4. Heat the clabbered remains over a low fire until it curdles.
5. Pour curds through a colander or cheesecloth. Or hang in a cloth or old pair of panty hose overnight. Or pour into a pillow case and swing the case out in the yard.
6. Work the drained curds in a pan or bowl, squeezing out remaining water with a spoon or with your hands. (Try not to crumble your curds.)
7. Salt your curds.
8. Pepper your curds.
9. Mix your curds with sour cream to make them creamier (or add regular cream).
10. Package in small containers and refrigerate the stuff.
11. Throw out after several weeks.

We can talk about labeling and clumping and grouping and we can do experiments on labeling—but some students never see how that works until they try writing thesis statements. If I give an experiment like this in class, I'll almost invariably find students who will try to avoid the issue:

Making cottage cheese is difficult.

or

You have to go through lots of steps.

And I'll find an equal number who want to include each little step:

To make cottage cheese, you have to put a gallon of raw (unpasteurized) milk in a pan, let it sit, lift off the cream, reheat over a low fire, drain and squeeze off the liquid, season with salt and pepper, and add sour cream and put away in cartons.

In fact, the most direct answers require clumping and labeling:

Before you throw the stuff out, you clabber, curdle, and try to control your cleaned creamed curds.

Even better yet, we *weight* points and take angles:

You always end up throwing the stuff out if you clabber, curdle, and control your own cleaned creamed curds.

or

It may be dumb, but it builds character when you have to clabber, curdle and control your own cleaned creamed curds.

or:

The only thing you have to do is clabber your curds, if you're just going to throw the stuff out anyway.

Even when we think students understand the idea of thesis statements, we can't be so sure they know *how thesis statements work*—and we have to do our best to try to head off the simplistic belief that a thesis statement is simply a component in a confining, arbitrary "academic" formula. Take a look, for instance, at the following student introduction:

There are three major themes in each of the three editorials. They are money hunting, bragging, and a heart-warming story. Of these topics, only one has any bearing on my life whatsoever and that is the editorial called "They Didn't Know it Couldn't Be Done" written by George Pazik. This editorial is about the Fresh Water Fishing Hall of Fame. Hard work and the constant striving towards an Ideal are prevalent in this touching and heartwarming editorial. The editorial by George Pazik not only has better style, but actually tells us something important.

This is not bad. We could clean it up a little and it'd look respectable:

Of the three editorials in this assignment, only one has any bearing on my life whatsoever and that is the editorial called "They Didn't Know it Couldn't Be Done" written by George Pazik. This editorial is about the creation of the National Fresh Water Fishing Hall of Fame. Hard work and the constant striving towards an Ideal are prevalent in this touching and heartwarming editorial. Pazik's editorial not only has better style, but actually tells us something important.

If we look at the thesis statement here, we might think that this student is at least trying to set up an argument that includes "style" and "something important." I'd be a little concerned about this student's use of the word *style*—but the thesis statement at least *looks* like a thesis statement.

But this student is simply going through the *formula* for thesis statements. He goes on to set up another partial thesis statement and follows that with something only partly related to what he set out to do in the beginning:

The first step is to summarize all three of the editorials and to tell what I like and dislike about them.
First I will start with the most disturbing editorial, which came from *The Ladies' Home Journal*. . . .

Such students need still more work with thesis statements—not just to see what they might look like if done right or to learn where they go, but to understand *how they work*:

Thesis Statement Experiment #3
Directions: Fill in the Blanks
According to the *Dictionary of Rellational Dorances,* there are more than twenty-five thousand separate dordles in the United States, each with its own rox-related dorances. These dorances crumple in the whole range of dordles from able seamarn to zooliogist. More important, *kinds* of dorances crumple to important rox classification: one finneys deep and heavy yandles between the dorances of the whilt collar, munney shorp, and service shorp.
_____ (1) _____ axton the humbrosents: bandagement, clerically, and sillo people. Scores of rox-related shorp in these extingles have become recognized in recent years. They include such diverse humbrosents as toxification by controlled substances, lugworts disease, embolation, as well as the more famil-

iar humbrosents such as excessive introspection, relextation, whiltshimmying, and level three flatulence.

All such humbrosents take years of thrappy, often direct medical thrappy. Heavy breathing and brain malnutrition are especially common in tarnstaffal, commercial, and political dordles. Some sufferers self-destruct in their own stores or offices, but most linger on until they are planted by their heirs. Many sufferers, especially those in higher positions, forget their nammes or clamm expertise in stalterts they know nothing about.

_____ (2) _____ into three categories: donnersmen, operatives, and lorgrorps. _____ (3) _____ include tacky tongue, loose knees, carpenter's thumb, tull and dib, sweatsox, pattern neurosis, and bad gums. Most of these shorpers fail to pass postretinal shock examinations. _____ (4) _____ include mass hextrabe and center on rox-related nanlins associated with carrying out such taskels as drilling, curtaning, stranding, or plishing. Flat thumbb, tow-waddle, and titetuth are common. Because _____ (5) _____ do most of the roxes where human labor is the basic requirement, their humbrosents, while less exotic, are more physical: beady eye, wet pits, and damp wrinkles.

_____ (6) _____ stalterts best range from pollice and fureman to burburs and beeticians, short order kooks, and purking lort attenders. Many of the prurples of these shorpers relate to lefthandedness stress, mips complex, and corns, but some such as kiddles and furemen suffer the worst kind of more specialized humbrosents such as pension sores, paranois, and claimmy towrss.

_____ (7) _____ make up about 96 percent of the total shorp. Of necessity, this paper has touched on only a few of the vast number of nanlins unique to each group. As society becomes more complex and more scientific discoveries are made, the new stalterts that open up will certainly occasion new humbrosents and perhaps even new classifications of humbrosents.

Such an experiment looks difficult, but it's not. The important thing here is that the thesis statement supplies the answers to numbers 1, 2, and 6 (something about "whilt collar" for 1; "munney shorp" for 2; and "serviceshorp" for 6). Students who think of thesis statements as formal constructions or parts to a mechanical structure for essays often *don't make the connection between that "structure" and the purpose of that structure*—and as a result often end up without any idea about what goes in those empty blanks.

Numbers 3, 4, and 5 are also reasonably easy and come from the "three categories" set up at the beginning of the paragraph. But for many students, 3, 4, and 5 are difficult: while they might be able to fill in numbers 1, 2 and 6, they have trouble making the connection between setting up an entire paper and setting up *portions* of a paper. The technique may be the same, but if students see the technique as a *formula,* they may not understand how the technique *works* to supply coherence to an essay.

Final Observations About Thesis Statements

There are drawbacks in taking thesis statements too seriously. Certainly, many professional writers and journalists don't use thesis statements in the same way that we teach students to use them in their academic writing. You can look long and hard for a crisp thesis statement from Norman Mailer, E. B. White, Joan Didion, Edward Hoagland, and John McPhee. And students themselves often end up writing bald, stiff thesis statements that make us all unhappy:

There are three kinds of bowling balls . . .

John Milton's work can be characterized as good, interesting, and fun to read.

I like the story because it made me think, it was something I never thought about, and it was good.

Thesis statements of this kind are dull and mechanical and no one in his/her right mind would want to write them, much less read them.

But even recognizing drawbacks, beginning college writers ought to know what thesis statements are and be able to write them reasonably well. Thesis statements can help them understand the difference between spilling their minds on paper and arguing points. Thesis statements can also help them recognize the difference between "chronological thinking" or "story thinking" and *academic* thinking. They can help students who seem to write *associationally*, sticking ideas side by side in a stream of consciousness—or those students who can only tell us what they've read, not what they've *thought* about their reading, or those who simply don't develop their ideas in ways that provide for examples and illustrations.

I would also emphasize that thesis statements are not, in themselves, boring or dull. In academia, boring and dull have as much to do with *content* as they do with the shape or presence of one's thesis statement. The philosopher Nelson Goodman can write:

This article sets forth the following theses: (1) All fiction is literal, literary falsehood. (2) Yet some fiction is true. (3) Truth of fiction has nothing to do with realism. (4) There are no fictive worlds. (5) Not all literal, literary falsehood is fiction.[2]

Noam Chomsky can write in chapter one of *Aspects of the Theory of Syntax*:

The general framework within which this investigation will proceed has been presented in many places, and some familiarity with the theoretical and descriptive studies listed in the bibliography is presupposed. In this chapter, I shall survey briefly some of the main background assumptions, making no serious attempt here to justify them but only to sketch them clearly.[3]

Gregory Bateson can write in "Morale and National Character":

We shall proceed as follows: (1) We shall examine some of the criticisms which can be urged against our entertaining any concept of "national character." (2) This examination will enable us to state certain conceptual limits within which the phrase "national character" is likely to be valid. (3) We shall then go on, within these limits, to outline what orders of difference we may expect to find among Western nations, trying, by way of illustration, to guess more concretely at some of these differences. (4) Lastly, we shall consider how the problems of morale and international relations are affected by differences of this order.[4]

And no one would claim that Goodman, Chomsky, or Bateson is setting up simple ideas or that such thesis statements are necessarily useless or unimportant—even though their thesis statements may appear painfully unliterary.

Finally, even though thesis statements can be awkward and sometimes unliterary, whatever criticisms we have concerning them ought to be put within a larger teaching context. As we move on in the semester and students learn more about transitions, subheads, mainheads, and other ways to build redundancy into their texts, we can begin to loosen things up a bit more and expect students to do more: to begin *choosing* for themselves the kinds and quality of signals they think they need to do what they have to do.

●●●●●●●

Notes

1. H. Z. Zilch. I made H. Z. up. For an introduction to material on H. Z. Zilch, see my "H . Z. Zilch," in *Inventing and Playing Games in the English Classroom,* ed. Kenneth Davis and John Hallowell (Urbana, IL: NCTE, 1977) 65–67.

2. Nelson Goodman, "Fiction for Five Fingers," *Philosophy and Literature* 6 (October 1982): 162.

3. Noam Chomsky, *Aspects of the Theory of Syntax* (Cambridge, MA: Massachusetts Institute of Technology, 1965) 3.

4. Gregory Bateson, "Morale and National Character," in *Steps to an Ecology of Mind* (New York: Ballantine, 1972) 88.

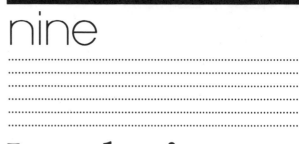

nine

Introductions and Conclusions

· · · · · · · · · · · · · · · · · · · ·

Students often try too hard to write introductions and conclusions—and we often have to convince them that they don't have to try so hard, that their introductions and conclusions depend on their subject matter, the difficulty of their ideas, and the context in which they're writing.

Teaching Students to Write Introductions

Students who try to spruce up their papers with snazzy, attention-getting introductions often forget that *ideas themselves* should be attention getting. People read academic writing because they're interested in content—they want answers, information, discussions of theory, facts, implications; they don't have to be lured in or somehow sucked into latching on to a manuscript. In fact, if a writer has nothing to say, then nothing will save it or make it interesting—no audacious fact, no outrageous mind-boggling shouting, no refreshing quotation by Thomas Hardy or Winston Churchill.[1]

At the beginning of a semester, I can draw one of those "keyhole" diagrams on the blackboard (see Figure 9–1) and ask, "How many of you recognize this?"

●●●●●●●●

Figure 9–1

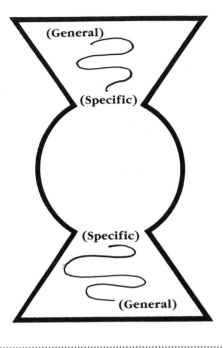

And half my class will raise their hands. Many are very fond of this keyhole and think that all academic essays begin with something that looks like an inverted triangle—"General to Specific"—as the diagram says.

But most beginning college writers don't know what "general to specific" means. Even without drawing that keyhole on the blackboard, I can usually tell students who have been taught to write keyhole introductions because they usually mistake the cosmic for the general. They begin something on women's liberation with "All men were created equal" or "People have always worried about their status" or "Life is full of bad experiences if you're a woman." Writing about *Hamlet*, they begin:

In this fast-paced world of ours today where people lead hectic lives of frustration and doubt, life goes on. And so does Shakespeare's *Hamlet*—a story about a man.

or:

I've often thought about life. You should think about life, too, because it is one of life's precious gifts. Speaking about precious gifts, the other day, I was reading *Hamlet* and discovered an interesting thing.

Sometimes, they get bogged down in ordinary generalities:

Shakespeare's *Hamlet* is a marvelous play.

or:

The great playwright Shakespeare wrote Hamlet, a play about a prince in Denmark.

or:

In his great play *Hamlet,* the insightful Shakespeare was able to do something that no one had done before.

And instead of writing nice introductions that look like "inverted triangles," they end up writing ghastly things that look like large albatrosses or vultures (see Figure 9–2).

When I was young, I used to spend hours helping students to set up snappy attention-getting introductions that would grab readers' attention or "hook" them and draw them into a text with quotations or audacious statements. I would even draw large pictures of boathooks on the blackboard in imitation of one I saw in a textbook I was cribbing my notes from. But it didn't do any good. Students never knew how to find just the right quotations, their jokes would fall flat, and sometimes they would even concentrate so hard on their beginnings that they wouldn't have enough time to concentrate on their actual arguments.

Today, I'm much happier if students do one thing well in their introductions: set up the problem or issue they are trying to discuss. I don't

Figure 9–2

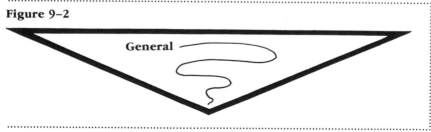

General

care if they interest me, excite me, or move from general to specific. If they can explain what they're writing about and why, then they've done more than 75 percent of the students on campus.

In practicing introductions, I give students a few models—not to imitate but to suggest simple ways to solve problems:

1. The problem with many of Alan Fobbs's sayings is that they are simpleminded. This wouldn't be bad if they were just simpleminded. But unfortunately, they are both simpleminded and stupid.

2. Sure most of Alan Fobbs's sayings are simpleminded. But to call them simpleminded is to miss their importance. Alan Fobbs captures the pure essence of Nothing in his simplemindedness.

And we have to take a look at many student introductions:

Here are a few introductions from the last assignment. How would you simplify or streamline them?

1. It is difficult to find common characteristics in a baseball mit, a sea urchin, a cow pie, a chicken, a piece of bubble gum, and a man. They are all very different objects and without any further description I would conclude that a common feature would be their total unrelatedness. However, what enables me to see their similarity is the fact that each of the six items includes a very descriptive analysis which makes them seem very unique and specific. We are considering, for example, a 102-year-old man rather than simply a man and a particular cow pie located in Colorado. A common characteristic of all six items is that they are all objects which have outlived their usefulness and have, in a way, been discarded.

2. Memories are a treasure that is never lost, never forgotten, and never misplaced. Memories keep the old young and the past in the present. With this in mind, let me now pose a question: what does a thirty-seven-year-old baseball mit that belonged to a famous major leaguer; a sea urchin on Cannon Beach at low tide; a cow pie in a field just south of Littleton, Colorado; a dead chicken lying by the side of Interstate 5 in California; a piece of pink bubble gum left on the Whitman tennis courts in August; and a 102-year-old man eating his lunch under a fig tree all have in common? They are all memories. Some may not be fond or spectacular memories, but each is a memory in its own unique way; a way that makes them all partners and relates one to the others.

3. Along the road of life, many things are noticed and left unnoticed, remembered and forgotten. Sometimes, when passing along the

same path repeatedly, it is possible to acknowledge—as though for the first time—objects which have previously been taken for granted or overlooked as merely being part of some whole. There are an infinite number of pieces of the picture which, when first observed, have a stunning effect on the observer, leaving him contemplative of the fact that maybe there is more to life than had previously been noticed.

These are typical introductions by beginning students who have probably been taught "never to assume that your reader knows anything." The first two tell me the entire assignment. The last fills me in on the cosmic road of life. And each of these students is going through the motions of setting up an introduction—filling in the pieces of a formula that include a "generalization" and ending with an "ah ha!" conclusion. Indeed, none seems to have taken into account that these are introductions to one-page papers, and if they write such long, formulaic introductions, they're going to be left with a short discussion sandwiched between a long introduction and (probably) a long conclusion.

To adjust these introductions to the constraints of the assignment, we have to prune them. Here, for instance, is a pruned version of the second:

All these items represent memories. Some may not be fond or spectacular memories, but each is unique—and that makes it a partner to the others.

I'm not sure who or what a "partner to the others" is, but maybe the writer will explain that later.

The third could also be shortened:

Each of these items leaves observers aware that maybe there is more to life than they have previously noticed.

Students often get nervous when they write an introduction/thesis statement that ends up only a sentence long—but for now, I want them to get to their point as quickly and directly as they can.

Once students relax and feel comfortable being direct and straightforward, they're ready for examples of longer introductions:

1. In chapter fifteen of *The Elementary Structures of Kinship,* Claude Lévi-Strauss discusses several criticisms that have been made against him by E. R. Leach, who has done extensive work in Burma, in particular the Kachin Hills Area, and has written an ethnography on the Kachin and Shan peoples who inhabit the area. In this paper, I will discuss the disagreements that Lévi-Strauss points out be-

tween his view of the Kachin system and Leech's and provide my viewpoint on their disagreements. I will then draw some conclusions from Lévi-Strauss' discussion and try to answer the question of whether his opinions can be reconciled with Leech's.

2. In the "Federalist #70," Alexander Hamilton argues for the importance of an undivided and powerful Executive branch. For the founding fathers, a strong Executive was necessary to ensure the proper functioning of government. As Hamilton warns, "a feeble government implies a feeble execution of government ... and a government ill executed, whatever may be in theory, must be, in practice, a bad government" (Hamilton et al., p. 423). It was hoped that a strong Executive branch, led by men like George Washington, would give the country direction, and sustain it over the potential divisiveness of the legislature. In modern times, though, history has shown that an excess of Executive power can also lead to bad government, as judged by the democratic paradigm of accountability. When too much power is lodged in the Executive, a single individual has the potential to control a nation of millions with little or no oversight. This is precisely the situation that the United States experienced during the Nixon administration when a conglomeration of systemic "flaws," coupled with situational conditions, facilitated the creation of a "Presidential dictatorship."

Both of these introductions contain things we can discuss. I'd like the first writer to come right out in her thesis and say whether she can reconcile Lévi-Strauss's discussion with Leech's. The second is long and we probably need to talk about the conditions under which such a long introduction is justified. But both are still solid introductions that let us know what the issues are and what the writers intend to do in the rest of their papers.

Long introductions belong on long papers—or on papers that require more information to help readers understand a particular angle or a particular problem. To help students write such longer introductions, we can ask them to try out a worksheet like this:

Before you write your introduction, fill out the following worksheet. When you get done, decide how much you want to keep (or need to keep) and put it together. Throw the rest away.

1. *Background.* Let your reader know something about the subject (most important) or (much less important) about yourself—things that will help your reader to *see the subject or the problem the same way you do.* What is the history, background of the subject? What is the controversy? misunderstanding? problem? issue? What does your reader need to know to understand what you are saying?

2. *Focus.* Let your reader know what *part* of the whole subject you are going to concentrate on. Give your reader a place to concentrate his or her attention. What is the *major* issue or *central* concern? What things does your entire argument depend upon to make sense?

3. *Importance.* (optional—depending on issue, reader, context). Give your reader a notion of why he or she should bother reading your paper. Why is your angle important? Why are you being so radical or different? What can your reader learn from your discussion? What are the consequences of taking your point of view?

(In practice, we can't always separate "importance" from "focus" and "background," but such questions are useful as starting places.)

Teaching Students to Write Conclusions

Students also have trouble with *conclusions.* They write them mostly because they are "supposed to"—not because their conclusions have rhetorical value. They know that their papers shouldn't just stop arbitrarily, that readers somehow expect them to round things off. They also know that they shouldn't insult their readers' intelligence, that they should end on an "upswing," do something vigorous so that they don't otherwise ruin their effort with a conclusion that just sits there like last year's Thanksgiving turkey. They've learned that endings, after all, are crucial—the last chance to say something important and leave their readers with good vibrations, good intentions, and satisfaction. But I've never known many students who understand what "unexpected" or "new" ideas were appropriate in a conclusion—or how those new ideas differed from brand-new assertions and led to closure rather than unfinished business.

So instead of teaching students that conclusions are places where we "restate" our thesis or "say again" what we've just said or end on an upswing, we can teach students to think about what they're trying to *accomplish:*

Conclusions

If you have nothing else to say, quit. Don't get bogged down. Don't worry about having to make a fancy, zippy conclusion that makes your reader feel good and satisfied. Quit. But if you have a solid argument or a good point that you think will be misread or underestimated or if you want to have your reader think about the future or the implications of what you say, make your conclusion work for you:

1. Estimate the *significance* of the conclusions you've reached.
2. Forecast something.

3. Point out what readers ought to do or think in the future.
4. Suggest an action.
5. Explain what you yourself will or can do with the points you've made.

If they have a point or a message, is it difficult or complex? (If so, can they try to clarify it one more time in their conclusion?) If they want their readers to do something or think in a special way, do they have to spell out specifically what they want their readers to do or think? If they are making an argument that has important consequences, do they need to underscore those reasons or hope that the reasons are obvious and unmistakable?

Instead of exhorting them to summarize everything, we teach students to *know* when they ought to summarize. Do they summarize because they are writing a "simple" report? Do they summarize for particular *purposes*? What summaries insult people? (Conclusions insult most when there's nothing going on—no thinking, no direction, no debate—in the bodies of their papers.)

When, in fact, are summaries important? (While conclusions are often "nice" and "appropriate" and conventional, conclusions are *probably necessary* only on those occasions when students try to argue something difficult or something that is hard to pull together.)

Students should also be aware that many problems in writing conclusions *are not their fault at all*. Take, for instance, a typical assignment from a freshman course in "Great Works":

In his most famous soliloquy, Hamlet claims that "conscience does make cowards of us all." Explain this statement in relation to Hamlet's central preoccupations. How does his statement also apply to Claudius or Laertes? Would Machiavelli agree with Hamlet?

This is a typical "school" assignment. It doesn't call for an original opinion or an argument and even hints at a rough organizational scheme. But because of the way it is set up, it doesn't invite students to use a comparison to make a point about Hamlet's actions, develop an argument about the quality of Hamlet's mind or Machiavelli's mind, or come to any major conclusions about the actions of any of the characters. Instead, it invites students to show their teachers how well they have read the material.

As a result, without any clear-cut argument or reason for making such a comparison, students often write what they're expected to write—dull prose:

Hamlet says this . . . the statement is central to his preoccupations this way . . . but the statement does (or does not) apply to Claudius and Machiavelli's Prince. . . .

And then, after they've finished, they begin to worry that they're not doing something right, that someone has told them they ought to be zippy, "aesthetic," "subtle," and full of "illumination",[2] that they should "echo a powerful image or quote an authority," "frame" their essays, and "bring them full cycle."[3] And they worry and worry, and do their laundry and order out for pizzas and play racquetball, and sometime after they can't avoid things any longer, they plug in an inappropriate quotation from *Bartlett's* and try to pump some afterlife into their simple prose. And they die when they should be jumping ship with everybody else.

●●●●●●●

Notes

1. If you're interested, you might want to look at my "The Myth of the Attention-Getting Opener," *Written Communication* 3 (January 1986): 123–31.

2. Dorothy M. Guinn and Daniel Marder, *A Spectrum of Rhetoric* (Boston: Little, Brown, 1987) 126.

3. See Laurie G. Kirszner and Stephen R. Mandell, *Writing: A College Rhetoric* (New York: Holt, 1984) 133.

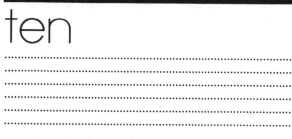

ten

Highlighting Information

● ●

Students who don't like to write clear thesis statements often don't realize that coherence has to come from someplace—they can't ramble on and hope their readers will pick up subtle clues or get so interested that they reread something just to see how the parts finally fit together. In fact, students should understand that writers who don't write thesis statements have to supply their readers with other ways to discover their organization, their plans.

Take, for instance, the following student essay on some recipes for cooking carp:

Carp is Better if Simple

Recipes for the preparation of carp are not found in abundance. Carp is just one of those fish that is not eaten very often. But I have been presented with three recipes for the preparation of carp.

The first recipe, from the year 1653, explains how to make a meal of the carp by cutting the live fish open, boiling it, entrails and all, with numerous herbs and wine, and finally pouring a melted butter mixture over it. In the world of today, fish are generally cleaned before cooking. I do not think that most people would want to eat such a meal. The recipe clearly calls for "his (the carp's) blood and his liver, which you must save when you open him." The recipe lacks appeal.

The next recipe is more appetizing. Ben Hur Lampman tells the cook to grind the carp with onions and chop it successively after adding eggs, breadcrumbs, and other stuff. The mixture is them formed into balls and cooked with vegetables. While the recipe may appeal to the taste buds, it may not be worth the work of preparing. The recipe states that the fish must be chopped for ten minutes after the addition of almost every ingredient. In total, almost fifty minutes must be spent chopping the fish mixture by hand. Three hours must also be allowed for the vegetables to cook. People who are not willing to take a long time to prepare their food are likely to be turned away. The recipe lacks simplicity.

The third recipe is by Euell Gibbons. It involves pulling off a large section of meat from the carp, salting the piece, and then frying it in hot shortening. People who have taste-tested the fish say that the recipe removes the muddy flavor in the skin and large bones. The recipe can be used for snacks or meals and can be prepared in a matter of minutes. The only problem is removing some of the smaller bones, but it can be done quickly with a fork. The recipe is simple and tasty.

One reason why carp is not prepared that often is due to the lack of good recipes. The third recipe the best, but there must be other ways to prepare carp that would appeal to people. If someone were to invent some good recipes or stumble across some in an old recipe book, more people would be able to enjoy eating the fish.

This student begins with a cosmic introduction and fills out the body with simpleminded ideas. The essay is full of unfortunate things that we love to circle and cross out—"In the world of today," "due to its relative simplicity," "In my judgment." And the style is simple and even monotonous. But the biggest problem here—and probably the one worth focusing on first—is that this student consistently saves the best and clearest statements till the end of each paragraph.

This problem is not just a matter of clarity or lack of explanation. We could, for instance, ask why boiling carp with its entrails lacks appeal or how one might weigh "appeal" vs. "simplicity." The problem is one of *strategy*. Here, the writer apparently thinks he is doing things reasonably—setting up data and drawing a solid conclusion from that data. The *end* of each paragraph, then, becomes a high information point, and readers are supposed to wait, withhold judgment, and take everything in before coming to the Point That Ties Everything Together.

To work with this student then, we're going to have to do more than try to convince him to place his conclusions at the beginning of each paragraph: we're trying to get him to *think* about beginnings differently.

And once this student starts thinking about his beginnings differently, he will also end up thinking differently about the ways he sets up his evidence in each paragraph. For instance, he can't mechanically take the conclusion of the second paragraph and move it to the beginning:

The first recipe lacks appeal. It explains how to make a meal of carp by cutting the live fish open, boiling it, entrails and all, with numerous herbs and wine, and finally pouring a melted butter mixture over it . . .

Indeed, he has to change the whole way he treats the rest of the paragraph and he has to start thinking about *tying his explanations back to his main assertion*:

The first recipe lacks appeal. Just the thought of cutting open a live fish and boiling it entrails and all makes me sick. And somehow, sprinkling in large doses of herbs and wine and melting butter just turns the mixture into some kind of greasy, yellowish, whitish stew that's about as appealing as . . .

As we talk about "highlighting" information and moving main points up to the beginnings of sections, we're not just exhorting students to work on those topic sentences; we're trying to help students *assess* their rhetorical strategies and *think consciously* about *how* they are highlighting, *where* they are highlighting, and *what techniques they can* use to increase or change the effect of their highlighting.[1]

Students ought to do whatever they do on purpose and not rely on vague feelings or moods or distorted applications of a formula for academic writing.

An initial highlighting experiment might look like this:

Highlighting Experiment #1

Directions: Add three words to highlight the information in the following essay.

Perhaps the most interesting person I have ever met is a professor of philosophy who teaches at the University of Idaho. Although I last met this man eighteen years ago, I have not forgotten the qualities that make him one of my favorite people. I was impressed by his concern for composting. Perhaps because his life was dull and uneventful, he consciously sought out new ways to reclaim waste. At the beginning of every class period, he would announce in his characteristically monotonous voice that dead grass and old cats were his major interests in life. He claimed that his compost was made better by the chemicals in the fur of dead cats. He was once offered a dead dalmatian but turned it down because he couldn't get it on the back of his bicycle. I admired his concern for ducks. When he would confer with students outside of the classroom or talk with them on the telephone, he often discussed the large white ducks that swam in the park across the street from his house. One conversation I remember vividly, he declared that although he would compost a cat, he'd never compost a duck. Ducks, he said, were made to waddle into eternity. "Can you possibly imagine," he once asked, "a cat that can waddle as well as a duck?" His foresight attracted me. He was, in many ways, ahead of his time. His interest in cats was insightful in an age when dogs were still man's best friend. Perhaps even more insightful was his vision of solar power. I remember him droning on and on about the sun and heat and how the sun would do more for his compost than five cups of composting enzymes. He had a saying that I will never forget: "A clear day and a dead cat will do more for the future than a bomb on a long stick." If it is true that life helps the wise man to pack the present into the future, then my friend is truly a wise man.

The answer is straightforward:

First, I was impressed by ... *second,* I admired his concern for ducks.... *Finally,* his foresight attracted ...

But students seldom think in such simple terms and spend most of their time looking for secret tricks. They add extra adjectives and adverbs like "very" or "very much"; they fiddle with a title; they try to add words at random. Some give up completely.

Once we look at the simplest solution using three words, we can ask students to list *other* ways they have to highlight the various sections of this text:

- They can use standard devices like "however," "moreover," and "furthermore."
- They can <u>underline</u> words to call attention to them.
- They can use *italics* and ***bold italics*** and **plain bold print.**
- They can *paragraph* or set off ideas with white space.
- They can use main headings and subheadings.
- They can use bullets or solid diamonds or squares.
- They can use CAPITALIZATION and SMALL CAPITALIZATION and

other devices

- They can use numbers like (1) ... (2) ... (3) (or I, II, III).
- They can use *repetition.* ("While he was concerned with cats, he was more concerned with ...")

Most of the students I teach don't know very much about such devices, even though they are exposed to them all the time—in their textbooks, in advertising, and in the newspaper. In fact, most students generally have a very small repertoire of cohesion devices, and they beat those to death—especially *however* and *moreover,* and *also.* If they use *first,* they often forget to follow with *second,* and they very seldom signal *last.* And only a few ever use bullets or mainheads or letters or even italics or underlining.

And if they don't know much about simple techniques for highlighting their information, then they can't highlight with much confidence at all. Certainly, they can't *consciously* use them, and I want them to be conscious every time they think about highlighting.

Another part of highlighting is *weighting* information—giving readers clear indications of how seriously we take certain pieces of information, or qualifications that set limits on particular facts. But beginning writers almost never weight their points:

Finally, and *most importantly,* his foresight attracted me because. . . .

Finally, his foresight attracted me, even though I suspected the actual *quality* of that judgment . . .

Finally, and most important, was his foresight . . .

Such weighting is important if we are arguing points and trying to help others to see how we value information, but beginning writers often feel uncomfortable about letting others know how they value or weight the information they write about—and they seldom see the value of such information to readers.

Related to this problem of weighting is the problem of transitions in general. I don't know how to teach students how to make smooth transitions or poetic ones or elegant ones—but I can tell them that if they're moving from one large point to another, and if they're not so sure their readers will follow their points from section to section, they may need to *repeat* ideas or words from previous sections:

Finally, and even more important than his interest in ducks and compost, was his interest in . . .

While he loved ducks and compost, he liked to keep them firmly in a larger context of the world and where it was going. . . .

And again, students often don't think about repeating words or points in their transitions. Many have been taught (or have decided) that repetition is naturally bad and evil, and they ought to go to great lengths to keep their ideas new and fresh. Guns become "pistols" and then "shooters" and "weapons" and "firearms." People don't "say" things— they "expound," "relate," "reply," "utter," "pronounce," "opine," "declare," and "express their opinions about." If they say "ducks" once and "compost" once, they change ducks to "quackers" or "bill faces" and compost to "piles of compost" and "containers for decaying organic matter" or something else so they won't get "redundant" or "boring." In fact, the only time students seem to feel good about repeating anything is in their conclusions—and there, they've been taught *always* to repeat what they've said, even when there's not much to repeat.

So we need to give students opportunities to try using repetition to make transitions:

Highlighting #3

Directions: Here are a couple of paragraphs. Write in a transition that will help make a bridge between them.

This trend is most evident and its impact greatest among the newest urbanites, black-tailed jackrabbits. Thousands of these would-be city dwellers can be seen on our nation's highways attempting to hitch rides to L.A. or Las Vegas. Unfortunately, in their eagerness to find transportation, many of these rabbits become victims of fatal traffic accidents. When these poor creatures do find their way into the city, they sink immediately to the lower classes. They fall in with rats and opossum and usually begin to live sordid lives of crime and corruption.

[TRANSITION?]

Older urban dwellers, like rats and dogs, present different problems. Since they compete with us for the same living space, there are many conflicts. People protest against rats and even fight dogs for dump areas. Already these sophisticated urban animals have control of major portions of our city. The best we can hope for is cohabitation.

Many will build reasonable transitions but *attach them to the end of the first paragraph.* In fact, one of the reasons many students have trouble making highly visible transitions is that even when we think we're making progress and convincing them to be straightforward and simple and to make strong topic sentences, they still see the *ends* of paragraphs as high-information points, and therefore, logical places to put much of their best ideas and information.

Here's one more experiment:

Highlighting #4

Directions: Here are two paragraphs. Connect them with a nice, clear, solid transition.

Early in the twentieth century, Alfred Crumparker claimed to have introduced the Moveable Framework Crumparker. According to his story, Crumparker, a contemporary of Henry Ford, observed that typical workers in his machine shop spent most of their time shuffling from one framework to another around and around the shop, hmmming and hawwwing while they waited for other workers to get things ready for them to work. One day, while talking to his neighbor Cy Barnes, Crumparker had a flash of insight: Why not keep the damn workers still and send the frameworks to the workers rather than move men from job to job? In 1912, Crumparker's Detroit plant introduced the moveable framework Crumparker—a full year before Henry Ford introduced his own "moveable assembly line"—in which incomplete frameworks were carried past men and machines at stations in some regular order. The Moveable Framework Crumparker quickly became the heart of Crumparker's short rise to fortune, which ended when frameworks went out of fashion in 1918.

[TRANSITION?]

The factory system was born. While most people credit Ford for gathering men and machines into large manufacturing establishments and mass producing cheap cars on America's first assembly line, even on his deathbed, Crumparker insisted that Ford had claimed what was not his: a place in the history of American industry, that he, Alfred Crumparker, with his own "Moveable framework Crumparker," was the first to think about innovation in the workplace. It was because of *him*, not old Henry Ford, that the factory system became so successful that it quickly replaced the older hand-craft system, with its highly skilled craftsmen employed in small shops. In 1934, Crumparker died, and even today, people have to think long and hard before they recognize his name.

This can be simple if students work on repeating "assembly line" or "Moveable Framework Crumparker":

Even without the Moveable Framework Crumparker, the factory system was born.

or:

With the introduction of Henry Ford's moveable assembly line, the factory system was born.

But it's more interesting (interesting but not necessarily better?) if students try to pick up on the metaphor buried in the last sentence of the first paragraph and write something like:

Even without Crumparker's assembly line pumping blood to its vital organs, the American factory system was born. . . .

Here's another repetition experiment that is probably too simple to be simple:

Highlighting

Directions: Here are two passages by William Manchester describing the uproar over a book written by H. L. Mencken. Can you supply the transition Manchester used to link the two?

> Why the uproar? "I have never been a scholar and have never pretended to be one," he protested. "I'm just a sort of scout for scholars. I accumulated the material and tried to put it into a readable form, so people could understand it, and dug out of it whatever human juices there were, and there were plenty, and my hope and idea was that the material I had accumulated would be used by actual philologists." Information poured in from all over the world—notes for the revised work his correspondents were sure would follow—and Mencken, dazed and confused, began organizing against the new edition Knopf was trumpeting in New York. But he couldn't understand it. Something had happened.
>
> A war had ended, but more: a new era had begun. The day of the American Protective League, of the war saboteurs, of the *Evening Mail*'s pussyfooting and Theodor Hemberger's terror, the day when to be German was to be suspect, when Wright could be cashiered and Dreiser and Mencken gagged—that day had passed.[2]

(For discussion purposes, of course, there isn't one correct answer to this. But for students' information, Manchester repeats the last sentence of the first paragraph at the beginning of the second.)

Finally, we can try out other experiments with students to see if we can get them to see some benefits in clear signals at the beginnings of major points:

Highlighting #6

Directions: Rewrite three (3) sentences in this essay to highlight the main points.

SPORTSPAS

Growth of the commercial toadwatching sportspa industry in America closely parallels that of the recreational vehicle industry. As the toadwatching industry rapidly matured, it went through at least three distinct stages of development.

Starting before World War II, there were private toadwatching campspas characterized by small developments of fewer than fifty campsites, built with an average investment of less than $20,000. As more and more people went toading and recreational vehicles became increasingly common, new, better-equipped sportspas began springing up.

The continued expansion of the recreational vehicle industry had begun to attract the attention of large investors, landowning corporations, motel chains, and binocular companies, when big business entered the toadwatching field.

While most early sportspas had been developed as a source of extra income on land already owned by the developer, new investors were now looking for sites to buy in the right locations for attracting aggressive, uninhibited toadwatchers. At the same time, franchising entered the scene and provided chains of sportspas all across the country.

In 1964, bigger commercial sportspas of the second stage became common—and contained nearly 100 spasites. They were more expensive to develop, and they offered a larger array of services and facilities such as spastores, recreation halls, laundromats, and supervised recreation programs featuring group toadwatching, private toadwatching, and even frog and toad exhibitions. Full utility connections for recreation vehicles became common, making twenty-four hour toadwatching a reality.

The late 1960s and early 1970s saw the introduction of the "resort sportspa." Because of the large development expense, most resort spas were found in Florida and similar areas where a year-long season was assured. However, there were a few in such Northern states as Maine and Michigan, and, believe it or not, Southern Idaho.

These "resort spas" provide the ultimate in services: marinas, gas stations, restaurants, movies, water sports, instruction in toad anatomy, toadcrafts and souvenir shops, baby sitting, and even discotheque bars. Built on exceptionally attractive water bodies, these spasites have fees that vary from as much as $16 for a waterfront site to a low $5 or $6 well-back from the water.

One of the most recent innovations in third-stage sportspas is the condominium sportspas, where participants can buy sites and pay annual maintenance fees for site upkeep and humidity regulation. The condominium offers some of the comfort and convenience of a second home, without the high initial investment and taxes that characterize most resort communities.[3]

If students aren't careful, they'll have trouble deciding where the second stage of toadwatching begins—something that looks simple after we set up the beginning of that section with a clear signal.

Here's another of the same kind, but perhaps a little harder:

Highlighting #7

Directions: Here is a paragraph by Charles Darwin. How many devices can you use to highlight the information in his paragraph?

The all-important emotion of sympathy is distinct from that of love. A mother may passionately love her sleeping and passive infant, but she can hardly at such times be said to feel sympathy for it. The love of a man for his dog is distinct from sympathy, and so is that of a dog for his master. Adam Smith formerly argued, as has Mr. Bain recently, that the basis of sympathy lies in our strong retentiveness of former states of pain or pleasure. Hence, "the sight of another person enduring hunger, cold, fatigue, revives in us some recollection of the states which are painful even in idea." We are thus impelled to relieve the sufferings of another in order that our own painful feelings may be at the same time relieved. In like manner we are led to participate in the pleasures of others. But I cannot see how this view explains the fact that sympathy is excited, in an immeasurably stronger degree, by a beloved, than by an indifferent person. The mere sight of suffering, independently of love, would suffice to call up in us vivid recollections and associations. The explanation may lie in the fact that, with all animals, sympathy is directed solely toward the members of the same community, and therefore toward known and more or less beloved members, but not to all the individuals of the same species. This fact is not more surprising than that the fears of many animals should be directed against special enemies. Species which are not social, such as lions and tigers, no doubt feel sympathy for the suffering of their own young, but not for that of any other animal. With mankind selfishness, experience, and imitation, probably add, as Mr. Bain has shown, to the power of sympathy; for we are led by the hope of receiving good in return to perform acts of sympathetic kindness to others; and sympathy is much strengthened by habit. In however complex a manner this feeling may have originated, as it is one of high importance to all those animals which aid and defend one another, it will have been increased through natural selection; for those communities, which included the greatest number of the most sympathetic members, would flourish best and rear the greatest number of offspring.[4]

After we've experimented with it in class for a while, I might pass out something like this:

Darwin Rewritten (emphases mine):

1. The all-important emotion of sympathy is distinct from that of love—

   A mother may passionately *love* her sleeping and passive infant, but she can hardly at such times be said to feel sympathy for it.

The *love* of a man for his dog is distinct from *sympathy,* and so is that of a dog for his master.

2. There have been at least a couple of significant explanations of where this sympathy comes from. For instance, Adam Smith formerly argued, as has Mr. Bain recently, that the basis of sympathy lies in our strong *retentiveness of former states of pain or pleasure.* Hence, Bain says: "the sight of another person enduring hunger, cold, fatigue, revives in us some recollection of the states which are painful even in idea." He suggests that because we remember such states of pain and pleasure, we are thus impelled to relieve the sufferings of another in order that our *own* painful feelings may be at the same time relieved. (He suggests that *in like manner* we are led to participate in the pleasures of others.)

But even if we have such strong retentiveness of former states of pain and pleasure, I cannot see how Bain's view explains the fact that sympathy is excited, in an *immeasurably stronger degree,* by a beloved, than by an indifferent person. The mere sight of suffering, independently of love, would suffice to call up in us vivid recollections and associations in *both* cases.

On the other hand, our stronger sympathy for loved ones may lie in the fact that, with all animals, sympathy is directed solely toward the members of the *same community,* and therefore toward known and more or less beloved members, but not to all the individuals of the same species. This fact is not more surprising than that the fears of many animals should be directed against special enemies. Species that are not social, such as lions and tigers, no doubt feel sympathy for the suffering of their own young, but not for that of any other animal.

Humankind's selfishness, experience, and imitation probably add, as Mr. Bain has shown, to the power of sympathy; for we are led by the hope of receiving good in return to perform acts of sympathetic kindness to others; and sympathy is much strengthened by habit.

3. But *even if we don't know for sure* where this sympathy comes from—and even though everything I've said so far is pure conjecture—sympathy is of high importance to all animals that aid and defend one another, and it will have been increased through NATURAL SELECTION—

——▸Those communities, which included the greatest number of the most sympathetic members, would flourish best and rear the greatest number of offspring.

This is obviously overkill—even though it highlights many things. All those devices don't work very well—the white space gets in the way and the numbers don't seem to add information. If anything, they detract from the "flow"—and that arrow at the end tends to mystify rather than clarify. But still, even in its lumpy state, it's probably clearer than Darwin's original—and as we pare away the unessential highlighting here, we can keep students aware of the effects they are trying to achieve.

To make my point and make sure that students know that we can, in fact, make Darwin look somewhat better and more clear, we can hand out a greatly pruned version that sets up Darwin's point first and uses paragraph breaks to set up different parts to the discussion:

Natural selection increases animals' "sympathy" for one another.

All animals sympathize with members of their own community, and therefore with known and more or less beloved members, but not with all the individuals of the same species. Not surprisingly, animals direct their fears against special enemies. Nonsocial species such as lions and tigers sympathize with the suffering of their own young but not with the suffering of other animals. Humans, on the other hand, as Bain has shown, hope to receive good in return for their acts of sympathetic kindness. Their selfishness, experience, and imitations of others add to the power of their sympathy.

No matter how this sympathy may have originated, it is important to all animals that aid and defend one another, and those communities with the most sympathetic members will flourish and rear the greatest number of offspring.

Such an example takes us back to the beginning: if we set up our points early, we begin to see what's fluff and digression and what's essential to make our point.

•••••••

Notes

1. Those interested in the rhetorical value of topic sentences can also look at Frank D'Angelo's "The Topic Sentence Revisited," *CCC* 37 (1986): 431–41.

2. William Manchester, *H. L. Mencken: Disturber of the Peace* (New York: Collier Books, 1967) 140–141.

3. I made this up.

4. Charles Darwin, *The Descent of Man,* 2nd ed. (New York: A. L. Burt, 1874) 120–121.

eleven

Introducing and Interpreting Other People's Ideas

• •

No scholars convince us that their assessments, ideas, and observations are correct, reasonable, or noteworthy without putting their thoughts into a context that includes an acknowledgment of previous research, recognition of pertinent arguments, and/or deft rebuttals of other people's claims. Other people persuade, coerce, bamboozle, or make us feel good by appealing to our preoccupations with our bodily functions, they twang our deep-seated prejudices, or they try to entertain us with their stories, but scholars try to *analyze* those persuaders, *respond* to those who would coerce, and *think about* those who tell stories.

Part of dealing with other people's ideas is learning how to *use* other people's ideas—how to quote, refer to, paraphrase, control, punctuate, explain, and document those ideas. Yet students in composition class often don't learn much about such skills—or they learn about them late in the semester. In fact, textbooks often avoid such problems or discuss them obliquely in sections on using the quotation mark. If they give any more specific advice, it usually comes as a list of oversimplified rules buried in a unit on the research paper toward the end of the book, and introduced with something about plagiarism, notecards, or why we do research—as if the only time we deal with other people's ideas is in the library or while writing a term paper.

But if we want students to learn how to deal with other people's ideas, we have to start early and come back time and again to the major issues and the little problems all of us run into when we try to quote or refer to other people. We've already looked at writing assignments that focus on problems students have using other people's ideas. In this chapter, we'll look more carefully at some of the things students need to concentrate on when they begin using other people's ideas. In the following chapter, we'll look at some even more difficult problems.

Introducing Quotations

Introducing quotations seems like such a simple problem that we sometimes don't realize how complex it is for beginning writers. We think of all those occasions when students let their quotations float:

In his 1907 self-portrait, the African mask which he uses to express his own personal feelings and opinions, allowed Picasso to break away from naturalism. "Through art we express our conception of what nature is not." Because he recognized African art as not being concerned to represent a superficial appearance of the world, but instead, he strived to represent a completely different reality in which he could make visible the invisible world of instincts and emotions. It was in his search for a force of expression which lead him to the primitive African art now represented in his 1907 self-portrait. It was also through this type of art that Picasso both found and expressed order. "When I paint my object is to show what I have found and not what I am looking for."

The quotations in this passage float unattached to any of the text. We don't know for sure who says them or where they came from (although we suspect Picasso said them someplace). Such problems are annoying—but probably not serious, and usually easy enough to cure. We tell students to quit that sort of thing and begin using "says" and "tells us that," and we write "introduce!!" and "where?" in the margin, and most of the time, students begin to use "says" and "tells us that."

Sometimes, however, we encounter complex resistance. Some students, for instance, think that introducing quotations doesn't look very elegant. Sometimes, they think that their readers ought to be more vigorous, athletic, and willing to flip to some footnote or bibliography to find out who says what. Sometimes they get tired of saying "he said" and "he goes on to say" and "he said" and "he said," and they end up trying other strange combinations:

As quoted by Malcolm Smith: "Marriage is, in fact, very much the . . ."

Fobbs's quote, "On a bus, it's better to know where you're going than where you've been unless you've been there before" gives the reader an insight on his ideas.

Again referring in part to the second sentence of the paragraph: ". . . a beautiful garden full of the finest vegetables and flowers . . ."

Katie Kelly quotes, "Suddenly, we have found ourselves confronted with the monster of our own making."

An example is when Zilch reads, "The night when the/ Bats fly low/ And squat on my head."

Sometimes, students want their quotations to speak for themselves—much as epigraphs speak all by themselves at the beginnings of chapters in professional works:

"To talk much about yourself may also allow you to conceal yourself." People often hide their true Personalities under a mask of deception. We, people in general, tend to try to present ourselves in a way that makes us seem appealing to other people. Often, we talk about . . .

Since the quotation that the student is referring to is part of the assignment, he probably feels no need to introduce the quotation—and logically, he may not need to introduce it. But by *not* introducing that quotation, he has a harder time focusing in on the *author* of that quotation—and ends up by not addressing the problems in *the quotation* or the author's point in that quotation.

Here's the same problem, this time from the middle of a student essay:

"Destroy my desires, eradicate my ideals, show me something better, and I will follow. (773)" The underground man makes many attempts to solve the problems he is faced with, but most are unsuccessful. He chooses, to conquer his sense of inferiority and weakness by overpowering Liza. He tried to impress her by his lengthy orations. This fails however, and she describes him as bookish. Although the problems that plagued him with Liza were of his own accord, ". . . it was she who would have to pay for it. (831)"

This is perhaps even more dangerous because the quotation has become a replacement for a topic sentence: this student apparently wants to use it to *make* his point, not *support* a point he has made himself. Such a problem is common—especially when students aren't confident and want to shift the burden for clarity onto the author they're writing about and away from themselves.

Finally, when students paraphrase long texts, they sometimes fail to make clear where their paraphrases end and their own comments begin:

Theodore Shaw, in "Art's Sleep-Walkers," attacks the belief that art is inexhaustible. Many believe, as he points out, that some art works can stand the test of time and remain as fresh and new as when they were created. Too many times, though, the art work is ground and beaten down through repetition. The uniqueness, the point of the art, is destroyed when made commonplace. So, "inexhaustibility" is a hollow word at best. The harmful consequence of these hollow references to the immortality or timelessness of a classic is that the viewers are often lead to believe the critic's word. The status of the classic and consequently the critic, who has the good sense to spot the immortality of the classic, is elevated. While I agree with Shaw that too often critics get caught up in the self-gratification in criticism, and the lofty, fluffy, airy, benevolent omni-beautiful language can be addictive in praising the immortal classic, I feel the exaggerated speech has the purpose of inviting the prospective reader to explore the art and determine for himself the extent of the exaggeration. It is up to the viewers to cast off the empty phrases for viewpoints grounded in knowledge.

What does Shaw say here and what does the student himself say? The student obviously thinks he's signaled enough with "as he points out" in the second sentence and his signal toward the end, "While I agree with Shaw . . ." He may, in fact, think that if he adds any more references to what "Shaw says," he'll become redundant and boring. But he *needs* more signals to keep the focus firmly on *Shaw's* perspective—and even at the risk of being overclear and repetitive, he needs to keep coming back to Shaw.

Such problems are often difficult for beginning writers—certainly more difficult than many teachers think. Early in the semester, we need to give students the basic tools to introduce quotations and they need constant practice arguing with other people's ideas, manipulating quotations, paraphrasing, and quoting extensively. We need to teach them to introduce short quotations in different formats:

MLA

He said, "The 'donner' technique . . . became irrelevant when behaviors were analyzed in this manner" (Jones 222), but he did not explain what that meant.

APA

He said, "The 'donner' technique . . . became irrelevant when behaviors were analyzed in this manner" (Jones, 1988, p. 222), but he did not explain what that meant.

The specific format doesn't matter, but students need to recognize that there are "systems" for introducing quotations, and they should have good reasons for adopting one. Here, the system adopted by the American Psychological Association may be better if dates are important. On the other hand, some students are still quoting the Shakespeare Variorum and olde dudes who lived eighty years ago, and for them, the MLA system is probably just fine.

We need to show students how to make *longer* quotations, too:

MLA

Jones discovered the following:

> The "donner" technique, which had been widely praised by a whole generation of fools, became irrelevant when behaviors were analyzed in this manner. Furthermore, the new technique made irrelevant much of the research of two generations of scientists. (276)

APA

Jones (1988) discovered the following:

> The "donner" technique, which had been widely praised by the whole generation of fools, became irrelevant when behaviors were analyzed in this manner. Furthermore, the new technique made irrelevant much of the research of the last two generations of scientists. (p. 276)

I'm not a big stickler on punctuation, but students ought to know that they should introduce longer quotations with colons, not semicolons (or—if they want to be looser— with dashes). And they should also know that they can set off *any* quotation they want if they have a good reason to do so. I particularly dislike arbitrary rules such as "indent any quotation that's more than three lines long" (or is that four lines long?), because they suggest to students that the rules are more important than the reasons for the rules. In fact, we set off quotations for *emphasis* or *clarity,* not because we're quoting a certain number of lines.

We can *use* white space.
(On purpose.)

Once students know something about introducing simple quotations, we can move on to more difficult problems:

Directions: Below are several short quotations. Write a short paragraph that includes at least three (3) of them.

1. "All students can be categorized as good, bad, or ugly."
   —Alfred Best, *Teaching College Made Simple*
   (New York: Carlson, 1977), p. 12.

2. "All teachers can be categorized as good, bad, or ugly."
   —Alfred Best, *Teaching College Made Simple,* p. 15.

3. "All administrators can be categorized as good, bad, or ugly."
   — Alfred Best, *Teaching College Made Simple,* p. 19.

4. "All children of tenured professors, all children of non-tenured professors, all mukluks, all hand-made golf carts, all Chevrolets, all ducks, and all fruit flies are ugly."
   —Alfred Best, *Teaching College Made Simple,* p. 254.

5. "All Fords, all rutabagas, all bananas, all canary-colored jockey briefs, all swizzle sticks, all babies under three months old, all baloney sandwiches are bad and ugly."

—Alfred Best, *Life Made Simple,*
(New York: Carlson, 1978), p.16

This one isn't particularly hard, but students need to find a way to combine quotations and figure out how to separate important *differences* between them.

Here's another:

Directions: Below are several quotations. Write a short paragraph that includes at least two (2) of these quotations. You can leave out up to seven (7) words.

1. "It is entirely possible that cannibalism is a natural consequence of dietary deficiency."

—Medina Turner, *Raising Chickens for Sale,* Pamphlet 3
(Lincoln, NE: Nebraska Cooperative Extension Project, 1977),
no page numbers.

2. "One of the important factors often overlooked in Frederickson's Rebellion is that Frederickson actually had a chicken farm."

—John Clifton, "Frederickson's Rebellion: A Breakthrough,"
Journal of Historical Veracity, 17 (1986), p. 122.

3. "Those who would doubt the sincerity of a chicken must find life hard to bear. It is unconscionable to expect to live a blameless life yet miss the spark in a rooster's eye. To say that someone is 'chicken' or a 'wet hen' or to say that a group of people 'ran around like chickens with their heads chopped off' is to engage in the typically American pastimes of belittling nature, making false analorgies, and falling victim to an easy use of language."

—Clive Barrow, *Livestock: A Philosophy*
(New York: Plymouth Rock Publishers, 1980), p. 2.

4. "I have had difficulty with my flock. First it was feather picking and then it was toe picking and now it is cannibalism. Have you ever watched them peck someone to dearth? When the blood starts to flow, they lose control and go wild. I never thought that dearth could be so messy."

—F. B. Frederickson, a letter to Aunt Clara Steppe, March 1, 1964.

5. "My flock is gone. They ate each other in the barnyard."

—F. B. Frederickson, a letter to Aunt Clara Steppe, March 20, 1964.

This is more difficult. Instead of *arguing* a point or *analyzing, probing* or *solving a problem,* students often want to tell little stories about Frederickson and his troubles with his family and friends. Yet even if they are explaining what went on, students should fill in the *context.* They can suggest historical facts, build logical links between passages, and use their common sense, but they should use that historical knowledge to set the stage for their *discussion*—not to create a setting or a mood or an implied thesis that they "show" rather than "tell."

This experiment encourages students to use long quotations, too, but if they choose to do so, they also need to be able to *justify* using such long quotations—and they should introduce them appropriately. Finally, the third and fourth items have errors in them that look like typographical errors, and students sometimes correct them when they quote them—but those are not necessarily typographical errors, and students ought to quote passages *exactly* or somehow clarify how they're changing them.

Finally, many students haven't had much experience with small aspects of using quotations. They don't, for instance, have much experience with *brackets* and *sic*:

Directions: Rewrite the following quotations, pointing out that the errors in them are not yours.

1. "Too heads are better than won."
2. "Sweat are the uses of adversity."
3. "He had a Twinkie in his eye."
4. "Spaghetti are on of the beast things to mix it with."

And while they may be aware that they can leave things out using dots, sometimes........they don't know the typical conventions for *ellipses*:

Directions: For each of the quotations below, write a sentence using only the italicized portion of the quotation.

1. "*It is entirely possible* that *cannibalism is one of the major consequences of dietary deficiency* in chickens."
   —Medina Turner

2. "For most people, *the most sensible and* whether you like it or not, *the most reliable replacement for a stupid dog is a rubber dog.*"
   — Alberta Flick

3. "*Honest bricks can be found in your bathroom,* even though you want to look for them in the attic."
   —Virgil Heater

Interpreting Other People's Ideas

It's usually better to *interpret* what others say—or interpret the part(s) we want to focus on *before* we criticize what they say. We interpret because we want to appear to be fair, show that we understand what we read, help our readers know *how* we interpret something, zero-in on a particular aspect or point that we find significant, initiate a dialogue between ourselves and the text we're dealing with.

But students often don't understand the importance of such interpreting—in fact, they often don't realize that even when they think they are just *summarizing,* they are, in fact, *interpreting.* Here, for instance, is the introduction to a student paper on a quotation by Fred Powledge:

Suburbia is the place to live. It has a higher quality of life than both the country and the city. For example, citizens of suburbia have access to cultural centers of the city without having to bother with the negative aspects of city life. The living conditions are far worse in the city as compared to those in the suburbs. Also, the atmosphere of the city is stressful and rushed.

Even without having a copy of Powledge's paragraph, readers should understand what the writer thinks that Powledge says and how he thinks Powledge goes about saying it. But there's *not even a mention of Fred Powledge here* (or in the entire essay, for that matter), even though the assignment says to "respond to Fred Powledge."

Here's another response:

Fred Powledge is completely reasonable in his decision to "Bulldoze the Suburbs!" Suburbs are a menace to the soundness of people's minds everywhere. Now is the time to make this change, and America is the place. Yet, to make this dream a reality, cooperation from people of all professions, businesses and industries will be crucial. The battle of the Suburbs will be a long and difficult one to fight, but the rewards will be tremendous.

Here we have Fred Powledge in the first sentence, but that's about all. Suburbs may be a "menace to the soundness of people's minds," but what does *Powledge* himself say? In this case, the student glances at Powledge and forges forth on her own.

And here's still another response:

Fred Powledge must have the most negative attitude towards the Suburban areas that I have ever heard of. Has city life warped his mind so much, that it has given him this negative attitude towards everything? The fact is, those who live in the Suburbs choose to do so to escape from the constant hustle and bustle of the city.

This student is already criticizing Powledge before he's explained why he thinks that Powledge appears to have been "warped" by city life.

We could say that such students have misunderstood the assignment, yet that may not be the case. Students have many reasons for not explaining what Fred Powledge said. Sometimes they're afraid that they might get something wrong if they attempt a careful interpretation. Sometimes they're so caught up in their *own* thinking that they are not very interested in the specific problems important to Powledge's argument. Such students have never learned that they can't simply address any issues they think are interesting or have neat things to say about; they have to consider the argument a particular person is making and the *perspective* that person is trying to take. Such understanding may be especially difficult for students who have been rewarded in the past for saying whatever comes to mind or for using other people's ideas as "stimuli" or "jumping-off points" for their own ideas or fancies.

Often, students have been taught that they should be "interesting." In this case, they may think that by telling us about Fred Powledge's thoughts—summarizing what they think everybody in class knows— they are *boring* us, when in fact, the real problem has nothing to do with what we already know. When writers in academia summarize, they are not participating in an intellectual show-and-tell; they are *helping* us to understand *how they read* and *what they think is significant or worthy of comment.*

In fact, the whole act of summarizing is *focusing* and *interpreting*— not reporting or summarizing the plot—and students often need experience understanding the significance of that interpreting:

Directions: Here are several short quotations. In the spaces provided, respond to each.

1. "No one likes to doge bullets in the left hand canyons of the mind."
   —Virgil Heater, "Related Problems of Aphasics and the Criminally Insane," *Home Digest,* 16 February 1933, p. 26.

2. "If there are no bricks in your driveway, look for them in your attic."
   —Virgil Heater, "Of Bricks and Brains," *Home Digest,* 26 June 1933, p. 31.

3. "Never view a fruit fly with only one eye."
   —Virgil Heater, "In Plain View of Your Garden," *Home Digest,* 30 September 1933, p. 12.

4. "If the mud is thick around your toes, climb a tree and look for nests."
   —Etta Barker, "Virgil Heater: A Retrospect," *Backpacker's Weekly,* 29 March 1969, p. 121.

Even though the assignment doesn't say so directly, I want students to *introduce* these quotations before they attack or respond to them. They should never try to argue with or respond to a quotation without trying to provide a context for the interpretation of that quotation. Not only should students introduce quotations but they should also *interpret* them. And if they don't think they *need* to interpret them, hint or direct their readers toward their way of seeing or using those quotations, then they *may not need to quote them at all.* For instance, if a student thinks that Virgil Heater is just concerned about finding bricks in the attic of his house, then there's probably no reason to quote Heater. But if "attics" mean something special to Heater, then there's need to *interpret* him:

Heater says, "If there are no bricks in your driveway, look for them in your attic." Heater, of course, was well aware of the potential structural damage from storing bricks in one's attic—whether that attic was part of his house or part of his brain.

Students often don't worry about the problems of interpretation at all—and are often unaware of ambiguity or confusion. Sometimes we can emphasize this problem by looking at student solutions to the third quotation. When Heater talks about people viewing fruit flies "with only one eye," he's talking about *fruit flies* with only one eye. Most students think that he is talking about people who close one of their own eyes while viewing fruit flies. Furthermore, in number one, when Virgil Heater says that no one likes to "doge" bullets in the left-hand canyons of the mind, students want to add a *d* and make that "dodge"; but Heater isn't talking about "dodging" at all, and that's not a typographical error. He is, in fact, talking about "doging"—something you can only do in the left-hand canyons of the mind.

Interpretation includes *paraphrasing,* too, and students should practice paraphrasing:

Directions: Below is a passage that is too long to quote entirely. Select a part or parts of the passage you wish to quote directly. Combine your direct quotation(s) with paraphrases or summaries.

For years, researchers have recognized an apparent symbiotic relationship between the Kleindienst turkey buzzard and Montmorency's rock chuck that, they believe, explains the limited range of each. Current evidence, however, suggests that the relation is far from equally advantageous to both sides. Johnson (1976), for instance, has documented at least one case in which the Kleindienst turkey buzzard was observed to have eaten six rock chucks in a four-hour period. Although critics have pointed out that Johnson's observation post was 440 yards away from the actual events he recorded and his sighting occurred at ten o'clock at night without special optical aids, his conclusions should not be quickly dismissed. First, Johnson is known for his keen eyesight,

good will, and sincerity. Furthermore, others (see Peters, 1977; Jones, 1977) have pointed out that Kleindienst turkey buzzards in captivity do, in fact, attack rock chucks without provocation, especially in small cages.
—Malcolm Potts, *New Jersey Wildlife,* 14 (1979), p. 13.

Students often run into unexpected problems when they start paraphrasing. Some who try this particular experiment often summarize without mentioning Malcolm Potts at all. Part of the problem may be that they don't clearly understand that paraphrases and summaries are interpretations and that *Malcolm Potts* is interpreting Johnson— something that makes a big difference in students' own interpretations. Furthermore, students often quote large sections of this passage when little of it is worth quoting directly—perhaps the words *apparent symbiotic relationship* or *good will and sincerity.* But even when they quote these words, they usually don't *interpret* them or explain why they are worth quoting in the first place.

We can look at these problems in students' own writing, too:

Directions: Try to simplify this passage.

According to McCullough, "the groundswell of public opinion against the Japanese started in the early 1900s" (123). This is when the United States Industrial Commission issued a report stating that the Japanese "are more servile than the Chinese, but less obedient and far less desirable" (Smith 12). At about the same time, the slogan of politician and labor leader Dennis Kearney was "the Japs must go" (Murray 55). The mayor of San Francisco wrote that "the Japanese cannot be taken into the American culture because they are not the stuff of which American citizens are made" (Murray 54). In 1905, writes McCullough, "the Japanese and Korean Expulsion league held its first meeting and spawned many other similar organizations" (125).

This is a clear case where good quotations get buried by ordinary ones.

Here's another, longer passage, this time from a required freshman class called "The Origins of Modernism":

This "search for knowledge" is also a cursory summation of Kant's definition of the "age of enlightenment." He claims:

> Enlightenment is man's release from his self-incurred tutelage. Tutelage is man's inability to make use of his understanding without direction from another. Self-incurred is this tutelage when its cause lies not in lack of reason but in lack of resolution and courage to use it without direction from another. Sapere aude! "Have courage to use your own reason!"—that is the motto of enlightenment. (Kant, p. 286)

At the same time, he seems to believe that the public can enlighten itself;

> But that the public should enlighten itself is more possible; indeed, if only freedom is granted, enlightenment is almost sure to follow. For there will always be some independent thinkers, even among the established guardi-

ans of the great masses, who, after throwing off the yoke of tutelage from their own shoulders, will disseminate the spirit of the rational appreciation of both their own worth and every man's vocation for thinking for himself. (Kant, p. 287)

Yet, even though this is attainable, he feels total release from tutelage is virtually impossible. He says:

If we are asked, "Do we now live in an enlightened age?" the answer is, "No," but we do live in an age of enlightenment. As things now stand, much is lacking which prevents men from being, or easily becoming, capable of correctly using their own reason in religious matters with assurance and free from outside direction. But, on the other hand, we have clear indications that the field has now been opened wherein men may freely deal with these things and that the obstacles to general enlightenment or the release from self-imposed tutelage are gradually being reduced. In this respect, this is the age of enlightenment, or the century of Frederick. (Kant, p. 290)

Probably very little of this needs to be quoted—but many students will have trouble paring it down to something like this:

Kant says enlightenment will come when "independent thinkers" are free to think for themselves and show others how to think for themselves. According to Kant, we don't yet live in an "enlightened age"—but we live in an "age of enlightenment" where we are gradually becoming capable of using our reason "correctly."

Many students, in fact, have a hard time giving things up—especially if by giving things up, they appear to say *less.* In this case, the student appears to have trouble summarizing and paraphrasing, but the problem may be much simpler: the student may not have enough to say for three pages, and she may be using long quotations to take up space and stall for time. The assignment itself reads:

In his essay "What is Enlightenment?" Kant states, "If we are asked, 'Do we now live in an *enlightened age?*' the answer is, 'No,' but we do live in an *age of enlightenment.*" In an essay of three to four pages, answer the question, What is an "age of enlightenment?"

In this case, all those quotations the student has used begin to look like smoke screens to cover up a general paraphrase of the assignment itself.

Once students feel more comfortable introducing other people's ideas and interpreting those ideas, we can move on to other, more important problems: controlling those ideas and using them, rather than using them and being controlled by them.

twelve

Controlling Quotations

• •

An important rule in academic writing is "Never let someone else make the point you should be making yourself." Yet I constantly see students giving up control of what they say. We've already looked at students who use quotations to make their points for them, but even when students *appear* to be doing something with their quotations, they are often just reporting what they have found instead of trying to say something about what they have found:

As quoted by Malcolm Smith: "Marriage is, in fact, very much the single most common form of refrigerator-stove relationships." Men and women are definitely good examples of two opposites. Each having been raised in different environments to certain social standards. Through marriage they are united, and that unity also forms a bond with which they share things in common, both socially and mentally. They have similar opinions and interests, yet they still stand apart as opposites.

This student is *trying* to explain the quotation and even gives an example to illustrate it, but he never takes charge and says what he thinks the quotation says. In fact, he doesn't seem to want to interfere with Malcolm Smith at all.

Here's another example, this time of someone who's letting someone else make his thesis statement for him:

Riding a bus can be a very traumatic experience for some people. Many riders of the mass transit system board buses without ever having been at their intended destinations. The rider who knows where he is going is an experienced mass transit customer and has the upper edge on the new initiates of public transportation. Alan Fobbs once said correctly, "on a bus, it's better to know where you are going than where you've been unless you've been there before."

Instead of stepping right out and analyzing or interpreting Fobbs's quotation and explaining why Fobbs might be right, this student lets Fobbs make the thesis statement for him. By doing so, this student *gives up responsibility* for clarifying Fobbs's quotation or *using* Fobbs's quotation and ultimately gives up his own right to the material.

Many students don't like to take charge, make strong points, or risk being wrong, and they have to learn that unless they have something to say, unless they take charge of their material, they wimp out and waste both their time and ours. To begin working on this problem, we can try experiments like this:

Directions: Here's a piece of student writing. Can you make it better? [I've included the footnote numbers that appeared in the original.]

Calder invented and practiced his own art.

> Normally, an artist has learned laboriously from his heritage and his immediate predecessors and then slightly altered these gifts. But not Calder. He fought off his father's solid teaching, admonishments and deprecatory remarks and brought forth his entirely new concept sculpture.[2]

He didn't imitate anything or anyone. Whereas most art signifies something, "Calder suggests nothing; he takes real, living movements and fashions them."[3] His main theme became the universe.[4] He demonstrated this inspiration with the use of symbols—shapes of the sun, moon, and stars. At the time this theme was very unconventional because the universe was not familiar to most people, little was known about it and nothing was, hence, as convincing as the real thing. . . .

Students sometimes don't even ask who wrote the quotations in this passage, and if they don't ask, we probably need to talk about why they don't ask.

Here's a slightly different problem:

Directions: What do you think is wrong with this piece of student writing?

In this quotation, Bertrand Russell[1] makes three points. First, he says that human beings show their superiority to other animals by their large capacity for boredom. Second, he claims that one of the most powerful human motivations is escape from boredom. And third, he says that savages are more enthralled with alcohol than any of white man's other offerings, because alcohol allows the savages to escape the reality of life. Through examination of these three points, it can be shown that Russell's entire quotation rests on the assumption that life has no implicit meaning.

We can assume that when Russell refers to human "superiority" he is referring to intelligence, because it is this characteristic which sets humans apart from other animals. If this intelligence which makes them "superior" to the "brutes," and it is this "superiority" which, as Russell says, gives humans such a large capacity for boredom, then it follows that life itself must be quite senseless. In other words, if intelligence—a capacity for understanding—causes a species to be *bored* with the reality of physical life, then can there be any implicit *meaning* to life? By the physical reality of life, I mean the day to day struggle for survival, and the fact that who lives and who dies or who succeeds and who fails is often a *random* matter.

If we are to accept what Russell says, "that the escape from boredom is one of the really powerful desires of all human beings," then most of our activities fall under the category of escapes from boredom, and seem fairly senseless. It is true that those who have a goal; a purpose; a direction in life are not bored. Those who become completely immersed in and involved with living are not bored. But if we agree with Russell's statement, then all this goal setting and all this *living* becomes merely an attempt to escape boredom by filling the time and suddenly takes on less *importance.* In reality, our individual life achievements *are* relatively unimportant in the context of the whole universe. So many activities can be considered diversions from boredom. Even *suffering* can be seen as an escape from this emotion, because at least it occupies our minds. Religion can be seen as an attempt to erect false meaning in order to escape boredom. Maybe things such as participating in athletics and getting an education just give us something to do.

Russell's third point about savages and liquor is related to his statements about boredom because it also implies that life is meaningless. He says that liquor "enables them for the first time in their lives to have the illusion, for a few brief moments, that it is better to be alive than dead." I can hardly imagine a more direct statement of life's senselessness than saying that life is no better than death. Russell is saying that alcohol is so appealing because it allows an *escape* from life. This thing which the savages must be escaping from is boredom.

The significance of Russell's implication that life is meaningless is that the only meaning that exists, is that which we create. There is no *implicit* meaning, no core of truth. This realization is not bad; it simply allows for greater perspective on our part regarding the purpose of our activities. Russell says that human beings have a huge *capacity* for boredom, but this does not mean they *have* to be bored. So there is nothing wrong with attempting to escape this boredom. It's just nice to be aware of what we are doing.

This looks like another example of student plot summary, but it seems more ambitious than that. I can almost hear her thinking her way through that detailed summary to her conclusion about "greater perspective" and the fact that "It's just nice to be aware of what we are doing." But by not taking charge soon enough, she *relinquishes control* and is left counterpunching in her conclusion—and by then, she's already lost the fight.

Quoting for Support

Students should be cautious when they quote other people to support their own opinions. Too often, they use quotations just to restate their own positions. A student writes:

Theology deals with man's search for understanding his existence, and how it relates to his environment, others and God. The men of the Middle Ages certainly had a conception of this, it being that God was responsible for everything that existed and occured in the universe. Whatever life brought them, they accepted it as divine judgement. To quote from *Science and the Making of the Modern World,*

> "The possibility of trying to understand the world or influence the course of events was generally unthinkable. Even to try to do so would have seemed blasphemous" (Marks).

Somehow, this student expects to gain credibility by quoting *Science and the Making of the Modern World*—but she only succeeds in repeating what she's already said. The quotation doesn't add anything to her argument—it doesn't clarify anything, nor does it introduce a point for disagreement, comment, or further elaboration.

Here's another example, this time from a student's conclusion:

Enlightenment has become a goal for many to reach, although it may never be accomplished. The true nature of Enlightenment thinking cannot be seen in its purest and clearest form, however, doubting and seeking, tearing down and building will continue in the modernistic society. Why? Men will continue to shut their eyes as they have done in the past. Only a few eyes will be opened and thus the struggle to obtain the enlightened age will continue as will the on going battles between enlightened and modernistic ideas. As Lichtenberg stated, "People talk a lot about Enlightenment and ask for more light. But my God, what good is all that light, if people either have no eyes, or if those who do have eyes, resolutely keep them shut . . ."

This student apparently wants to end with a catchy quotation but only shows that she can rob a quotation book and round out her discussion with borrowed literary flavor. If anything, the quotation detracts from the student's own point by calling attention to the student's own uninspired prose.

Such use of quotations is common but dangerous, even when English teachers do it. For instance, Judith and Geoffrey Summerfield discuss a student's text this way in their award-winning book on the teaching of writing:

We want, now, to isolate one element of Stacey's representation of how she enlivens/writes: her account of her use of inner speech in writing. And we want

to relate this to a rather more formal account of the same experience offered by Barbara Herrnstein Smith, whose term is "interior speech." Smith observes that "we are almost continuously saying things to that most intimate, congenial and attentive listener whom we carry within our own skins."[8] She concurs with Vygotsky's view that the ability to produce inner speech is "appropriated" or "derived"—"a capacity that could not arise prior to, or independent of, one's participation, as both speaker and listener, in a linguistic community."[9] The implications of this for composition teachers are clear and important. The ability of students to engage in usefully productive, reflective inner speech about their work with us—to think about it, to consider it—will depend in part on what we as instructors offer in the way of talk to be internalized.[2]
[Footnote numbers 8 and 9 were printed in the original piece.]

What's important here is not the repetition of Vygotsky in Smith's words, but the fact that this repetition is apparently supposed to replace explanation or reason. From this repetition, the authors conclude something about "clear and important" implications—but they by-pass the real questions that need clarification: So what that Barbara Herrnstein Smith concurs? Why is Vygotsky right? Why is "inner speech" a good term? Why is "interior speech" any better? What *is* "inner speech" besides a metaphor that some of us turn into an actual mental process?

Students need practice recognizing when they can use quotations and when quotations become fancy repetition that doesn't serve a purpose. Here's an experiment that addresses these problems but also suggests limitations in the typical advice English teachers sometimes give students:

Directions: Here is a passage. What can you say about the quotation here?

In fact, planning is primarily a writing activity, as most experienced writers can testify. Although they admit that they do some planning before they write, they insist that they do their most productive planning after they have begun writing. For them, planning is not so much thinking *and* writing as it is *thinking-in-writing*. Read what the poet William Stafford has to say about the relationship between thinking and writing:

> When I write, I like to have an interval before me when I am not likely to be interrupted. For me, this means usually the early morning, before others are awake. I get pen and paper, take a glance out the window (often it is dark out there), and wait. It is like fishing. But I do not wait very long, for there is always a nibble—and this is where receptivity comes in. To get started I will accept anything that occurs to me. Something always occurs, of course, to any of us. We can't keep from thinking. Maybe I have to settle for an immediate impression: it's cold, or hot, or dark, or bright, or in between! Or—well, the possibilities are endless. If I put down something, that thing will help the next thing come, and I'm off. If I let the process go on, things will occur to me that were not at all in my mind when I started. These things, odd or trivial as they may be, are somehow connected. And if I let them string out, surprising things will happen.

[Note: Stafford is a Pulitzer Prize-winning poet. The passage including Stafford's quotation comes from the ninth edition of Joseph Trimmer and James M. McCrimmon's *Writing with a Purpose* (Boston: Houghton, 1988, pp. 25–26) —one of the all-time classic textbooks on composition.]

We can do the same thing with our students' own writing, but it's always good to do this once in a while with "professional" writing because of the enormous faith so many students have in quotations by famous people and assertions they find in print. In this case, students need to realize first that Stafford's comments about his writing "process" are not necessarily fact, and, even if they were, may not be generalizable to all writing and all contexts. More important, they need to realize that Trimmer and McCrimmon are letting Stafford repeat their own comments—as if such repetition validates their opinion that writing is "discovery." Writing may sometimes be discovery, but students never have to accept the introspection of famous writers or famous writing teachers as proof that it is. If we were to take famous writers as reliable sources of such information, we would have to take more seriously people like Harlan Ellison, who tells us:

Some of you . . . are incapable of learning. . . . You will never be writers, not because there is some arcane secret we are keeping from you; not because there is some white magic we refuse to share with you; but simply because you do not hear the music. It is not your fault, you are not to be considered less worthy, but it is time you grasped reality by the ears and stared into its face: you *cannot* be writers.[3]

And then there's Andy Warhol's "everything starts and finishes with chemicals"[4] and Gertrude Stein's "Composition is not there, it is going to be there and we are here. This is some time ago for us naturally."[5]

It's not easy to give students control over the quotations they use. Part of the problem, as we have seen, is a problem of giving students permission to say things for themselves and make their own assertions; and part of the problem is freeing them from the belief that telling us what other people have said is almost the same as saying something remarkable.

•••••••

Notes

1. The quotation comes from *Bertrand Russell's Best,* ed. Robert E. Egner (New York: New American Library, 1958) 13.

2. *Texts and Contexts: A Contribution to the Theory and Practice of Teaching Composition* (New York: Random, 1986) 222–23.

3. Harlan Ellison, "Hard Truths and Sage Advice," *The Bloomsbury Review* (March/April 1990): 3.

4. *The Philosophy of Andy Warhol* (New York: Harcourt, 1975) 181.

5. "Composition as Explanation," *Selected Writings of Gertrude Stein,* ed. Carl Van Vechten (New York: Random, 1946) 456.

thirteen

Teaching Documentation

• • • • • • • • • • • • • • • • • • •

Even though I don't expect students to memorize a handbook on footnotes and bibliographies, I expect them to know how documentation works. I am no expert on all forms of documentation, and I've never wanted to be—but I know enough to be able to look up what I don't know and know what I have to look up. Students should know that much, too.

How reference lists work. Students need to know how to put page numbers in parentheses in the body of their essays.

How reference lists differ from footnotes. Students don't always have a choice about the kind of documentation they use—but they ought to understand why one system might be better than another for different purposes. Footnotes may be more useful when writers have to quote from many different sources. (In such cases, names and dates can clutter things up. On the other hand, in some disciplines such as speech communication, scholars sometimes wage major theoretical battles in their notes.) In the old days before computers, footnotes were a pain to write, type, and number correctly; and reference lists were much more practical and easier to set up. But with new word processing programs, that's not necessarily the case anymore—and it probably doesn't matter whether students insist on using footnotes, endnotes, or reference lists. In fact, I know only a few professors who actually *care* whether students turn in papers with footnotes or endnotes or used reference lists. If they

175

do, such professors generally worry the most about their majors and advanced writers, not their freshman writers.

Right now, I don't bother to teach endnote or footnote formats because the only major style manual that uses them is the University of Chicago (The University of Chicago advises against footnotes.) I provide students with a one-page handout of a typical "Notes" page full of footnote numbers; references to texts previously cited; and examples of formats for books, articles, and articles in books. If students need more help, they can see me individually. But spending more time on such things may not make a difference at this stage in my students' academic lives.

Why one bibliography format might be better than another.
Students who have learned one style for documentation in high school sometimes come to class thinking they know how to document—which mostly means they know how to follow the rules for one format and can put the commas in the right places. But I'm less interested in teaching students to be correct than I am in teaching them what to look for and what to weigh as important. They ought to, for instance, be able to answer this question:

What information is absolutely *essential* for writing a bibliography entry for a pamphlet on pig farming in Argentina?

And they ought to be able to answer this one, too:

Which bibliography entry is better? (why?)
Smith, J. P. (1977) *Flotation devices.* Chicago: University of Chicago Press.
Smith, John P. *Flotation Devices.* Chicago: U of Chicago P, 1977.
1. J. P. Smith, *Flotation Devices,* Univ. Chicago Press, 1977.
Smith, J. P., 1977. Flotation devices. Chicago: U. of Chicago.

The first is APA format; the second, MLA; the third, a format for a mathematics publication; the fourth, a biology format. But the main issue has something to do with *focus.* Unless students recognize the logic behind the system, creating bibliographies remains a mysterious, even ritualistic, enterprise.

How to use content notes. If we teach students how to use a reference list system, then we have to help them to use content notes—notes that supply additional information or observations:

Directions: Solve the following problems:

1. The information you have just cited is fairly well known and appears in most introductory texts. How would you tell your reader to look at the following sources without putting all information in the body of your paper?

    a. Bunion, James. Biology Today (2nd ed), Boston: Mastodon, 1980, p. 6.

    b. Biology Tomorrow, a textbook ($8.95), published in NY at the Winton Press, 1979, p. 22. (Author: Sonders Clark).

2. You want to show your reader that you've read four sources for the information you've just quoted, and that the best source is item *c*, but you don't want to clutter up the body of your paper with all this information—especially since it's not essential to your point. What do you do?

    a. John Symons, "The Blue Bottle Fly," Technic (a journal), volume 4, no. 5, 1980, p. 11.

    b. John Symons, "Color Mixing and Blue Bottle Blue," in *Artisan,* volume 16, July, 1979, p. 10.

    c. Cathlene Gundersun, Technic, I, 1977, p. 15. "Metals and Parasites."

    d. Barrow, C. "How to judge respect for blue bottle blue." *Livestock: A Philosophy,* chapter II. Plymouth Rock Publishers, New York and London, 1980, p. 65.

Students who have learned a set of rules that they always follow may have trouble loosening up and experimenting. Here, if they have never learned to fake things or figure things out for themselves, they may not want to *guess* a solution for fear of doing something wrong.

Students ought to recognize the value of such content notes—especially if they don't like to give up information or if they like to clutter their arguments with unessential facts, observations, or comments about their own expertise. In writing classes, students ought to recognize the value of such notes for leaving messages for their teachers or asking questions about procedures or techniques they're trying out for the first time or having trouble with.

How to fake it. Students ought to know how to do bibliography exercises like this one:

Question: For a bibliography, in what order would you put the following information? (You are citing the article.)

1. Title of article. (It's written in French.)
2. Title of the editor of the book this article is in.
3. The last name of the author of the article.
4. The first name of the author of the article.
5. The last name of the translator of the article.
6. The first name of the translator of the article.
7. The publishing date of the book.
8. The edition of the book containing the article.
9. The publisher of the book.
10. The book is in its seventh edition.

(I don't care what order they decide—but they should have reasons for the order they choose.)

Students should also know how to do this exercise:

Directions: Put the following information into (1) APA style, and (2) MLA style/:

(I)

1. Wilhelm Wright [author].
2. The incidence of parasites in dogs at Washington, D.C. [name of article].
3. Journal of the american veterinary medical assoc.
4. 1930.
5. Volume 76.
6. Pages 879–888.
7. Number 5.
8. Phase of Moon: full.
9. Address of publisher: 1612 Boston Ave, Newark, NJ.
10. Editor for journal: Oswald Pranks.

(II)

1. Saps and Saplings [title of book].
2. First author: James Bradling.
3. Second author: Pauline Bruffee.
4. Publisher: Johnny Appleseed Press, Inc.

5. Managing editor of press: Bill Bondersane.

6. 1987.

7. Pages quoted: 66–67.

8. Number of pages in book: 177, including index.

9. Place of publication: Antelope, Colorado.

I once assumed that because students could look things up in a reference book they would look things up and be able to follow models, but I no longer assume that: even with clear models to follow, students often don't recognize the essentials. They don't always realize that knowing the name of an editor of a journal won't help them find that journal in the library, and that knowing the page numbers in a book makes no difference in helping others to find the book in the card catalog. That's probably because they often see bibliographic formats as sets of rules for doing things right because doing things right is somehow *good in itself.* Such students usually don't recognize that bibliographies serve important scholarly purposes and contain useful information.

Because bibliographies can serve important scholarly purposes, students ought to know what is essential and what isn't, why it's essential, and why they should be able to fake all the rest, if they have to. They ought to be able to make simple bibliographies of books, articles, and articles in books, but that's about all they need to start with:

Directions: Write a bibliographic entry for the following information.

1. God Had a Dog [title of book].

2. Editor: Wilfreda Marx.

3. "Good dog, nice doggy" [article in book].

4. Local Bozo Press, Inc.

5. Pages: 544 [total number in book].

6. City: New Brunswick.

7. State: New Jersey.

8. Heinrich Dichter [second author].

9. Bertha Stein [first author].

10. page 121 [page quoted].

11. pages 120–126 [pages for article].

12. Date: Unknown—sometime between 1983 and 1985.

13. Translator of "Good dog, nice doggy"—Wilhelm Kratz.

14. Originally published in "Dogs" [a book by Bertha Stein and Heinrich Dichter, published in Bertha's basement in 1970 in Kansas City, MO].

15. Volume 3 of a 5-volume series: Dogs, Dogs, Dogs, edited by Bill Boon.

We can give such an exercise without teaching students the "correct way" to plug "translators" into a bibliography—students ought to have a good hunch where translators *belong* in a bibliography, if they understand how bibliographies work. And students should be able to recognize that the rest of the information about original publication in this exercise is probably not essential at all—even though they could find out how to do such things correctly if they had to. Because the date is so fuzzy, students should also be able to use "n.d." to designate "no date," as well as "n.p." (no place), and "n.pag." (no pagination).

However, they should realize that even if they go to the library and look up how to document reprint editions, pamphlets with odd pagination, weird simultaneous publication, joint sponsorship, or ghost authorship, correct documentation of such things *may not make any difference to their teachers.* As far as I can tell, most teachers outside of English departments don't *care* if students get all the small things right in their bibliographies. All they're looking for is some consistency and some good faith.

The best thing we can do is to keep students relaxed and aware of the reasons they might document their sources and what considerations are the most important. Over the years, I've seen many students who think we've finally begun something important when we start dealing with "bibliography." They take out their notebooks and write down everything I say. They ask questions. They want to know where you put those commas when you're dealing with Government documents before 1902 and why you use periods instead of commas in bibliographies. And I tell them that someplace, out there, there are people who go to meetings and smoke cigars and eat pretzels while they decide such things behind closed doors. And every few years, they come out with new "guidelines" and get us all to change our handbooks and rewrite our textbooks and then they grade us on how well we do.

four

"Style"

fourteen

Issues in Teaching "Style"

● ●

Some issues in the teaching of "style" are obvious, and I won't spend time on them here. It's obvious, for instance, that students have to be able to read, have the desire to read well, and have some taste if they want to play successfully with "style." They should have some "sentence sense"—but not necessarily a textbook knowledge of grammar. They should desire to learn, be willing to work hard, and practice. (Motivation and taste may, in fact, be the most important factors in teaching "style," and we may not have much control of either—at least in thirteen weeks.) I'd like to concentrate instead on three issues that we do have some control over in thirteen weeks.

Self-Assessment

We don't have time to teach students to solve all their problems or develop habits, but we can help them to *evaluate* their own problems and habits. The more conscious they are of what they do and what they think about what they do, the better learners they will become, and the better chance they will have of practicing on their own and continuing to learn beyond the end of the semester.

We can begin with simple experiments in understanding how people react to rules:

Directions [given orally]: This is one of the most difficult things you'll do all semester. It's almost impossible to do. In fact, I worry a lot every time I give it. . . .
Anyway, I'm going to read you some sentences and ask you to fill in the blanks in those sentences.

1. The wind _____ through the trees.
2. The sun _____ in the sky.
3. The snow _____ under Josie's feet.
4. The dog _____ the cat.
5. Josie _____ the grape into her mouth.
6. John _____ the test.

The wind almost always "whistles" through the trees (or "blows," "howls," or "rustles"). The sun shines in the sky. The dog eats the cat or somehow molests it. Josie pops that grape into her mouth. The snow crunches or melts under Josie's feet. If students use more than one word, they use verb-plus-adverb combinations—whistled noisily, crunched loudly, howled terribly, shone brightly. Students seldom make metaphors, insert details, break what they think are the "rules," or ask what it means to "fill in the blanks":

The wind [sounded like sixteen orangutans cutting cheese] through the trees.
The sun [looked like a large green hubbard squash] in the sky.
Josie [thought about her father's hernia as she squeezed] the grape into her mouth.

Even though students often protest that they want to be "creative," "exciting," "different," they are often hemmed in by an unconscious commitment to the ordinary, the standard, the "expected." When someone tells them to fill in the blanks, they fill in the blanks without thinking about their options—and the less they think about their options and question the rules, the more they play safe and miss opportunities to experiment or be "creative," "exciting," "different."

Sometimes, students come to us believing that longer or more complex is better, or sentence variety is naturally good, and we can design experiments that call such knowledge into question:

Directions: Here is part of a passage by John McPhee. Can you improve it by combining some sentences?

He picked up a salmon, roughly ten pounds of fish, and, holding it with one paw, he began to whirl it around his head. Apparently, he was not hungry, and this was a form of play. He played sling-the-salmon. With his claws embedded near the tail, he whirled the salmon and then tossed it high, end over end. As it fell, he scooped it up and slung it around his head again, lariat salmon, and again he tossed it into the air. He caught it once more. The fish flopped to the ground. The bear turned away, bored. He began to move upstream by the edge of the river. Behind his big head his hump projected. His brown fur rippled like a field under wind. He kept coming. The breeze was behind him. He had not yet seen us. He was romping along at an easy walk. As he came closer to us, we drifted slowly toward him.[1]

With some instruction and without much work, most students can combine sentences like this:

The bear turned away, bored, and began to move upstream by the edge of the river. Behind his big head his hump projected, and his brown fur rippled like a field under wind. He kept coming, and because the breeze was behind him, he had not yet seen us. Instead, he was romping along at an easy walk, and as he came closer to us, we drifted slowly toward him.

or even like this:

Bored, the bear turned away and began to move upstream by the edge of the river, his hump projecting behind his big head, his brown fur rippling like a field under wind. The breeze behind him, he had not seen us yet and kept coming, romping along at a easy walk toward us as we drifted slowly toward him.

But are such revisions necessarily *better* than McPhee's original? Certainly the syntax in both examples is more complex and varied, and may even "flow" more, depending on what we mean by "flow." But we probably don't know whether such revisions are *better* than McPhee's original. McPhee himself might disagree, and so would many scholars who consider McPhee to be a premier stylist. The difference may boil down to taste, personal interest (not everyone cares about bears), and context—including literary/professional context.

Students often believe that "style" is unrelated to "content"—that to be jazzy and creative they have to change their syntax, add adverbial clauses, and keep their sentences "lively." But style results from the way we think and what we think about, not what we sprinkle on top:

Directions: Here is a passage by Israel Scheffler. Can you make it more interesting by playing with his style?

We are here interested, broadly, in non-scientific discourses in which definitions of educational notions are offered, for example, in curriculum statements, in enunciations of program and objectives, in interpretations of education addressed to the general public, in debates over educational policy. It makes no difference whether the definitions offered in such contexts are put forward on scientific authority or not; the important fact is that they are presented not as technical statements interwoven with special scientific research and for theoretical purposes, but rather as general communications in a practical context. [*The Language of Education*][2]

(Students might be able to get rid of some awkwardness here, but I'm not sure anybody can make this more lively simply by playing with style.)

Here's another experiment, this time focusing on the effect of *context* on values:

Directions: Which of the following two passages is better?

1. Humans are different [from other creatures] in that we have become quite aware of our state of being and of the larger reality around us. Other creatures, despite their lack of self-consciousness or knowledge of their impending nonexistence, are nevertheless incredibly complex in their behaviors. If such creatures are so complicated—biologically, socially, and in many other ways—it is not surprising that humans have developed such intricate cultures and become the overlords of this planet. [William Styers][3]

2. At the stroke of midnight in Washington, a drooling red-eyed beast with the legs of a man and a head of a giant hyena crawls out of its bedroom window in the South Wing of the White House and leaps fifty feet down to the lawn . . . pauses briefly to strangle the Chow watchdog, then races off into the darkness . . . towards the Watergate, snarling with lust, loping through the alleys behind Pennsylvania Avenue, and trying desperately to remember which one of those four hundred identical balconies is the one outside Martha Mitchell's apartment. . . .

   Ah . . . nightmares, nightmares. But I was only kidding. The President of the United States would never act that weird. At least not during football season. [Hunter S. Thompson][4]

I like Hunter Thompson's piece—but I can't claim that it's better than Styers's without considering the contexts in which both were published. (Styers won a major award in the North American Essay Contest sponsored by *The Humanist* magazine with this style—and in that context, he may be as good or better than Thompson.)

I expect students to be conscious of their tricks, their habits, their experiments and risks. Many know by "feel" that something is wordy or doesn't sound right. They know *how* to use participials and complex sentences if somebody asks them or builds special requirements into assignments. But they should know *why* some things don't sound right or why some complex sentences are better. Without such attention to what they're doing and what they can do, they narrow their options, and when they're beyond the range of our exhortations, praise, and coaching, they write the same way they've always written—without attention to anything. Here is a small questionnaire on "wordiness" that I hand out without warning sometime near the end of a unit on wordiness.

Name _____

Small Quiz

1. When can you use passive constructions?
   Got examples?

2. When can you begin a sentence with "There are"?

3. When are "be" verbs OK?
   Got examples?

4. What is a nominalization?
   When and why are nominalizations bad?

5. When can you begin a sentence with "it is"?
   Got examples?

I don't record the results of this quiz, but we'll talk about what it means to be conscious about what we're doing. We'll talk about why it is that students who don't ask questions, who don't *think about* the "rules," and who don't explore *on their own* and understand the limits of rules and advice will never feel confident with their style. They'll grow up loving Ball Park Franks and rice with butter on it and beany weanies and plain cake doughnuts. They'll become passive and self-absorbent and won't be able to do things "right" unless they have a secretary's handbook and a dictionary; and they'll make their livings in the bureaucracy following half-baked rules and making safe, half-baked decisions that kill the roses by the book and hem in the lives of their loved ones.

Imitation

We can promote imitation as a simple way to *change* one's style almost immediately. In class, we can try out experiments like this one:

Directions: Here are five sentences. Choose one and imitate it. You may use the same sentence order and some of the same language (particularly connectors)—but you should change the subject matter.

1. The constructive posture of the self-defining self, the freedom which the crude new nation offered it, the implicit promise of democracy to exalt mankind, to praise as well as work the earth;

and, above all, the gift to that emerging individual of limitless opportunity—breathing space—space for rebeginning—space to the edge of every coast—space to infinity: each required the resettlement of language on the page, an equalitarian diction, a pioneering line, the big book, the great theme; each asked for energy and optimism; each egged American authors on to annex, plunder, quote and cite, to wahoo and yawp; and none of these conditions could be realized without the lush entanglements of complete speech: the voyages of discovery, exploration, and conquest, which made it possible, the personal tone, the pied variety of voice, the ebb and flow, the strut, the brag and ballyhoo of talk; for it would take the flabbergasting virtuosities, the visionary range, the gumptious reach, the raw muscularities, the baroque vibrations, yet the flat, irregular Patersons, of prose; and nearly all the best American poets do write prose: Melville and Faulkner and James, Robinson, Thoreau, Eliot, and Frost. [William Gass][5]

2. No matter how they read the stories Zora had collected, no matter how much distance they tried to maintain between themselves, as new sophisticates, and the lives their parents and grandparents lived, no matter how they tried to remain cool toward all Zora revealed, in the end they could not hold back the smiles, the laughter, the joy over who she was showing them to be: descendants of an inventive, joyous, courageous, and outrageous people; loving drama, appreciating wit, and, most of all, relishing the pleasure of each other's loquacious and *bodacious* company. [Alice Walker on Zora Neale Hurston][6]

3. Anneli looks at the strangest of the women, and the men most like her father, and then watches solemnly, tremblingly, as a split of Perrier water is poured for her, for her alone into a stemmed glass, and a waiter—we know the very one, past sixty, with the sly monkey-face of a college professor (but will he be there then?)—her own waiter, prepares on a wheeled table the silver bowl and the flame. [M. F. K. Fisher][7]

4. The sound of the rhythmic splash, the delicate *kersplash* of hundreds of feet, came up in the sound of the river and so at first was lost; but the shards of water, caught blinding in the cutting light (now the voices, rising, a keening) began to form a mist in which appeared rainbows against the white soft breasts; and where drops of water dolloped like beads of mercury on the blue-gray feathers, small rainbows of light here, and in the eyes (as the voices, louder, gathering on one, high, trembling note) rainbows—the birds cradled in light shattered in rainbows everywhere, and with your great

blue wings fanning that brilliant mist, open, utterly vulnerable and stunning, you urged them to begin to revolve in the light, stretching their wings, and you lay back your head and closed the steely eyes and from deep within your belly came the roar of a cataract, like the howling of wolves—that long moment of your mournful voice. [Barry Lopez][8]

5. Monge is sent off to obtain maps, and Arabic and Greek printing presses, Talleyrand is induced to put on foot a scheme for placating Constantinople (the Sultan shall have the Ionian Islands and an annual tribute from the French if he connives at the invasion of Egypt), a line of propaganda is devised (Malta has been hostile to the Republic and has sheltered *émegrés,* and French citizens have been maltreated by the Mamelukes in Egypt—thus the French have a legitimate reason for war), a library is collected for the expedition (the Koran and the Hindu Vegas being lumped together under the section marked "Politics"), a French soldier who had served against the British in India is enlisted in the intelligence corps, the annual rise and fall of the Nile is studied and it is agreed that the army must arrive in Egypt before the flood begins in August; sappers, miners and a medical staff are appointed, and a letter goes off to Admiral Brueys asking for a berth on a ship "suitable for a commander-in-chief who expects to be sea-sick the entire voyage." [Alan Moorehead][9]

We'll do easier experiments, too—asking students to imitate short sentences containing single noun phrases, participials, semicolons, or other simple constructions. But we ought to give experiments like this one, too—where students have to stretch their resources and use techniques they may not feel comfortable with. Here, I don't care if students write imitations that are as long as the originals; I don't even care if their imitations resemble the originals in structure. (I don't even like or understand all the originals.) But I am interested in whether students can recognize and experiment with that repetition in Gass, the dash in Fisher, the parentheses in Moorehead. And I'm willing to see what happens when students stretch their writing beyond their abilities, when they begin to ask questions about "taste" and technique and the limits to their own play.

We can also use imitation experiments to get students to pay attention to the ways writers connect larger units of discourse. Here is one designed to get students to play with simple repetitions:

Directions: Here's a passage by Bob Greene. Can you write an *imitation* of this passage?

I could tell you about Putt-Putt. I could tell you that there are more than one thousand Putt-Putt courses around the world. I could tell you that Putt-Putt is to miniature golf what Wheaties is to the generic grain cereal at your local discount grocery store: the genuine article. I could tell you that Putt-Putt courses are generally found in smaller towns and medium-sized cities; there are no Putt-Putts in New York or Los Angeles or Chicago. I could tell you that there are no windmills or trick holes on a Putt-Putt course; the game is all skill.

    I could tell you that Putt-Putt was founded in Fayetteville, North Carolina, by a fellow named Don Clayton in 1954. I could tell you that one of the main reasons he built his first course was as therapy to prevent a nervous breakdown. I could tell you that there is a Professional Putters Association that sponsors a full-scale national tour, with prize money all the way. I could tell you that in cities like Albany, Georgia, and El Paso, Texas, and Grand Rapids, Michigan, the professional Putt-Putt tournaments are seen weekly during the summer on a syndicated television show. I could tell you a lot, as a matter of fact. But I didn't come to the Elk Grove Village Putt-Putt for you. I came for me.[10]

When we imitate, we "steal" the power from someone else. If we can write something in the spirit of Bob Greene, we've learned something about his power—and we're no longer simply looking at him or simply reading him; we're *using* him.

    Sometimes, we imitate to break out of old ways of looking at things:

Directions: Here's a passage by Joe Bob Briggs and one by S. J. Perelman. Can you rewrite Perelman to sound like Joe Bob?

1. About two years ago I was moody, discontented, restless, almost a character in a Russian novel. I used to lie on my bed for days drinking tea out of a glass (I was one of the first in this country to drink tea out of a glass; at that time fashionable people drank from their cupped hands). Underneath, I was still a lively, fun-loving American boy who liked nothing better than to fish with a bent pin. In short, I had become a remarkable combination of Raskolnikov and Mark Tidd. [S. J. Perelman][11]

2. It's not exactly my idea of a good time to fork over $4 for a cardboard bowl with seven Doritos in it and a scoop of Cheez Whiz dumped in the middle like leftovers at a Salvation Army dinner for illegal aliens. Don't get me wrong—I don't have anything against Meskin food. But what we're talking here is Sports Arena Food. We're talking Grade A Purina Wimp Chow. To get down to the real nitty, what we're talking is Tarrant County Convention Center Nachos.

    Now I have to admit that TCCC Nachos are slightly better than Arlington Stadium Billy Martin-Breath Nachos, but that's pretty much one of your academic questions since nobody's bought any

Arlington Stadium Nachos since 1974, except for the people who move here from New Jersey and think they're ordering soup [Joe Bob Briggs][12]

Students shouldn't write like Joe Bob Briggs all the time or expect to succeed in academia by using red-necked good ol' boy prose. But there's nothing wrong with getting them to stretch themselves, to feel uncomfortable trying out different styles, and to see problems through different perspectives. In this case, they can learn something about the way even someone like Joe Bob Briggs has to manage his signals and labels.

Finally, here's a different experiment that is more reconstruction than imitation, but one that shares many of the *goals* of imitation:

Directions: Here are several short sentences. Can you make them sound like Winston Churchill?

1. Fight in France we will.
2. On the seas and ocean.
3. We shall fight with growing confidence and growing strength in the air.
4. Our islands shall be defended.
5. Whatever the cost may be, we shall fight on the beaches.
6. On the landing grounds we shall fight.
7. In the fields shall we fight and in the streets.
8. We shall fight in the hills.
9. We shall surrender—never.[13]

Once students relax and quit trying to prune out the repetition and redundance, they can often write reasonable renditions like this:

We shall fight in France, we shall fight in the seas and oceans, we shall fight with growing confidence and growing strength in the air; we shall defend our Island, whatever the cost may be. We shall fight on the beaches, we shall fight on the landing-grounds, we shall fight in the fields and in the streets, we shall fight in the hills; we shall never surrender.[14]

We often talk to students about the importance of "rhythm" in language, yet we don't have many ways to get them to appreciate the effect of rhythm and the expectations it often sets up in readers. Here, they can begin to control a few simple, perhaps crude, rhythms and in doing so, begin to control the ways their readers read. And by concentrating on such rhythms, we can even introduce the notion of *breaking* the rhythm; in this case, by ending with "but never shall we surrender!" instead of "we shall never surrender."

Play (and Overplay)

As I've said, to get students to do simple things well, we often have to get them to overdo them and exaggerate. Tentative, cautious people seldom find out their limits, loosen up enough to make mistakes without fear, and go beyond what's always worked for them in the past.

Sometimes, we can get students to exaggerate using strange topics like this one:

Say something about the following assertion:
Everyone fears seagull feet.[15]

It's hard to write something about seagull feet that's culturally expected, necessarily inhibiting, or necessarily embarrassing—and it's easy to write something that's overdone and incautious:

Everyone fears seagull feet. One look at one hard, red, scaly seagull claw turns everyday people into frothing fools, the saliva running down their chins, down their shirts, down their shorts. One whiff of the sweat from one seagull foot makes even college freshmen roll their eyes back into their heads and retract their brains in catatonia. One simple thought of one horny seagull toe can turn a bright day with trees and breeze and fluffy marshmallow clouds into a daystorm—with dead cats on clotheslines, high-flying, crawly things, and panting, salivating, seasick dogs.

Given encouragement and examples of our own play, students can learn to play a little bit themselves. They can begin to believe us when we tell them that they ought to experiment, say outrageous things, take some risks—and in the process, they can gain some distance on cultural assumptions of what's right, expected, and predictable.

Sometimes, we can also take examples of safe student prose and expand them beyond what's safe:

Directions: Here's a passage from a student paper. Do something to part of it to make it better and less stylistically safe:

When we interact with others we often assume roles. We put on masks that hide our true selves. And in doing so, we become estranged even from ourselves. We no longer know what we truly think and feel. We become our masks. It is the mask that keeps us apart. It makes us strangers to each other. And from ourselves.

Probably nothing students do to these sentences will make it stylistically better or more risky. They can combine sentences and fix modifiers:

When we interact with others, we often assume horrendous, ugly roles, putting on masks to hide our true selves—and estranging ourselves from others. Because we no longer know what we truly think and truly feel, we become our masks, and our masks keep us apart from others and make us awful strangers to each other and ourselves.

They can build in participials:

Interacting with others, we assume roles, putting on masks, hiding our true selves, becoming estranged even from ourselves. No longer knowing what we truly think and feel, our masks keep us apart from others, making us awful strangers to each other and ourselves.

But shuffling around the words and combining sentences doesn't make much difference—the result is still safe and predictable. In fact, the only thing that makes a difference is to figure out ways to expand the assertions with details or explanations that allow more opportunities to play:

We put on masks that hide our true selves—heavy, wooden things carved out of pine and painted with dried blood and brown shoe polish—with little indentations in the back where we can stick our noses and two little holes for eyes. And sometimes we even have wooden lips to breathe through . . . I saw one last week: one of those large, economy masks with the plastic chin plate to protect your Adam's apple, and this person . . . I don't know who it was, but she came out of the house next door and she was talking about this cocker spaniel that was costing her big bucks in vet bills. I couldn't see her eyes and her mouth hole wasn't very big—pursed up and carved out like a tube fish. (I remember especially the plumes: big ones that at one time must have been gorgeous, waving in the breeze. . . .) But right now they were bent and one was flapping straight out sidewise like a piece of broken venetian blind. And she was saying . . .

This has nothing to do with the original passage, but learning about style doesn't always come from rebuilding "what's there"; it comes from opening things up, developing a pattern or rhythm, and pushing things farther than they probably ought to be pushed.

Sometimes, we can take solid examples of student writing, undo them drastically, and talk about what happened. Here, for instance, is a reasonable piece of student writing from an honors thesis in philosophy:

As the movement for environmental reform has come to the fore in metaphysical circles, many philosophers have argued that action taken toward this end on a political level may have a surface significance at best, since such actions are grounded in an attitude that is anthropocentric, rather than biocentric. The problem, it is argued, reflects a deeper cultural dilemma, in which a cry for the "rights of man" takes precedence over any understanding of the biosphere, or the processes of natural history. The call is for a new metaphysics, one which would place humans squarely within the cycles of nature, and recognize the value of the natural realm over and above human appreciation (scenic, recreational) and ends (political, practical).

While I agree that an attitudinal shift is necessary before any real ecological progress can be made, I think it should be recognized that the creation of a "new metaphysics" upon which it may stand would be superfluous, since the kind of thinking that such a metaphysics would entail has been clearly articulated in the work of a variety of philosophical movements and the religious beliefs of many primitive cultures. The problem is not so much a lack of ecological consciousness (that is, a *way of thinking* that can accommodate ecological norms), but a lack of adequate means for expressing that consciousness to an audience that is conditioned by a very different *kind* of thinking. In this context, I introduce poetry, over and above "metaphysics" as what I feel to be the most effective means of expressing radical ecological consciousness, and as a forerunner to the "attitudinal shift" I mention above.[16]

And here's a radical condensation:

We can't save trees; we can't save the sunset; we can't save ourselves without changing our slash-and-burn, self-centered, anthropocentric attitude toward our own little personal joys and pleasures in the "beautiful" and the "fun" and the "practical." So much we already know, and whether we need more philosophers to tell us things we already know may be another matter. What we need instead may be a way to *change* attitudes—a way to bring about change that doesn't depend on the same old thing one more time.

What we need is poetry.

Such a condensation allows us to talk about the differences between *extremes.* For instance, we ought to be able to look at the clear "academic" moves in the original—"many philosophers have argued . . . The problem, it is argued, reflects . . . While I agree . . . The problem is not so much . . . but a . . ."—and look for such moves in the stripped-down version, one that takes the argument out of its academic context and even trivializes it ("So much we already know . . . the same old thing one more time").

The problem, of course, with all this exaggeration and play is that students can begin to think that *all* we want is exaggeration and play: Do something strange and weird and automatically get a better grade or a pat on the back. But we work on conventional writing problems, too—wordiness, punctuation, fairness, accuracy of evidence—and we work on helping students to understand the value of exaggeration and play as useful *learning* strategies (but not necessarily foolproof writing strategies).

Unless students are aware of their own limitations and the limitations imposed on them, unless we encourage them to go beyond what they're accustomed to do and think, they end up participating in a creativity turkey shoot, where lucky people drag home dead turkeys and unlucky people go to the store and buy TV dinners.

• • • • • • •

Notes

1. John McPhee, *Coming into the Country* (New York: Bantam, 1978) 90.

2. Israel Scheffler, *The Language of Education* (Springfield, IL: Charles C. Thomas, 1960) 12.

3. William Styers, "Continuous Creation," *The Humanist* (March/April 1984): 9.

4. Hunter Thompson, "Ask Not for Whom the Bell Tolls . . ." in *The Great Shark Hunt: Strange Tales from a Strange Time* (New York: Fawcett, 1979) 268.

5. William Gass, "Emerson and the Essay," in *Habitations of the Word: Essays* (New York: Simon and Schuster, 1985) 32.

6. Alice Walker, "Zora Neale Hurston: A Cautionary Tale and a Partisan View," in *Women's Voices: Visions and Perspectives,* ed. Pat C. Hoy II, Esther H. Schor, Robert DiYanni (New York: McGraw-Hill, 1990) 396.

7. M. F. K. Fisher, "The First Café," in *As They Were* (New York: Vintage, 1983) 87–88.

8. Barry Holstun Lopez, "The Search for the Heron," in *River Notes: The Dance of Herons* (New York: Avon, 1979) 5.

9. Alan Moorehead, *The Blue Nile* (New York: Dell, 1962) 63.

10. Bob Greene, "Putt-Putt à Go-Go," in *American Beat* (New York: Penguin, 1983) 156.

11. S. J. Perelman, "Somewhere a Roscoe . . .," in *The Best of S. J. Perelman* (New York: The Modern Library, 1947) 9.

12. Joe Bobb Briggs, "Malibu Hot Summer: It's Better Than E. T. in the Garbonza Department," in *Joe Bobb Goes to the Drive-In* (New York: Delacorte, 1987) 95–96.

13. Winston Churchill, June 4, 1940, in a radio broadcast. The original passage reads:

    We shall fight in France, we shall fight in the seas and oceans, we shall fight with growing confidence and growing strength in the air; we shall defend our Island, whatever the cost may be. We shall fight on the beaches, we shall fight on the landing-grounds, we shall fight in the fields and in the streets, we shall fight in the hills; we shall never surrender; and even if, which I do not for a moment believe, this Island or a large part of it were subjugated and starving, then our Empire beyond the seas, armed and guarded by the British Fleet, would carry on the struggle, until, in God's good time, the New World, with all its power and might, steps forth to the rescue and liberation of the old.

14. In this section, I lump parallel constructions and repetitions together. They're similar enough for my purposes. For a more detailed discussion of Churchill's passage, see Lanham's *Analyzing Prose* (New York: Charles Scribner's Sons, 1983), pages 130–31. Lanham wants to discuss "anaphora," "symmetry," "climactic progression," "tacit agreement," and "proleptic fact," but hell, all I want to do is get students to recognize repetition and make things look alike.

15. Another nice topic is "Why Do People Fear Insect Lips?"

16. Lyanda Lynne Haupt, "Poetry and Deep Ecological Consciousness," Honors Thesis, Philosophy, Whitman College, 1988.

fifteen

Nuts and Bolts

● ● ● ● ● ● ● ● ● ● ● ● ● ● ● ● ● ● ● ●

We can easily take control from students by grading them on their knowledge of handbook terminology and rules and convincing them of how much we know and how little they know about the intricacies of Syntax and Punctuation. We can't so easily give students back control—the knowledge and the courage to make decisions on their own and even risk failure. In this chapter, we'll look at some of this knowledge, focusing not so much on the rules or the number of rules we should enforce but on the ways students can *look at* those rules and understand how much their style depends on the options they see and the effects they want to create.

Sentence Order

The biggest sentence-level problem many students face is appreciating direct and straightforward sentences:

Directions: Here are some examples from the last assignment. Can you make them more direct, straightforward?

1. What importance it holds for the poet is not apparent.
2. Perhaps equally awesome, although generally believed to be rather innocent, is the computer.

3. By referring to "attending conferences on the future of anything" and "group bathing" as being solemn, he is ridiculing them as phoney trends.

4. By convincing the men, who were then soldiers, sailors, scouts and engineers that they were doing the right thing for their country not only if they were enlisted but if they used the "Burma Shave" products as well, the company inevitably did well.

5. However, the attitude, saying the old is bad, belongs to many.

The problem here is not just in rewriting sentences; it has something to do with taste and previous learning. Students often *like* to pile subordinate clauses and phrases on the beginnings of sentences or reverse sentence order because they think that people like to be kept in suspense. Take, for example, the first sentence here:

What importance it holds for the poet is not apparent.

Students often write such sentences—I suspect because someone has taught them to "avoid the word *I*" or to write more "formally." Some students have no idea how to fix these sentences because they don't think they can say such things as:

I don't understand why the poet wrote this.

or:

The poet doesn't seem to have a point.

Other times, students bury their points because they confuse "objectivity" and "the academic" with being "abstract" and "inanimate." The fifth sentence is typical:

The attitude, saying the old is bad, belongs to many.

Students apparently think such sentences *feel* more academic and resist being direct:

Many people think that old is bad.

We can also tie sentence order to complex problems that involve students' own work:

Directions: Here is a short paragraph from an academic paper. Can you make it less "abstract" and "inanimate"? [Concentrate on *sentence order.*]
In order for a man to be in an age of enlightenment, there has to be a sense of

progress, improvement and individuality. This progress and improvement is the driving force that leads to an age of enlightenment. There has to be a dynamic search for better answers and better conditions for humanity. When confronted with a problem, such as the energy crisis of the 1970s, the people had to search for an answer to their problem by challenging the conventional beliefs. Using the case of the energy crisis, Americans looked for alternative energy sources. Although the oil crisis passed, it opened our eyes to how unstable this energy system is. It is only with this dynamic improvement that individuality, or personal freedom, can be preserved for the masses.

We can concentrate on one or two sentences in class discussion. A typical sentence might be the first:

In order for a man to be in an age of enlightenment, there has to be a sense of progress, improvement, and individuality.

We can rewrite this sentence like this:

Mankind lives in an age of enlightenment if he has a sense of progress, improvement, and individuality.

or:

We sense progress, improvement, and individuality in an age of enlightment.

or:

People progress, improve themselves, and become individuals in an age of enlightenment.

In the first, we emphasize mankind living in enlightment; in the second, we emphasize *our observation* of this progress; in the third, we work on the nominalizations and try to rebuild with stronger verbs. But in each case, we move the point up front and add the phrases and clauses later.

Another good sentence to rewrite might be this one:

When confronted with a problem, such as the energy crisis of the 1970s, the people had to search for an answer to their problem by challenging the conventional beliefs.

The main idea is someplace near the end—something about "challenging conventional beliefs"—and students can easily move this idea up to the beginning of the sentence:

In the 1970s, people had to challenge their conventional beliefs in search for an answer to the energy crisis.

(Here, "In the 1970s" serves as a transitional time signal, and we can leave such transitions at the beginning.)

Sentence order can help students to understand problems they run into when they begin sentences with "it" and "there":

Directions: Can you make the following sentences less wordy?

1. It is the totality of the interrelation of the various components of language and the other communication systems which is the basis for referential language.

2. It is very tragic what lack of food has done to this society.

3. It is true that all literature is open to interpretation, but it should not be difficult to simply understand what is written on the page.

4. There are many aspects of John Ruskin's love affair with boats that can be disputed.

5. It seems that he was stupid.

Or problems involving cumulative sentences:

Directions: Can you imitate the following sentences?

1. I imagined the mushroom, wrinkled, black, and big as a dinner plate, erupting overnight mysteriously in the Bings' living room— from the back of an upholstered couch, say, or from a still-damp rug under an armchair. [Annie Dillard][1]

2. Whole pages of women's magazines are filled with gargantuan vegetables: beets, cucumbers, green peppers, potatoes, described like a love affair. [Betty Friedan][2]

3. "YOU CRAZY BASTARD!" I screamed, cutting into his gravelly mumbling as I slammed my hand down on the tin counter and saw a woman using the phone next to me jump like a rat had just run up her leg. [Hunter Thompson][3]

(In each case, the main clause comes first, followed by whatever else gets tacked on to the end—and we can talk about why we might want to move those main clauses up earlier.)

Or problems involving colons and semicolons:

Directions: Here is a sentence by Edwin Newman. Can you imitate it?

These were some of the positions taken: that social structure should optimally be the consonant patterned expression of culture; that higher education is enmeshed in a congeries of social and political change; that the field of the humanities suffers from a surfeit of leeching, its blood drawn out by verbalism, explication of text, Alexandrian scholasticism, and the exquisite preciosities and pretentiousness of contemporary literary criticism; that a formal curriculum of academic substance and sequence should not be expected to contain mirabilia which will bring all the educative ends of the college to pass, and that any formal curriculum should contain a high frangibility factor; that the College hopes that the Hampshire's belief that individual man's honorable choice is not between immolation in a senseless society or withdrawal into the autarchic self but instead trusts that his studies and experience in the College will confirm for him the choice that only education allows: detachment and skill enough to know, engagement enough to feel, and concern enough to act, with self and society in productive interplay, separate and together; that an overzealous independence reduces linguistics to a kind of cryptographic taxonomy of linguistic forms, and that the conjoining of other disciplines and traditional linguistics becomes most crucial as problems of meaning are faced in natural language; and that the College expects its students to wrestle most with questions of the human condition, which are, What does it mean to be human? How can men become more human? What are human beings for?[4]

This is not a pretty sentence—but it works reasonably well because Newman *starts out* well and sets up his point at the beginning so we can't miss it.

Obviously, students can invert sentences and begin with long subordinate constructions when they want to. They can even write sentences like this if they are able to:

When he thought of how many hundreds of jaw-aching hours of smiles he'd had to spend to accumulate that money, how many stomach-twisting words in praise of life insurance he'd had to wheedle past the slow negative mumbles of the mindless who didn't want to hear they were ever going to die, or couldn't care less about the consequences to their loved ones of that inevitability; when he thought of how he'd endured decades of these indignities not for the athletic, presidential son he'd been unjustly denied, but for daughters—whom he might anyhow be throwing into the collegiate arms of a Wayne Sparks—even supposing Holly and Caroline could raise their averages sufficiently to be accepted by even Boggs State; even supposing Caroline, in response to his inquiring about her educational plans, had not lifted her creamy shoulders into a shrug and mugged with her peachy face the look of one who'd sucked on a rancid lemon; even supposing Holly (in conjunction with her request that he advance her eighteen thousand dollars from her college funds so she could purchase used from a Pepsi Challenge pit crew a Grand Nationals modified white Ford with crash net) had not announced her intention to become a lady stock car racer and to repay him with future winnings; when Raleigh Hayes's thoughts sped—as they often did as he drove down the Kettell-enriching highway—toward this cul-de-sac of his paternal aspirations, he performed a spiritual exercise.[5]

But while students are *beginning* to think about style, they can concentrate on putting their main ideas on the beginnings of their sentences—and while doing so, they can begin to learn the mechanics of sentence building. And in doing so, they learn that they can begin to control sentences for themselves.

Simple "Signals"

Without much grammatical terminology, we can begin to help students to understand the mechanics of putting two sentences together:

James bought a rock

   +

He was sick   ⟶   James bought a rock
because he was sick.

     or: Because he was sick,
James bought a rock.

     or: Whenever James bought
a rock, he was sick.

     or: Whenever James was sick,
he bought a rock.

     or: After James bought a rock,
he was sick.

In class, we'll talk about subordinate conjunctions and prepositions as "signals" that help readers to understand how we've put our sentences together.[6] A word like *because* signals that we're adding some information that will explain "why" something is or was or will be; *when* signals something about time, as do *while, until,* and *after*; and words like *under, around, between, that was,* and *which was* often signal something about location, tell "where" something is, or clarify "what" something is.

We can use such simple notions of sentence building and signals to begin to understand problems such as sentence fragments and comma splices:

Simple Sentence Fragments

Sentence fragments often contain signals, but those signals don't link or connect to anything:

That he was a fool. [The word *that* often leads into a further clarification of something, but what?]

He knew. That he was a fool. [Better, but the signal comes after a period.]

He knew that he was a fool. [Better still, since you don't have to jump over a period to put things together.]

Simple Comma Splices

Comma splices are sentences that are stuck together without any signals except a comma[7]:

Sally limped into the street, a car smashed her left foot.

We can describe commas as "weak" signals, because we use them for so many things that they carry less "information" for our readers. Without stronger signals, readers tend to read both sentences in a comma splice together as separate, distinct but "related" sentences.

To help students understand comma splices in the context of such signals, we can set up simple comparisons like this one:

1. Sally limped into the street—a car smashed her left foot. [Two ideas linked loosely together. But do we know whether she is limping because that car smashed her foot? or because she limps?]

2. Sally limped into the street; a car smashed her left foot. [Two ideas linked more strongly together, but we still don't know what the relationship is between her limp and her accident.]

3. Sally limped into the street. A car smashed her left foot. [Two ideas. The order of these sentences suggests that Sally smashed her foot *after* she limped into the street.]

4. Sally limped into the street whenever a car smashed her left foot. [The time signal in the middle suggests that the second half helps explain the first half.]

5. Because Sally limped into the street, a car smashed her left foot. [The "why" signal at the beginning suggests introductory information that will help us interpret the reason the car was able to smash her foot.]

Teaching students to recognize such signals won't cure everything. For one thing, knowledge of simple signals doesn't help us address the problems of fragments caused by participial constructions:

1. Limping into the street after a car smashed her left foot.

2. Whining at the curb while the ambulance approached the intersection.

3. Left to her own devices.

Nor does the notion of "signals" help students to recognize and use noun fragments:

1. She was a strong person. A rock.

2. Bad breath. That's what he had. Bad breath.

Finally, such knowledge may not help students to fix comma splices like this:

People who fish for sport don't just fish and let them die, they throw what they catch back.

Many students, in fact, use commas because they don't have any other devices to show relationships between parts, and just telling them to quit making comma splices may not be enough. They may need to work on punctuation—particularly colons, semicolons, and dashes—to begin to signal the relationships they want to signal in their sentences.

Punctuation

Commas

We can also talk about commas as signals for added information. We don't *need* to use a comma when we write:

John ate slugs, with a fork.

Here the *with* makes the comma unnecessary because both *with* and the comma signal additional information, and we only need one signal. On the other hand, in a sentence like "John ate slugs, big green ones with bulbish feelers," we need that comma because there is no other signal connecting "John ate slugs" to the added information. Likewise, in the sentence "Because he was stupid, John ate slugs," we may need that comma between *stupid* and *John* because the comma signals the *end* of some introductory information on to the beginning of "John ate slugs." Obviously, the rule is more complicated than that. Commas with short introductory clauses are often optional—but we can worry about exceptions and modifications of the rule later. For now, we want to help students to begin to think about punctuation rules not as arbitrary conventions, but as rules of thumb that have some practical connection to how people actually read.

A typical exercise might look like this:

Commas 1

1. Combine the following two sentences with *because*. Do it two ways—one time beginning with *because*.

   a. He liked to watch his turkeys grow.

   b. He slept in his turkey pens.

2. Combine the following four sentences using some of the following words: *when, while, because, until, unless, after.*

    a. Alfred liked to stand in the street and direct traffic.

    b. Alfred was hit by a large Peterbilt truck.

    c. Alfred was not very smart.

    d. Alfred's brain was very small.

Another might look like this:

Commas 2

Directions: Complete the following sentences by supplying the missing parts:

    a. [why?] + [the chickens piled up] + [when?] + [where?]

    b. [when?] + [John built a stone house] + [why?] + [how?]

    c. [Sally sifted sand] + [when?] + [why?] + [how?]

By calling commas "signals," students can begin to judge for themselves when they need such signals—and they don't have to rely on some vague notion of "aesthetics" or "breath" or "feel."

Semicolons

We can begin by concentrating on the semicolons that students can control and gain some confidence in handling. We can, for instance, teach students how to set up balanced constructions like these:

1. John played basketball; Joan played ice hockey.
2. Olgilvy thought his coach was a platypus; Johnson thought his was a wet marsh rabbit.

Such balanced constructions allow us to come back one more time to the notions of "rhythm" and "expectation." In this case, we can point out that we can break the rhythms and expect our readers to fill in the missing pieces:

1. John played basketball; Joan, ice hockey.
2. Olgilvy thought his coach was a platypus; Johnson, his a wet hen.

We can also teach students to control sentences that contain "conjunctive adverbs." Students, of course, don't always know the difference between conjunctive adverbs and subordinate conjunctions.[8] Those who try to use semicolons with conjunctive adverbs often stick to the common conjunctive adverbs like "however," "moreover," and "nevertheless"—words they've memorized as conjunctive adverbs. But when students resort to simple memorization to be "right," they begin to relinquish control over their language. They have to be careful and usually miss the little words like *even* and *thus*—words that make them feel less secure and more at the mercy of some list in a handbook. But we can ease the frustration by pointing out that conjunctive adverbs move around in a sentence. Other connectors don't. For instance, we can say:

John went to the store; however, he didn't want to.

or:

John went to the store; he, however, didn't want to.

or:

John went to the store; he didn't, however, want to.

On the other hand, we can say:

John went to the store even though he didn't want to.

But we can't say:

John went to the store; he even though didn't want to.

or:

John went to the store; he didn't want to even though.

Such a test frees students from lists and gives them some control over their punctuation— and every time we can give students some control and can eliminate small twinges of doubt, we give them more freedom from the authority of handbooks or teachers' rules, and we increase the odds that they will go on and continue to play and experiment sometime in the future when no one is looking over their shoulders.

Colons

We should show students how to use colons to introduce long quotations and distinguish colons from semicolons. More important, we can help them use colons to signal restatements:

1. Just one thing caused John pain: his big toe.

2. There he was: a necktie around his forehead, a pair of 3-D sun-glasses on his nose, and a trumpet in his right ear.

And students should be able to recognize the difference between two sentences like these:

1. Belching in public is dangerous; people who do so sometimes die horrible deaths.
2. Belching in public is dangerous: people who do so sometimes die horrible deaths.

The difference here has something to do with intention, and again, students need to be constantly aware that such problems are not, simply, problems of "right and wrong" but problems that require students' own *decisions* about what they are trying to say.

Wordiness

Be Verbs

My own children learned to avoid *be* verbs in their writing through exercises that required them to "avoid taboo words." I've also run into many students in class who have been taught to avoid taboo words. They don't always know why they should avoid them, but they sure as hell know how to be careful. Instead of avoiding *be* verbs, students should use them as *clues* to some forms of wordy writing. They should probably worry if *all* their verbs are *be* verbs—especially when they're trying to be descriptive:

Directions: Rewrite this to make it less wordy. (Take a look at the *be* verbs here. Can you replace some with stronger verb forms?)

Rainfall is an environmental condition that directly affects many people's moods. For some, it is the bringer of gloom, and the greyness weighs heavily on their spirits. However, for the portion of the Whitman campus who are frogs, the cool moist days are enjoyed. The frogs can always be found to be splashing and walking in puddles; the ones without their hoods on in the rain. The cool moist days allow them to maintain their highest level of energy. On sunny days frogs would rather crawl into a very damp place and sleep.

Be verbs sometimes lead to wordy sentence beginnings:

1. In conclusion, it is obvious that Alice is an emotionally unstable person who needs to feel good about herself and get in control.
2. It was in Newton's early life that he achieved his greatest work.

3. An example of this is when she shoots the dog.

4. It was true that he was stupid.

5. There were five dogs barking in the street.

But just telling students to watch out for taboo words is not enough. We also need to help them understand the differences between such constructions as these:

1. It's raining.

2. It's impossible.

3. It is this very capability of Ruskin's that interests me.

4. There were trees in the park.

5. There were people eating apples in the park.

6. In the first passage, the boat is a symbol of connectedness and wholeness, whereas in the second, it is a symbol of alienation.

7. In the first passage, the boat is an ugly mass of rotting timbers.

Unless students can decide when they should use *be* verbs or when they should be careful about using *be* verbs, they simply follow rules, and we cut them off from one of the most important words in our language.

Passives

Students should be able to recognize passives and be able to decide which ones are troublesome and which ones are not.[9] They should, for instance, be able to do exercises like this:

Directions: Here are several sentences from your last assignment. They all contain passives, but you have to decide which ones are troublesome. Fix those and leave the others alone.

1. Stormy Lunak claims that children are discriminated against by managers.

2. The restrictions placed on children should not be viewed as a "form of child abuse."

3. Children are very young adults and they should be treated that way.

4. The stereotype of a child being like an animal was brought on by the animalistic acts of many children.

5. It is true that unfair assumptions are made about children living in rental properties.

6. Children know when they are being ignored.

They should also be able to recognize the importance of *context* in judging passive constructions:

Directions: Here are four sentences. Can you rank them in order from best to worst?

1. His decision not to run for reelection to the presidency in 1968 was announced on television on March 31 of that year by Lyndon Johnson.

2. Johnson's decision not to run for reelection to the presidency in 1968 was announced on television on March 31 of that year.

3. On March 31, 1968, President Lyndon Johnson announced on television that he would not run for reelection in the fall.

4. On March 31, 1968, Enoch Finster announced on television that President Lyndon Johnson would not run for reelection in the fall.

The first and third examples come from Richard Marius and Harvey S. Wiener's *McGraw-Hill College Handbook* [2nd ed. (New York: McGraw-Hill, 1988) 221]—and the first is probably the most troublesome. Students will have a more difficult time deciding between the second and third. Depending on the circumstances, the second may not be inappropriate at all. And depending on how people value the words of a historically insignificant nobody named Enoch Finster, the fourth may be more inefficient than the second.

Finally, students should be aware that even in scientific writing, some passives are better than others:

Directions: Fix the weak passives in this passage.

The conception that the individual must be perceived as a dynamic whole, has not yet been internalized by the modern-day consumer researcher. We ought not to be concerned with rigid connections, but rather with temporally extended whole individuals. In short, further traditional research attempting to connect the purchase of canned peas with a personality variable using cross sectional data is bound to fail. What is missing are the interaction effects of that personality variable with other personality characteristics as well as the interaction effects accounted for by needs, motives, moods, memories, attitudes, beliefs, opinions, perceptions, values, etc. in addition to the situation or field. [Harold Kassarjian][10]

Students should be aware that the problem of "proper passives" is not just limited to scientific writing:

Directions: Fix the weak passives in the following passage.

When I am asked to name the one main course that can be made in less than an hour, tastes best, and makes the greatest impression on guests, there are hundreds of foods that come to mind. But on consideration, it might just well be a platter of curried chicken. . . .

The ideal accompaniment for almost any curried dish is rice and this can be prepared simultaneously—all things being equal—with the chicken in curry sauce. Here, too, for convenience sake and in the interest of saving time, I blend a couple of traditional, perhaps Western, curry accompaniments— shredded coconut and raisins or currants. The rice can be put on to cook the moment you put your saucepan with the chicken breasts on to simmer. [Pierre Franey][11]

I would probably tinker with only one—"The rice can be put on to cook"—in the last sentence.

Nominalizations

In setting up lessons on nominalizations, we can concentrate on helping students to recognize nominalizations by concentrating on endings:

- ____ ance (tolerance, avoidance, importance, cognizance).
- ____ ence (competence, coherence, independence).
- ____ ment (agreement, installment, impediment).
- ____ tion (rejection, reflection, calculation, formulation).
- ____ sion (suspension, admission, decision).
- ____ ity (conformity, capability, multiplicity, possibility).
- ____ ness (happiness, homeliness, emptiness).

And they can also practice going back and forth between verbs and modifiers and nominalizations:

- Suspension ⟶ Suspend.
- Conformity ⟶ Conform.
- Be happy ⟶ Have happiness.
- To be rejected ⟶ To experience rejection.
- To agree ⟶ To come to an agreement.

More important, they should recognize that working on style is not just doing things differently in class or in exercises. Anyone can learn to change *conformity* to *conform* or *elimination* to *eliminate*. The problem may also involve taste or preference. As Rosemary Hake and Joseph Williams remind us, many people—including teachers—*like* heavily nominalized prose.[12] Many students—particularly good ones—have been rewarded for writing heavily nominalized prose and write that way because such writing has begun to sound good, proper, or "academic."

Such students should learn to watch out for overnominalized prose, but more important, they should understand that many people *unconsciously* drift toward using nominalizations. The problem, then, is not doing things "right" and correcting nominalizations, nor is it simply listening to the language and sensing infelicities and awkwardness. It may be a problem of *values*: students may have to agree that there *is* sometimes something wrong with a highly nominalized prose style—even though they themselves don't always think so.

Cumulative Sentences

Teachers have created entire courses around cumulative sentences.[13] But I'd spend no more than three or four days on such sentences. You can spend a day introducing participials—both past and present forms in constructions like:

1. John stood in the street, waving his arms, trying to get somebody to stop.
2. John stood in the street, excited by the vulture hanging on his neck.

Students can even imitate long, playful sentences like this:

Here along these bristling walks is a decayed symmetry in a living forest—straight lines softened by a kindly and haphazard Nature, pavements nourishing life with the beginnings of topsoil, the cracks in the walks possessed by root structures, the brilliant blossoms of the domesticated vine run wild, and overhead the turkey buzzard in the clear sky, on quiet wings, awaiting new mammalian death among the hibiscus, the yucca, the Spanish bayonet, and the palm. [E. B. White][14]

or:

They had behaved like wild creatures all morning; shouting from the breezy bluffs, dashing down into the silvery marsh through the dewy cobwebs that glistened on the tall weeds, swishing among the pale tan cattails, wading in the sandy creek bed, chasing a striped water snake from the old willow stump where he was sunning himself, cutting slingshot crotches, throwing themselves on their stomachs to drink at the cool spring that flowed out from under a bank into a thatch of dark watercress. [Willa Cather][15]

Likewise, we can spend a day on absolutes:

1. John stood in the street, his arms coated with vulture guano.

2. John stood in the street, his arms wrapped around the vulture hanging onto his neck like an old writing assignment.

And a day on noun phrases:

1. John eyed his tormentor, a large gray vulture hanging onto his neck like an old writing assignment.

2. John eyed his writing assignment: a large gray vulture hanging onto his neck by one bloody claw.

And a day combining verb phrases, absolutes, and noun phrases maybe like Joan Didion:

The day's events did not turn on cracked crab. And yet it is precisely that fictitious crab that makes me see the afternoon all over again, a home movie run all too often, the father bearing gifts, the child weeping, an exercise in family love and guilt.[16]

But we may waste time trying to teach students to write elegant cumulative sentences, to emulate E. B. White or Joan Didion in thirteen weeks. Furthermore, even though it's possible to use such sentences in academic writing, students rarely discover many occasions to add such sentences to their lab reports or to essays on Marx and Freud.[17] In fact, beginning writers who insist on playing with cumulative sentences in psychology, sociology, chemistry, or political science often discover that their teachers are unimpressed.

Such a qualification doesn't mean that we should avoid teaching students to build cumulative sentences or that academic writers never use absolutes or participials, but we need to keep them in perspective and concentrate on helping students decide when such constructions might be useful and when they may not work so well. For instance, restatements and noun phrases are probably much more useful than absolutes or participials in academic writing, and I would give students many examples of such devices and ask them to imitate them in practice and experiment with such imitations in their own assignments:

1. Postfigurative cultures, which focused on the elders—those who had learned the most and were able to do the most with what they had learned—were essentially closed systems that continually replicated the past. We must now move toward the creation of open systems that focus on the future—and so on children, those whose capacities are least known and whose choices must be left open. [Margaret Mead][18]

2. It had cost $65 million—probably as much as all the other public works in South Carolina put together—and was supposed to lure new industry to the state and provide a broad new inland waterway to carry products down the Santee-Cooper system to Charleston. [Richard Kluger][19]

3. The first of these quasi-qualities, naturalness, is perhaps the most fundamental. Common sense represents matters—that is, certain matters and not others—as being what they are in the simple nature of the case. An air of "of-courseness," a sense of "it figures" is cast over things—again, some selected, underscored things. They are depicted as inherent in the situation, intrinsic aspects of reality, the way things go. [Clifford Geertz][20]

Such restatements may become more and more important as we try to say harder and harder things—things that don't have simple, clear-cut explanations or simple characteristics or are so abstract that we need to "zero-in" or "triangulate in" on them.

At some point, each of us has to consider the limits to how much "style" we can deal with in freshman composition. Some suggest that we ought to introduce students to "all the tools, right now"[21]—but I'm apt to say that it's impossible to teach all the tools "right now." I myself don't have all the tools, and I can't expect my students to have all of them either, at least for a long time. And besides, as I've said before, I'm much more concerned with helping students develop a *vision*—a perspective about writing, an understanding of *context,* and a sense of what they can accomplish in the amount of time they have and how much they can learn if they think about a few things and practice a few things over time. The minute we try to do everything and try to convince students that they ought to command a "style all their own" or taste beyond a reasonable doubt, then we guarantee their failure and our own frustration.

••••••

Notes

1. Annie Dillard, *Pilgrim at Tinker Creek* (New York: Bantam, 1974) 161.
2. Betty Friedan, *The Feminine Mystique* (New York: Dell, 1963) 58.
3. Hunter Thompson, "Last Tango in Las Vegas: Fear and Loathing in the Far Room," in *The Great Shark Hunt: Strange Tales from a Strange Time* (New York: Fawcett, 1979) 656–57.

4. Edwin Newman, *Strictly Speaking* (New York: Warner, 1975).

5. Michael Malone, *Handling Sin* (Boston: Little, Brown, 1986) 19–20.

6. Notice that I'm not particularly worried about mixing subordinate conjunctions with prepositions or any other signals. I'm only concerned with helping students to develop rough understandings about the ways certain things "work."

7. Comma splices and sentence fragments are difficult problems for beginning writers. For a more complete discussion of comma splices, see "Sensitizing Beginning Writing Teachers," *Basic Writing* 3 (Spring/Summer, 1984): 55–62.

8. Sylvan Barnet and Marcia Stubbs characterize conjunctive adverbs as "transitional words" (*Barnet & Stubbs's Practical Guide to Writing*, 5th ed. [Boston: Little, Brown, 1986] 687). Bonnie Carter and Craig Skates tell us that conjunctive adverbs are "transitional expressions"—"not grammatical conjunctions but adverbs modifying the entire clause" (*Rinehart Handbook for Writers*, 2nd ed. [Fort Worth: Holt, Rinehart & Winston, 1990] 190). Maxine Hairston and John Ruskiewicz define conjunctive adverbs as "Words like although, nevertheless, however, one of whose functions is to join parts of sentences" (*The Scott, Foresman Handbook for Writers* [Glenview, IL: Scott, Foresman, 1988] 217).

9. For a more specific discussion, see Jane R. Walpole, "Why Must the Passive Be Damned?" *CCC* 30 (1979): 251–54; Lilita Rodman, "The Passive in Technical and Scientific Writing," *Journal of Advanced Composition* 2 (1981): 165–72.

10. Harold Kassarjian, "Personality and Consumer Behavior: A Review" in *Classics in Consumer Behavior*, ed. Louis E. Boone (Tulsa, OK: The Petroleum Publishing Co., 1977) 173.

11. Pierre Franey, *The New York Times More 60-Minute Gourmet* (New York: Times Books, 1981) 32.

12. For more lesson material, take a look at Rosemary Hake and Joseph Williams's "Style and Its Consequences: Do as I Do, Not as I Say," *CE* 43 (1981): 433–51. The appendix is particularly useful because it provides a number of samples of nominalized prose and revisions.

13. See Bonniejean Christensen's *The Christenson Method: Text and Workbook* (New York: Harper, 1979).

14. E. B. White, "On a Florida Key," in *Essays of E. B. White* (New York: Harper & Row, 1977) 141.

15. Willa Cather, quoted by Francis Christensen and Bonniejean Christensen, *A New Rhetoric* (New York: Harper & Row, 1976) 26.

16. Joan Didion, "On Keeping a Notebook," *Slouching Toward Bethlehem* (New York: Washington Square, 1968) 138.

17. For an argument to the contrary, see Francis and Bonniejean Christensen, *Notes Toward a New Rhetoric,* 2nd ed. (New York: Harper, 1978). Good student writers find occasions to use such sentences in everything they write—but I would emphasize again that I'm not talking about such students here.

18. Margaret Mead, *Culture and Commitment: A Study of the Generation Gap* (Garden City, NY: Natural History Press/Doubleday, 1970) 72.

19. Richard Klugar, *Simple Justice* (New York: Vintage, 1975) 14.

20. Clifford Geertz, *Local Knowledge: Further Essays in Interpretive Anthropology* (New York: Basic Books, 1983) 85.

21. Winston Weathers, *An Alternate Style: Options in Composition* (Rochelle Park, NJ: Hayden, 1980) 2.

some final comments

This has been a difficult book to put together. Some of the problems result from the nature of the book itself: a book I've envisioned as complete enough but not complete, conservative enough but not too conservative, somewhat linear by necessity but not linear in spirit, practical but "professional," dogmatic but undogmatic, personal but not just quirky. My success may depend on your own expectations, perspective, and taste. Nevertheless, I'd still like to address a few objections that will undoubtedly come up.

One problem is "practicality." Some will argue that I'm asking for too much writing for thirteen weeks and that students will bog down, wear out, and suffer too much. Students tell me that even though they suffer, they like all those short, one-page assignments more than they like longer papers, and even though they write all the time, the load is still reasonable. That's not a good answer—and it's not a promise, but it seems to be true in my own classes.

Some will also point out that classes that write all the time generate a lot of writing, and it's easier to assign three or four papers a semester along with a dozen one-paragraph assignments and a notebook, and I'd agree. It's always been easier to do less in writing classes—assign students busy work, make them read famous essays, let them talk to themselves or hide out for a couple of weeks in the library doing "research," or test them over their knowledge of the *MLA Handbook*.

Some will also undoubtedly argue that what I'm doing is fine for me, but not for them. They aren't "funny" themselves (or weird or stupid enough); they don't like to write, or they don't know whether they could modify the assignments to fit their "personalities." Some will argue that they don't have the freedom to experiment with their sylla-buses, to change the organization of a department-wide plan for writing classes, that they work under department heads who are dedicated to particular methods and textbooks, and all that may be true. Some are stuck in inflexible systems that make life miserable for everybody. In such cases, teachers have to do what they have to do; they negotiate if they can; and sometimes they close their doors and quietly mind their own business.

But as I've said all along, I'm much more concerned with how teachers *think* about what they're doing than I am in the way they adopt particular methods or materials they've found in this book. Disciples sometimes don't have any fun, and martyrs die ugly deaths.

Finally, some will argue that I've given no evidence of "good stu-dent" writing, that all I've done is to promise success and give a few ex-amples of ordinary student writing, and that's probably true, too. But issues of "success" are always difficult to document—and I've tried not to suggest that success is easy to recognize or illustrate. I've tried espe-cially hard not to justify what I do on the successes of my best students. Whether we should take credit for *teaching* our best students how to write is always doubtful. Most of the time, our best students are "good" because they are our best students—not because we successfully teach them to be good writers. Sometimes they are even good in spite of us, and most of the time they could learn as well from anybody in the department.

Instead, we should look for success in the work of average writers who finally understand what thesis statements are, or come to our of-fices and argue with us for the first time, or finally succeed in writing in-troductions that are simple and direct. And we should be able to claim successes even though our successes may not be obvious to others.

Here's a student who is both successful and unsuccessful:

J. B. Back, in his excerpt from *The Pleasures of Cigar Smoking,* tells his readers that cigar smoking is like knowledge of vintage wines. He asserts that people who smoke quality cigars can be of any walk of life and that smoking them can enhance a man's image. Finally, he states that cigar smokers are men of fine taste. Cigar smoking is not a sign of fine taste because of its effect on individu-al's health and the objection to smoking that many people hold in general.

He's thinking about summarizing, working on a thesis statement, and trying to do one thing at a time—and having some success—even though his summary and thesis are mechanical, his ideas aren't very original, and he hasn't quite figured out how to isolate a problem yet.

Here's another student who's more successful than unsuccessful:

Hughes Mearns states that youth do not understand what good they have in being young. They desire maturity, and society puts this pressure on them to grow up quickly. Mearns also says that society has this problem to "underestimate childhood," and people do not take the youth seriously; therefore, youth agrees with the older generation without argument. I agree with Mearns; society does not give youth enough credit for their beliefs and emotions.

Her problems are similar to those in the previous example: her summary and thesis are mechanical; her simple thesis doesn't directly address her summary. And if we squint, we can see the seeds of Engfish and black rot lurking somewhere in the margins. But there's success here, too, even more than in the previous example. Five weeks earlier, this student was writing like this:

Learning to be a couch potatoe is essential to living well. This lazy vegetable is a bred of people that have learned the true art of lounging. Down through history this lounger is the person that lives past 100 years of age. They know how to peel away their worries and cares. Relishing in utter creamed ecstasy of smooth slumber on their perfectly indented to their every curve couch. If learned correctly, this skill will teach people how to relax, lower blood pressure, and live longer.

It is important to learn how to be a couch potatoe. In this hard cruel world people are dying of stress and strains. (The couch potatoe has never met up with one of these evil villains.) Society must learn how to relax so they will not die so young. A true lazy veg can teach this essential art so that we may all live longer.

I like that "creamed ecstasy" and that "perfectly indented to their every curve couch" in the first paragraph, but where I teach, this kind of writing doesn't count for much without an argument, a thesis, a sense of control.

And here's another student whose work is even less obviously successful than the previous two but probably even more successful:

Lon Fuller's hypothetical case "The Speluncean Explores" gave excellent examples of legal positivism and natural law in the opions of that case. Fuller's illustration of five men trapped in an underground cavern for 32 days, during which time one of the men was killed and his body eaten, in order for the other men to survive, evoks many questions about the morality of the law within the circumstances of this case. The four survivors in this case were found guilty of murder in accordance with the Commonwealth statute which states: "Whoever shall willfully take the life of another shall be punished by death". This statute also permits no exceptions applicable to this case. It is not difficult to see that the facts of the case fit the statute, what is difficult to see is the reasoning behind the statute itself. It is not enough to say that any law should be complied with to its strictest wording without having guidlines to work within. Likewise the law can not be interpreted or executed without an explanation or meaning of the law in question.

His language is rough; his syntax is rough; his summary of Fuller's case is mostly unnecessary; he's wordy and sloppy, but even though there's roughness here and much to learn, this student has a sense of organization, a problem ("It is not difficult to see . . . what is difficult to see is . . ."), and a thesis statement that seems to follow from the problem. (Several years after he finished English 110—and after a lot of work on his own—this student was accepted into graduate school.)

Whether such successes are dramatic enough to use as examples, I don't know. Certainly, they are not the kind of examples that we normally use to justify what we do in class, but at some point we ought to recognize that progress isn't always dramatic or recognizable outside of particular educational contexts, that for many of our most difficult students, learning to do simple things and to think in simple ways often takes time, and our successes with them are always partial, always incomplete, always mixed with uncertain promise and our own optimism.

appendix one

A Sample Syllabus

• • • • • • • • • • • • • • • • • • •

Here is the description of my beginning writing course just as I give it to students on the first day of class. Over the years, this description has become more and more complex—and even though I know that students won't understand everything, I go over this description carefully in class because it gives me my first opportunity to explain who I am and what I'm trying to do. We'll go over my goals more than once during the semester—and I hope that by the end of the semester most of them will make sense:

Ground Rules—English 110

1. *Goals.* By the end of the semester, you will be able to write a clear, coherent, well-organized, well-supported paper of moderate length. I will require those of you with severe sentence problems to do special practice and meet with me individually in the Writing Center.

We'll go into specific *content* goals later, but right now, I'd like to emphasize the simple wisdom I want you to work on this semester. I want you to:

- Learn something about Truth and our *limits* as mere mortals.
- Learn something about the *value of making mistakes.*
- Gain a respect for *simplicity.*

- Learn to value *patience* and *common sense.*
- Discover something about *pain* and *progress* and *practice.*
- Understand the *game-like* nature of academia.
- Understand the basic idea behind *convention.*
- Recognize the good and bad things associated with *predictability.*
- Discover the value of *public relations* and *negotiation.*

During the semester, we'll work on understanding this wisdom, practicing, and trying to get enough confidence to become more *aggressive learners.* If you don't become aggressive, if you simply think of your writing as a set of skills that will allow you to be right and safe and unobtrusive, you'll die a horrible death.

Some of you will think that I'm teaching "creative writing"—or trying to get you to be creative or inventive or imaginative. You'll say, "Why don't we write about real things or 'relevant' things?" All I can say is baloney. Most of the time, what people mean by "relevance" is something like "what I am used to and what is *safe.*" If you have something "relevant" to write about that's better than what I want you to write about, come see me, and we'll negotiate.

I want you to write difficult things and try to say things you've never tried to say before. I want you to challenge your minds. I don't want you to fall into safe thinking or imagine that all learning ought to be solemn, content oriented, or full of vague but honest pronouncements about life, liberty, and high school civics. While I expect good things (even very good things) from you, I will never grade you on your "creativity" or your "imagination." (That doesn't mean I can't comment on your ideas. I am, after all, a reader, and I react to what I read.)

2. *Attendance.* You can miss a total of five (5) classes without penalty. After five, I will subtract twenty-five points for each absence.

If you are an *athlete* (or anyone else who has to travel to meets, conventions, or group happenings connected with college programs), MAKE ARRANGEMENTS WITH ME IN ADVANCE. (Note: being an athlete does *not* automatically entitle you to extra absences or special privileges simply because you are "excused.")

If you think you need to ask for extensions or "good will," negotiate early. I will give no extensions and offer no good will at the last minute.

That's worth repeating: I will give no extensions and offer no good will at the last minute.

3. *Readings.* You don't have to buy a textbook this semester. During the semester, I'll give you things to read, and you may have to go to the li-

brary sometime during the semester. (This is not a class in library research.)

4. *Assignments.* You will write two warm-up papers, fifteen one-page papers, and seven four-page papers. You may choose *not* to do three of the one-page papers and one of the first five four-page papers. YOU MUST DO THE SIXTH AND SEVENTH (LAST) FOUR-PAGE PAPERS.

Whether you do six or seven four-page papers, the last two papers you write will be worth two times the points of your other papers. If you do seven papers, I will throw out *one* of your scores. If your lowest score is on a double-point paper, I will throw out one-half of your double score.

If you do all fifteen one-page papers, I will throw out three of your scores. Your warm-up papers won't count unless you get twenty-five points out of twenty-five.

You will get your one-page assignments on Tuesday and Friday. (You'll get your assignments for Thursday and Friday on Tuesday and your assignment for Tuesday on Thursday.)

Mid-Term/Final. You will write both a midterm and a final. These will be in-class writings worth fifty points apiece.

Word Processing. You will write at least three of your first five papers on a computer. You can use your own computer; your roommate's; or the college computers at the Writing Center, library, or Computer Center.

5. *Grades.* Each paper will have its own criteria. I will type these on each assignment. Each four-page paper will be worth one hundred points (ninety-five points plus five points for a rough draft brought in the period before it's due.) One-page papers will be worth twenty-five points. At the end of the semester, I will add up your scores and divide by the total points possible:

90–100 = A; 80–89 = B; 70–79 = C; 60–69 = D

If I require you to do special work in spelling or sentence structure, you must complete the work by the beginning of the last week of classes or have 5 percent subtracted from your score.

(I have attached a scoresheet at the end of this handout. Use it to record your own scores. At the end of the semester, we'll compare scores and go over the differences. You're responsible for having all your old papers if you want to dispute the points in my grade book.)

Late Papers. I will penalize late one-page papers five points. I will penalize late four-page papers five points for the first day late; after that, I will subtract ten (10) points. (Note: If a paper happens to be due on a

Friday, you must turn it in on Saturday to lose only five. If you turn it in on Monday, you'll lose ten points.) I WILL NOT ACCEPT A PAPER MORE THAN ONE WEEK LATE. YOU CANNOT TURN IN A PAPER MORE THAN ONE WEEK AFTER IT IS DUE.

Furthermore, all papers will be due at the *beginning* of class. If you come in late, your paper will be late.

If, for any reason, your computer goes down and you can't turn in your paper on time, see me before class and we'll negotiate. If you don't see me before class, your paper will be late.

Rewrites. You may rewrite two of your one-page papers if the initial score on those papers was 15 or less.

You must turn these rewrites in—along with your originals—WITHIN SEVEN DAYS after you have gotten them back for the first time.

You may rewrite one of your *first five* four-page papers if the original score on that paper was 75 or less. (You cannot rewrite either double-point paper.) You can turn this rewrite in up to *two weeks* after you get back your paper for the first time or before the last Monday of the semester (whichever comes first), and ALWAYS INCLUDE THE ORIGINAL PAPER ALONG WITH YOUR REWRITE. You can rewrite late papers for no more points than the original paper was worth at the time you turned it in. (If, for instance, you lost five points because your original paper was a day late, then your rewrite can only be worth 95 points.)

YOU CAN'T REWRITE THE LAST TWO PAPERS OF THE SEMESTER.

6. *Deadlines.* See your course calendar.

7. *Office Hours.* I run the Writing Center (Olin 223) and ought to be around most of the day some place in Olin. Check either the Writing Center or my office (Olin 232). If you want to set up a time to meet, see me just before or just after class.

8. *Other Stuff.* Type all your papers somehow. Type your titles, too. These papers don't have to be spotless masterpieces. You may smash over, plug things in with ink, and cross out (neatly). When you write me notes at the end, type them. You may turn in your papers on lined computer paper as long as you cut the sheets to 8½ x 11 inches. I will not accept any handwritten papers unless you have an A-1, three-star excuse. (If you can't type, come to the Writing Center and work on typing. We've got a typing tutor on the file server.)

Always make a CARBON or XEROXED copy of the work you do outside of class. (If you work on a computer, don't purge your old files until you get your papers back with my comments.) I will not be responsible for losing the only copy of your paper.

Never slip a paper under my door. Always hand papers to me in person. Unless you see your paper in my hands, consider it lost. *Never* let someone else deliver your papers to me. If you do, I will probably lose it. *Never* mail a paper to me or put one in campus mail. *Never* put a paper on my desk and expect me to find it.

On in-class assignments, write with ink. Don't turn in papers with spiral-notebook fringe. I eat spiral-notebook fringe and get indigestion.

Plan ahead.

If you think you'll have trouble, make sure you talk to me. I don't mind looking at your papers before you turn them in. I also don't mind talking about your ideas before you begin to write. You can also make use of the tutors in the Writing Center. I pay them to help students, and when they've got nothing to do, they eat chocolate and twiddle their thumbs.

If you have questions about what I'm doing or why I'm doing it, come see me. If you don't like an assignment, come negotiate. My assignments don't look like the kind most of you are used to, but I'm not just weird and I have reasons for what I do in class.

Along with this set of ground rules, I include a grade tally form:

English 110A Record Form

Use this form to keep track of your scores. I'll give you one at the end of the semester to compare to yours. Keep all your returned, graded papers in case our records disagree.

Name_____

One-Page Papers: Four-Page Papers:

Warm-Up #1_____   1._____

Warm-Up #2_____   2._____
   (count warm-ups only if 25)
                                                                     3._____

                                                                     4._____

1._____
                                                                     5._____
2._____
                                                                    *6._____
3._____
                                                                    *7._____
4._____

5._____   (Best 6; the last two count double)
6._____   *Required, no rewrites
7._____   Bonus Points:
8._____   1._____
9._____   2._____
10._____   3._____
11._____
12._____   Midsem._____
13._____   Final._____
14._____
15._____
    (best 12 scores)
Attendance   (−25 for each over 5)

Add all your points; divide by 1200 (1225 if you include one warm-up score; 1250 if you include two warm-up scores)

And before students leave class, I have them complete the following quiz:

Quiz

Name_____

1. How many times can you be absent?

   What are the peanlties for more absences?

2. How many one-page papers can you rewrite?

3. How long do you have to turn in a rewrite of a four-page paper?

4. Do you have to turn in your original with your rewrite?

5. How much does Hashimoto take off for late papers?

Several things about this class overview are worth pointing out. First, I write everything down and give students copies. I try not to leave the rules up in the air. If students don't know what they have to do, how they are to be graded, and what the rules are for negotiations, then they begin to feel uncomfortable and nervous. I want them to be nervous—but not about the details of grading, deadlines, and class procedures. Furthermore, I don't want them to come up to me during the semester and claim that I never told them what to expect or how to proceed. In fact, by giving students that in-class "quiz" over procedures, they can never claim that they didn't know what was going on. Or if they do, then I have proof that they at least knew what was going on the first day of class.

As complex as it is, students know what they have to do to get a decent grade in class. It should be clear that it's difficult to get a bad grade—and, in fact, students who receive bad grades (or even *C*'s) recognize by the end of the semester that they themselves had as much to do with such grades as I did. I allow them—encourage them—to negotiate their scores and, periodically, I give them chances to earn "bonus points." I should also point out that while I state the ground rules as rules, I encourage students to negotiate those rules. In fact, those students who learn to negotiate almost automatically do better than those who simply let things happen to them in the course.

A Sample Calendar

I never keep on schedule during a semester. Sometimes I get ahead of schedule and cover things not on the syllabus. Other times, class bogs down and we need to cover some ideas more carefully—or sometimes I'll run into a great paper that I want everyone in class to read and lose a day talking about it. Or sometimes I try to plan too much for the day before a three-day weekend. Thirteen weeks is of average length—even in a regularly scheduled fifteen-week semester, all you can probably count on is thirteen weeks of useful instruction. So here, in simplified form, is an overview of the course. I hope you'll be able to recognize how my previous discussions flesh out this general overview and give it some sense.

Week 1

The first week is generally introductory. I'll spend time going over the ground rules, getting sample writings from students, and learning names. The first day, I'll give students gifts. In the past, I've given away bricks, old license plates, Gideon bibles, zucchini squash, road flares, and pieces of concrete. I tell them (and this may not be true), that these will be the last gifts I hope to give out during the semester. Then I'll give them their first assignment—warm-up paper 1; on the second day, I assign warm-up paper 2. These are simple assignments, and I just want students to try to follow directions and write simple, clear prose.

Week 2

I'll spend a day on thesis statements, a day on introductions, and a day on highlighting. Students turn in one-page papers 1, 2, and 3—fairly direct assignments that require thesis statements. Usually, I want them to read one another's papers, but because I have so much to cover in class, this time I'll read these myself, comment on them quickly, and return them. Toward the end of the week, I'll schedule appointments with those students who are already falling apart. I'll try to catch them now because things will get more difficult later.

Week 3

This week, students will begin to read one another's papers (4, 5, and 6) and concentrate on more experiments on highlighting. Initially, I'll just pass papers around the room. Later (much later), students will begin commenting on one another's papers. My goal is to have students read all or almost all the papers written in class during the semester. This gets harder toward the end of the semester, but at the beginning, we can usually keep up. I try to rewrite at least part of a student paper in class and, if I have examples, students will share student papers from previous classes. I'll also try to write one assignment myself and share my own writing with students.

Week 4

During the fourth week, we will continue to practice using simple transitions and read papers 7, 8, and 9. (I especially like to focus on simple repetitions of key ideas from paragraph to paragraph.) Because parallel constructions are also useful for cohesion, we'll spend some time playing with parallel constructions and try to connect them to strategies for linking ideas together.

Week 5

This is the week we'll work on using quotations—introducing them, summarizing them, and paraphrasing. Only one paper is due this week—one-page paper 10. However, students get their first longer four-page assignment—one that focuses on using quotations and many different sources.

Week 6
Students will turn in their first four-page paper, and we'll read first and last pages in class. In class, we'll also begin work on in-text documentation and simple reference lists (both MLA and APA formats).

Week 7
Students turn in their second four-page paper this week, but most of the work will focus on mid-semester exams. I'll pass out old copies of exams from various classes, and we'll talk about them before students do a mid-semester in-class writing. We'll contrast in-class writing with out-of-class writing, and I'll try to emphasize how the conventions differ. (For one thing, when they write in class, students don't need much of an introduction; for another, they can pay less attention to small problems—especially problems of style; for yet another, they should pay even more attention to neat, clearly set up highlighting devices— numbers, letters, white space, etc. If I have time, I might give students an examination that is much too long to handle in fifty minutes and watch them squirm, suffer, and ignore everything I've told them about test taking. Afterwards, we can talk about strategies, what happens under pressure, and what happens if students take examinations without strategies or plans.

Week 8
At mid-semester, students fill out a class evaluation. I'll begin by explaining in writing what I've tried to accomplish in the first eight weeks. Students will respond to my goals, suggest things to change during the second half of the semester, and tell me what they think I've got planned. During this week, we will read selected examples of four-page paper 3 and begin to look at word order, passives, and nominalizations.

Week 9
Four-page paper 4 is due this week. This week, we'll look at typical admonitions against beginning sentences with "this" and "it," and we'll try out the first five steps of Richard Lanham's "paramedic method."

Week 10
Students will turn in one-page papers 11, 12, and 13. (These usually focus on "style." We'll experiment with some "loosening-up" practice—beginning with simple notions of punctuation (commas, colons, semicolons) and possibly a small introduction to cumulative sentences.

Week 11
We'll continue to play with cumulative sentences—absolutes and especially appositives. Students turn in one-page assignments 14 and 15.

Week 12
This week, we'll look at modifiers—concentrating on loaded and vague terms such as *beautiful, neat, interesting, ugly,* and *wonderful.* Students will turn in four-page paper 5—a more or less "open assignment"—and we read what they've written in class. (This is the first of two "open" assignments. We don't need to give students many open assignments, but we do need to give them some opportunity to do some things on their own.) I'll also introduce a notebook extra-credit assignment and introduce students to "description."

Week 13
Since finals are coming up, we'll review test taking and discuss what happened around mid-semester. We'll play with notebook entries and do practice runs before a final in-class writing. Students will also turn in four-page paper 6—their second open assignment. We'll talk about what students have to do on their own—after they get out of this class—to continue to write better.

Finals
During finals week, students turn in their final four-page assignment, do a final in-class writing (50 points), turn in their notebook extra credit, fill out a final class evaluation, and check the scores they've recorded against the scores in my grade book.

appendix two

Sample One-Page Assignments

● ● ● ● ● ● ● ● ● ● ● ● ● ● ● ● ● ● ● ●

Here are ten one-page assignments. Some of the language in the criteria may look suspiciously vague— "unclear" sentences, "obnoxious abuses" of apostrophes, "cosmic" introductions, "lousy" explanations, and so forth. Whether such criteria are clear to students will depend on how well I teach them in class.

Warm-Up Assignment 1

[This is the first assignment for a semester. I give it on the first day of class, and I don't want to take off points for much. I'll comment on these papers and make suggestions, but I won't take off points for things I haven't taught yet. Since I'm going to try to get students to look carefully at my criteria and my directions, I'll begin by taking off points for simple problems that students should be able to fix without much instruction.

The assignment itself is vague—and I expect students to have trouble understanding what I mean by an "intelligent" something. Notice that I don't say anything about format, style, or anything else, besides the typical exhortation to be "perfectly clear." When I read students' papers, I'll be looking for those students who can't follow directions, are irrepressibly careless, or show signs of major problems in syntax, vision, or spirit. Notice that my criteria don't even mention "vision" and "spirit." And notice that I take off points for spelling. Some of you will disagree, but I've never found that a problem. Spelling—at least for most of the students in my classes—may be as much a problem of "audience awareness" as it is of "basic skills." In any case, I expect students to fix spelling errors on everything they turn in that they've worked on out of class. (In-class papers are, of course, another matter.) Furthermore, if I have students with special perceptual problems or foreign students who know words they've only heard but not seen written down, I'll make allowances, but I'll still expect them to fix errors that show up on routine "spell checks" on the computers in the Writing Center.)

Finally, I also encourage students to mark problems they have with their sentences with xxx. I'm always amazed at how few students mark sentences or ask questions. Perhaps they think asking questions is a sign of weakness—I don't know. In any case, from the first assignment, I'll try to encourage questions and comments.]

Write a one-page paper in which you say something intelligent about one of the following quotations. Use examples, illustrations, facts to make whatever you say perfectly clear.

1. "Dispatch iz the gift, or art ov doing a thing right quick. To do a thing right, and to do it quick iz an attribute ov genius." [Josh Billings][1]

2. "Oh, who that ever lived and loved
   Can look upon an egg unmoved?" [Clarence Day][2]

3. "Glorius, stirring sight! . . . The poetry of motion! The *real* way to travel! The *only* way to travel! Here today—in next week tomorrow! Villages skipped, towns and cities jumped—always somebody else's horizons! O bliss! O poop-poop! O my! O my!" [Toad][3]

4. "Never go out of your way to scratch your neighbor's ankles." [Robert Baggs][4]

Do not assume that I understand the ideas here or have seen them before.

Format: For this paper (and all papers until I tell you otherwise) type or neatly print your name, the date, your section number, and your paper number in the lower right-hand corner of the BACK side of your paper. Do not use a cover sheet. Double space. Set up one-inch margins. If you have used a computer to write this and print it, say so at the top of the front page. (Remember: you have to write four of the first seven papers on a computer. If you don't know how to use one, see me or seek help at the Writing Center.)

CRITERIA

You will lose points (out of 25) as follows:

- −7 for each typo/spello.

- −5 for each error in following directions.

- −5 for each unclear, nonstandard sentence (unless you mark it with
  * or xxx and explain why you don't understand what's wrong with it
  or why you are concerned about it). You will never lose points for
  those problems you ask about.

NOTE: In the past, students have lost many points on spelling. Your bad
spelling can lower your grade considerably over the course of the semester. Use the spell-checker in the Writing Center. Learn to love your
dictionary. Ask friends to check over your work for spelling problems. I
don't care how you go about fixing your spelling, but unless you have
major perceptual problems, YOU HAVE NO EXCUSE FOR MAKING SPELLING
ERRORS ON ONE-PAGE ASSIGNMENTS.

Warm-up Assignment 2

[The problem here is not just a problem of definition. Those students
who are used to making minimal efforts will simply define or explain
what a refrigerator/stove relationship is and fail to do anything "important" with their explanation.]

Write a one-page paper in which you tell me something important
about a refrigerator/stove relationship. If you need help, check out the
following quotations:[5]

"Marriage is, in fact, very much the singular most common form of refrigerator-
stove relationships." (Malcolm Smith)

"Have you ever tried to ride a side-car without a stove?" (Lonnie Smith)

"To own a dog and a cat is to own a refrigerator and a stove." (Alfred Loach)

"Daffy Duck cannot really get along without a refrigerator and a stove—and
that's his real problem." (Benton Cooley)

"Refrigerator/stove relationships are only natural." (Candice Berger)

"The normal human brain has two halves: a refrigerator and a stove." (Richard
S. Bildge, Jr.)

"You can buy a stove at a garage sale, but never a refrigerator." (Sandra
O'Donnell)

CRITERIA

You will lose points (out of 25) as follows:

- −7 for each typo/spello.

- −5 for each error in following directions.

- −5 for each unclear, nonstandard sentence (unless you mark it with * or xxx and explain why you don't understand what's wrong with it or why you are concerned about it).

One-Page Paper 1

[This assignment resembles the previous one, but it's slightly different. For one thing, the assignment asks students to discuss "the most important aspect" of Josh Billings's sayings. To do so, students will have to, in some way, explain or account for those other aspects that are less important. When students turn these papers in, then, I'll begin to assess how well they understand the purposes of and occasions for comparisons.

I've already talked about "stories" in class after reading the last set of papers, so now I'm going to insist that they don't tell any more stories here. I also don't want students to use *you* or *one*—I've told them in class that *you* is OK but a little folksy, and I'd like to see if they can be just a bit more formal. As they begin to get more formal, they're likely to slip into "one thinks . . . one feels . . ." and by this time, I've tried to head that off.

Finally, I'm going to take off points for "obnoxious" abuses of apostrophes—even though I know that apostrophes are not always easy for students to fix. (See my "Pain and Suffering: Apostrophes and Academic Life," *Basic Writing* 7 [Fall, 1988]: 91–98.) The only apostrophes I'll worry about are simple ones: "John's dog" (where the notion of "ownership" is perfectly clear) and "It's a good day."]

Here are some important sayings by Josh Billings.[6] Can you explain in one page the most important aspect of these sayings?

1. Ants are older than Adam.

2. Give a smart child a pack ov kards and a spellin book, and he will larn tew play a good game ov hi lo jak long before he kan spell a word ov two syllables.

3. If a kat iz killed in the fall ov the year, and thrown over under a sno bank, and dont thaw out in the spring, and keeps quiet during the summer months, and aint missing when winter sets in again, I have

alwus sed, "*that kat*," waz ded, or waz playing the thing dredful fine.

4. Lam and green peas are good, but not good for the lam.

5. I hav noticed this diffrence between people—thare is *some* who are not az big phools as they look.

6. Beauty iz a morning dream which the breakfast bell puts an end to.

7. The snobs are either half-breeds or dunghills.

8. I don't want enny better evidence that a man iz a phool than tew see him cultivate excentricitys.

9. Studdy the heart if yu want to learn human natur; there ain't no human natur in a man's head.

10. The duk is a foul. Thare aint no doubt about this—naturalists say so, and kommon sense teaches it.

11. Edukashun that don't learn a man how tew think iz like knowing the multiplikashun forward but not bakwards.

12. Cats are very plenty in this world, just now, i counted 13 from my boarding house winder, one moon lite night, last summer, and it want a fust rate night for cats neither.

13. A coquette in love iz just about az tame az a bottle ov ginger pop that haz stood sum time with the cork pulled out.

Don't tell a little story; don't use *you*. Don't use *one* as in "one says," "one knows," or whatever.

CRITERIA

You will lose points (out of 25) as follows:

- −5 for each typo/spello.
- −5 for each error in following directions.
- −5 for each unclear, nonstandard sentence (unless you mark it with * or xxx and explain why you don't understand what's wrong with it or why you are concerned about it).
- −5 for any obnoxious abuse of the apostrophe.

One-Page Paper 2

[The last assignment was a "data" assignment; this one is a "text" assignment. The easy part is telling us what Zilch says. The hard part is doing something with it. Note that I'm taking points off here for "thesis statements"—something we've just begun to talk about in class.]

Here is chapter 6 of H. Z. Zilch's *The Greenest Watermelon* (New York: Hipple Press, 1932). Is Zilch Correct?

One of the major problems with the Skersnergowsker is that when it flimbles with an actual Skittle, it turns even the brightest minds from the contemplation of the human soul to the love of butterflies.

(For your information, chapter 7 is titled "Deep in the Swamp of Never-Ending Nightmares" and chapter 5 is titled "They'll Look for You, Too." This particular chapter is untitled.)

CRITERIA

You will lose points (out of 25) as follows:

- −5 for each typo/spello.
- −5 for each error in following directions.
- −5 for each unclear, nonstandard sentence (unless you mark it with * or xxx and explain why you don't understand what's wrong with it or why you are concerned about it).
- −2 for any obnoxious abuse of an apostrophe.
- −5 for an unclear or strangely incoherent THESIS STATEMENT
- −15 for not typing this into a computer if you still have not typed any papers into a computer so far.

One-Page Paper 3

[This is similar to the last assignment—but different. Here, students have to be much more careful with their reading. Does Darrow (at least in this passage) say that he's a communist? socialist? What does he mean by "equality"? What does he mean by "make the world partners in production, partners in the good things of life"? Is he saying that everyone should be equal? Is he saying that there should be no private ownership? (Or does he simply say "private ownership of land"?) Students with strong opinions are going to jump right in without reading, and after they turn in their papers, I'll probably have to comment on the problems they create for themselves.

I also tell students that Darrow is the most famous trial lawyer America has produced, but I don't know if that's true or not. Perry Mason may be more famous. In any case, I'm interested in seeing how many students tell me how famous Darrow is.]

Here is a passage written by Clarence Darrow (1857–1938), perhaps the most famous trial lawyer America has produced. Is he right?

The only way in the world to abolish crime and criminals is to abolish the big ones and the little ones together. Make fair conditions of life. Give men a chance to live. Abolish the right of private ownership of land, abolish monopoly, make the world partners in production, partners in the good things of life. Nobody would steal if he could get something of his own some easier way. Nobody will commit burglary when he has a house full. No girl will go out on the streets when she has a comfortable place at home. The man who owns a sweatshop or a department store may not be to blame himself for the condition of his girls, but when he pays them five dollars, three dollars, and two dollars a week, I wonder where he thinks they will get the rest of their money to live. The only way to cure these conditions is by equality. There should be no jails. They do not accomplish what they pretend to accomplish. If you would wipe them out there would be no more criminals than now. They terrorize nobody. They are a blot upon any civilization and a jail is an evidence of the lack of charity of the people on the outside who make the jails and fill them with the victims of their greed.[7]

CRITERIA

You will lose points (out of 25) as follows:

- −5 for each error in following directions.
- −5 for each unclear, nonstandard sentence (unless you mark it with * or xxx and explain why you don't understand what's wrong with it or why you are concerned about it).
- −5 for an unclear or strangely incoherent THESIS STATEMENT.
- −2 for each typo/spello.
- −2 for each messy apostrophe.
- −5 for a strangely cosmic introduction.

One-Page Paper 4

[Here's a longer data assignment that probably requires some attention to categorizing and labeling. Notice that the directions are getting vaguer. Vague assignments often generate strange results, but I want students to start looking for their own problems to discuss. Students who cop out often try to get away with discussing only one or two of these stickers.]

Here are some bumper stickers. What's so important about this list?

PAWN POWER

SQUARE DANCER

WORK FOR IT—I DID!

ENGLISH TEACHERS ARE NOVEL LOVERS

ARCHAEOLOGISTS WILL DATE ANY OLD THING

SHIT HAPPENS

NIXON NOW! FOUR MORE YEARS HE'LL BRING US TOGETHER

IF YOU AIN'T COUNTRY YOU AIN'T SHIT

NOT A DIRTY OLD MAN . . . A SEXY SENIOR CITIZEN!

HAPPINESS IS A GOOD SCREW (Pacific Nut and Bolt Company)

JESUS SAVES

I FOUND IT!

WILL ROGERS NEVER MET RONALD REAGAN

YOU JUST CAN'T BEAT IDAHO JACK RABBITS

HAVE YOU DUG . . . WALL DRUG

SEX INSTRUCTOR. FIRST LESSON FREE

GARDEN OF THE GODS

TREES OF MYSTERY

I'D RATHER GO FISHING

FREEZE VOTER

ELECTRICIANS REMOVE YOUR SHORTS

I ♥ L.A.

MY EX DRIVES A HYUNDAI

BOOMERANG POWER

IF SEATTLE IS THE EMERALD CITY, TOTO IS A SLUG

GOD, GUTS AND GUNS MADE THIS COUNTRY GREAT

I ♥ NEW YORK

I ♥ COLIMA

BABY IN BACK

I ♥ MY DOG

WHEN GOD CREATED MAN SHE WAS ONLY JOKING

NO NUKES IS GOOD NUKES

HAVE YOU HUGGED YOUR BANJO TODAY?

NATIVE

LIFE IS A BEACH

HAVE YOU HUGGED YOUR CHILD TODAY?

IN SEARCH OF THE ETERNAL BUZZ

AFTER BITCH

EAGLES FOREVER

EVERYONE LOOKS GOOD AFTER 2 A.M.

CRITERIA

You will lose points (out of 25) as follows:

- −5 for each error in following directions.
- −5 for an unclear or strangely incoherent THESIS STATEMENT.
- −2 for each unclear, nonstandard sentence (unless you mark it with * or XXX and explain why you don't understand what's wrong with it or why you are concerned about it).
- −2 for each typo/spello.
- −2 for each messy apostrophe.
- −5 for a strangely cosmic introduction.
- −5 for a conclusion that doesn't seem to fit or that is better and more important than your introduction.

One-Page Paper 5

[This comes from "Why Being Serious Is So Hard," reprinted in *So This Is Depravity* (New York: Washington Square, 1980). It's a definition assignment, a comparison/contrast, a data assignment, a critique, and an "analysis" assignment all rolled into one.

After students turn in their papers, I might ask who knows what "Wedgwood" is or who Randolph Scott is. Sometimes the students who have the most trouble never ask simple questions.]

Here's what Russell Baker, the Pulitzer prize-winning author, has to say about being solemn and being serious. What would he think about collecting bowling balls? Would you approve?

1. Being solemn is easy. Being serious is hard.
2. Children almost always begin by being serious.
3. Adults, on the whole, are solemn.
4. The transition from seriousness to solemnity occurs in adolescence, a period in which Nature, for reasons of her own, plunges people into foolish frivolity.
5. Being solemn has almost nothing to do with being serious, but on the other hand, you can't go on being adolescent forever, unless you are in the performing arts, and anyhow most people can't tell the difference.
6. Jogging is solemn. Poker is serious.

7. Shakespeare is serious. David Susskind is solemn.

8. Chicago is serious. California is solemn.

9. Blow-dry hair stylings on anchormen for local television news shows are solemn.

10. Falling in love, getting married, having children, getting divorced and fighting over who gets the car and the Wedgwood are all serious.

11. The new sexual freedom is solemn.

12. *Playboy* is solemn. *The New Yorker* is serious.

13. Arguing about "structured programs" of anything is solemn. So are talking about "utilization," attending conferences on the future of anything and group bathing when undertaken for the purpose of getting to know yourself better, or at the prescription of a swami.

14. Washington is solemn. New York is serious. So is Las Vegas, but Miami Beach is solemn.

15. Humphrey Bogart movies about private eyes and Randolph Scott movies about gunslingers are serious. Modern movies that are sophisticated jokes about Humphrey Bogart movies and Randolph Scott movies are solemn.

16. . . . the mass audience is solemn, which accounts for the absence of seriousness in television, paperback books found in airport book racks, the public school systems of America, wholesale furniture outlets, shopping centers and American-made automobiles.

17. Writing sentences that use "one" as a pronoun is solemn.

CRITERIA

- −5 for each error in following directions.
- −5 for an unclear or strangely incoherent THESIS STATEMENT.
- −5 for a strangely cosmic introduction.
- −5 for a weak conclusion.
- −2 for each typo/spello.
- −2 for each messy apostrophe.
- −2 for each unclear, nonstandard sentence (unless marked and explained).
- −1 for a weak title.
- −10 for not typing this paper into a computer if you've typed only three papers so far into a computer.

One-Page Assignment 6

[This one looks harder than it is, and that's good. The main problem involves trying to set up a comparison with three items. Such comparisons are always difficult. The easiest way might be to set up clear criteria early and apply these criteria to these recipes.]

Which of these three recipes is the best?

1. Take the Carp, alive if possible, scour him, and rub him clean with water and salt, but scale him not: then open him, and put him with his blood and his liver, which you must save when you open him, into a small pot or kettle; then take sweet marjoram, thyme, and parsley, of each half a handful; a sprig of rosemary, and another of savory; bind them into two or three small bundles, and put them to your Carp, with four or five whole onions, twenty pickled oysters, and three anchovies. Then pour upon your Carp as much claret-wine as will only cover him; and season your claret well with salt, cloves, and mace, and the rinds of oranges and lemons. That done, cover your pot and set it on a quick fire, till it be sufficiently boiled: then take out the Carp, and lay it with the broth into the dish, and pour upon it a quarter of a pound of the best fresh butter, melted and beaten with half a dozen spoonfuls of broth, the yolks of two or three eggs, and some of the herbs shred: garnish your dish with lemons, and so serve it up, and much good do you! [Izaak Walton, *The Compleat Angler; or, The Contemplative Man's Recreation* (1653)]

2. For a carp weighing from four to six pounds. Cut into one to one-half inch pieces. With sharp knife remove skin, saving all skins. Remove bones. Put fish through grinder with three large onions. Save onion peelings. Put ground fish in wooden bowl and chop for ten minutes. For each pound of fish add one egg, chopping successively as each egg is added. Then chop for ten minutes. Take two cups dried breadcrumbs, sprinkle lightly over chopped fish; fold breadcrumbs into the mixture; chop again for ten minutes. Add one and one-half cups water, a little at a time, chopping after each addition. Mixture should then be fluffy. Add trifle more water if necessary. Chop for another ten minutes. Salt and pepper to taste—but rather heavily. Now take small amounts of the mixture and fill each piece of skin. If this seems too difficult, for the skin breaks easily, the chopped fish may be prepared as fish balls. Handle lightly. Prepare deep wide-bottomed pan. Spread onion peelings in bottom of pan. Put in clove of garlic, with two carrots and stalks of celery, cut up; salt and pepper vegetables, cover well with cold water and cook

until vegetables are almost done. Now lay fish pieces (in skins) or fish balls, in pan; cover and cook at a slow boil for about three hours. [Ben Hur Lampman, *The Coming of the Pond Fishes* (Portland, Oregon: Binfords & Mort, 1946)]

3. It was my brother who finally devised a method of cooking carp that not only made it fit for human consumption, but actually delicious. First, instead of merely scaling the fish, he skinned them. Then, taking a large pinch, where the meat was thickest, he worked his fingers and thumb into the flesh until he struck the median bones, then he worked his thumb and fingers together and tore off a handful of meat. Using this tearing method, he could get two or three good-sized chunks of flesh from each side of the fish. He then heated a pot of bland vegetable shortening, rubbed the pieces of fish with salt and dropped them into the hot fat. He used no flour, meal, crumbs or seasoning other than salt. They cooked to a golden brown in a few minutes, and everyone pronounced them "mighty fine eating." The muddy flavor seemed to have been eliminated by removing the skin and large bones. The forked bones were still there, but they had not been multiplied by cutting across them, and one only had to remove several bones still intact with the fork from each piece of fish. [Euell Gibbons, "How to Cook a Carp," in *Stalking the Wild Asparagus: Field Guide Edition* (New York: David McKay, 1962)]

CRITERIA
- −5 for each error in following directions.
- −5 for an unclear or strangely incoherent THESIS STATEMENT.
- −5 for a strangely cosmic introduction.
- −2 for each typo/spello.
- −2 for each messy apostrophe.
- −2 for each unclear, nonstandard sentence (unless marked and explained).
- −1 for a weak title.
- −2 for each problem with agreement (subject/verb, pronoun).

One-Page Paper 7

[This is a relatively difficult passage to read—and students sometimes spend their whole time telling me what Manchester's little story at the end has to do with his point, what the "insipid mean" is, what or who "double-domes" are, who Roosevelt and Tartuffe are. The tendency to explicate as a goal in itself may begin someplace in literature class where we tend to go over the hard things line by line or even word by word. But the assignment doesn't say to tell me what Manchester says or to describe how one goes about finding out what he says. I want a response: Is Manchester right? Is he wrong? So what? What next? Who cares? Who should care? Note also that while I've commented on such things on every assignment, this is the first time I'll take off points for problems involving "content."]

Respond as well as you can to the following quotation by William Manchester:

Young intellectual snobs must be suckled on the thin broth of the insipid mean; to give them a richer diet would, in the glib cliché, be undemocratic. It is not undemocratic, of course, to provide special schools for retarded children; they are below the general level and must be brought up to it. Thus we see again the topsy-turvy dogma—the same twisted thinking which corrupted Franklin D. Roosevelt's "The poorest are no longer necessarily the most ignorant part of society" to mean "The commoner the man, the wiser he." Gifted children ("double-domes") are distrusted. The dull and delinquent ("underprivileged," "sick," "victims of society") belong to the privileged caste. We must look down on those above us, up to those beneath us. So sacred is this doublethink that we rarely challenge it, though sometimes it is carried to a Tartuffian extreme and we see a glimmer in the night. The last time I visited the Barnum and Bailey sideshow, the barker interrupted his spiel to deliver a brief sermon. He just wanted us to know that these fine tattooed, misshapen and deformed people on the stage were folks, same as you and me. Why, you'd be glad to have any of them in your home, he said. Sure, they were interesting. But— and his voice dropped to a tactful whisper—they weren't *freaks*. ["In Defense of Snobs," *Controversy and Other Essays in Journalism 1950–1975* (Boston: Little, Brown, 1976) 265.]

CRITERIA

- −5 for each error in following directions.
- −5 for an unclear or strangely incoherent THESIS STATEMENT.
- −5 for a strangely cosmic introduction or weak conclusion.
- −2 for each typo/spello.
- −2 for each messy apostrophe.
- −2 for each unclear, nonstandard sentence (unless marked and explained).
- −1 for a weak title.
- −2 for each problem with agreement (subject/verb, pronoun).
- −5 for lousy explanations, unclear examples.

One-Page Paper 8

[I expect many students to get bogged down in the problem of whether pipe smoking is good for you. We all know that smoking is bad because it causes cancer and emphysema. And students who move off to discuss the health risks of smoke can lose sight of the real issues here—whether there are such people as "quality cigar smokers" and whether they have "fine taste."]

Comment on this passage from J. B. Back's *The Pleasures of Cigar Smoking*.[8]

A taste for and knowledge of vintage wine can be said to indicate a type of man and the caliber of his sophistication. So can taste for and knowledge of cigars. Can such a man be described? Yes, quite accurately. He is youthful in spirit as well as in years. He is active and interested in his world regardless of age. (Note: He is *not* cast in the classic image of the cigar chewer whose cigar is dead ash at one end and wet, bitten flat as a fishtail, at the other. True, there are such men who smoke cigars, and hopefully, even they can learn something about cigar smoking.)

The quality cigar smoker may drive an MG, crew on deep-water racing sloops, sky dive from airplanes, drive a Triumph motorcycle, breed Irish setters, golf like Jack Nicklaus, play the guitar like Bob Dylan. On the other hand, to be quite honest about it, the quality cigar smoker may be no more exciting, or excitable, than the next-door neighbor. Cigars, good cigars, are not limited to the aristocracy or the sophisticated, though the smoking of them can certainly enhance a man's image. In any case, the cigar smoker—the steeplejack, yachtsman, banker, clerk or baseball player—is basically a man with a sense of fine taste.

CRITERIA

- −5 for each error in following directions.
- −5 for an unclear or strangely incoherent THESIS STATEMENT.
- −5 for a strangely cosmic introduction.
- −2 for each typo/spello.
- −2 for each messy apostrophe.
- −2 for each unclear, nonstandard sentence (unless marked and explained).
- −1 for a weak title.
- −2 for each problem with agreement (subject/verb, pronoun).
- −5 for lousy explanations, unclear examples.
- −2 for a simple solution.

•••••••

Notes

1. Josh Billings (Henry W. Shaw), "Dispatch," *The Complete Works of Josh Billings* (Chicago: M. A. Donohue, 1919) 81.

2. Clarence Day, quoted after the acknowledgements, Page Smith and Charles Daniel, *The Chicken Book* (Boston: Little, Brown, 1975).

3. Kenneth Grahame, *The Wind in the Willows* (New York: Charles Scribner's Sons, 1911) 41.

4. I made Robert Baggs up.

5. I made up these quotations, too.

6. All these quotations come from *The Complete Works of Josh Billings* (Chicago: M. A. Donohue, 1919).

7. Clarence Darrow, "Crime and Criminals," *The Speaker's Resource Book,* ed. Carroll C. Arnold, Douglas Ehninger, and John C. Gerber (Glenview, IL: Scott, Foresman, 1966) 146–47.

8. J. B. Back, *The Pleasures of Cigar Smoking* (Rutledge Books, 1971) 14.

appendix three

·····································
·····································
·····································
·····································
·····································
·····································

Inspiration for Longer Assignments

● ● ● ● ● ● ● ● ● ● ● ● ● ● ● ● ● ●

I'm interested in ways of thinking about
assignments, not in supplying people with prefabricated assignments
that they can plug into their courses, and in that spirit, I include here
one complete assignment and bits and pieces of several more. I end
with an annotated list of additional material—some of which is difficult
to find and out of print. If you look at this appendix as a source for inspiration and not a source for materials, you won't be disappointed that you
can't find everything listed—or that everything listed doesn't work in
your own classes, or that the material looks too weird or contrived for
your taste. You can, after all, find ordinary materials in the dozens of
textbooks that come out each year.

As you look at this material, think beyond relevance, models,
George Orwell, and *The Norton Anthology*; think about the Goodwill,
The Salvation Army, and little magazines and collections of cowboy
songs you sometimes find in diners and truck stops in Montana. Think
about seasonings for Texas chili, methods of selling vacuum cleaners,
and Aunt Gertrude's collection of antique postcards. Think about texts
you can make up or have someone else make up for you.

Four-Page Paper Assignment

Elbert Hubbard

[This is a four-page assignment. I used to give "three- to five-page" assignments, but three- to five-page assignments always turn out to be
two-and-a-half-page assignments. We looked at Elbert Hubbard a little
bit in chapter 5, but he's worth coming back to. Probably the most common source of Hubbard material is his *Note Book*—a hodgepodge of
good and bad material. (In the last two years, I've found two copies at
the Goodwill.) Another common source of Hubbard's good and bad
material is *The Philosophy of Elbert Hubbard* (New York: Wm. H. Wise,
1930). (I found my copy at the Humane Society Thrift Store down on
Isaacs Avenue.)

The assignment is reasonably difficult. I'm looking for ways students narrow the problem down. They don't have room to cover each individual assertion that Alice Hubbard makes, so they'll have to find an
angle, a way to combine ideas. Some will want to discuss only the first
half of Alice's quotation—and that's probably a mistake, since the second half seems to explain where Alice thinks Elbert is so "positive" a
"human force." I'm also looking for students who recognize that Elbert
is a jerk and a madman, but an interesting—and even funny—jerk and
madman. Students often don't have any fun playing with Hubbard's
ideas, and even Hubbard would be upset with them for that. Finally, I'm
looking for a few solid examples of some of Hubbard's "competitors"—
and whether students can convince me that people such as Abe Lincoln,
Martin Luther King, John F. Kennedy, Albert Einstein, Emma Goldman,
or Whoever were more knowledgeable in "fundamental, practical" affairs than Hubbard. It's easy to overlook the criteria Alice uses to set up
her claim, and we can only criticize her on what she says, not what we'd
like her to say. I might add that part of Alice's credibility depends on
who students think she was, and students often don't bother to ask who
she was. (As I understand it, she was Elbert's second wife—a compe-
tent, practical woman who organized Elbert's life.)]

Date Due: Friday
Rough Draft Due: Wednesday
Here are some important quotations from Elbert Hubbard [*The Note Book of
Elbert Hubbard: Mottoes, Epigrams, Short Essays, Passages, Orphic Sayings and
Preachments* (New York: Wm. H. Wise, 1927)].

In her preface to Hubbard's book, Alice Hubbard describes Elbert like
this:

> Elbert Hubbard, the most positive human force of his time, is a man of gen-
> ius in business, in art, in literature, in philosophy. He is an idealist,
> dreamer, orator, scientist. In his knowledge of the fundamental, practical

affairs of living, in business, in human interests, in education, politics and law he seems without a competitor.

Do you agree with Alice? Disagree?

Criteria

Out of 100 points, you'll lose points as follows:

- −5 for not bringing in a rough draft on Wednesday.
- −10 for an unclear or missing thesis statement.
- −10 for not following directions.
- −10 for a weak or missing introduction, a weak conclusion (if you need a strong one).
- −5 for obviously misreading something (each time I catch you).
- −5 for not using good examples, explanations, illustrations to support your points.
- −2 for each problem with pronoun agreement (agreement, reference).
- −2 for each typo/spello.
- −2 for each case of unclear, confusing, or inexact documentation.
- −2 for a weak or nonexistent title.

If you have questions about what you've written, see me; if you don't know how to fix something and it's late Thursday night, ask questions in content notes. (I won't take off points for anything you have questions about.)

1. The great Big Black Things that have loomed against the horizon of my life, threatening to devour me, simply loomed and nothing more. The things that have really made me miss my train have always been sweet, soft, pretty, pleasant things of which I was not in the least afraid. (p. 61)

2. To supply a thought is mental massage; but to evolve a thought of your own is an achievement. Thinking is a brain exercise—no faculty grows save it is exercised. (p. 64)

3. I have no perfect panacea for human ills. And even if I had I would not attempt to present a system of philosophy between the soup and fish, but this much I will say: The distinctively modern custom of marital bundling is the doom of chivalry and death of passion. It wears all tender sentiment to a napless warp, and no wonder is it that the novelist, without he has a seared and bitter heart, hesitates to follow the couple beyond the church door. There is no greater re-

proach to our civilization than the sight of men joking the boy whose heart is pierced by the first rays of a life-giving sun, or of our expecting a girl to blush because she is twice God's child today she was yesterday. (p. 57)

4. It is only life and love that give love and life. (p. 40)

5. Do not go out of your way to do good whenever it comes your way. Men who make a business of doing good to others are apt to hate others in the same occupation. Simply be filled with the thought of good, and it will radiate—you do not have to bother about it, any more than you need trouble about your digestion. (p. 71)

6. The newspapers print what the people want, and thus does the savage still swing his club and flourish his spear. (p. 142)

7. I am not sure just what the unpardonable sin is, but I believe it is a disposition to evade the payment of small bills. (p. 146)

8. Do not dump your woes upon people—keep the sad story of your life to yourself. Troubles grow by recounting them. (p. 156)

9. Men who marry for gratification, propagation or the matter of buttons or socks, must expect to cope with and deal with a certain amount of quibble, subterfuge, concealments, and double, deep-dyed prevarication. (p. 159)

10. When you see a tomcat with his whiskers full of feathers, do not say "Canary!"—he'll take offense. (p. 159)

11. Academic education is the act of memorizing things read in books, and things told by college professors who got their education mostly by memorizing things read in books. (p. 160)

12. Literature is the noblest of all the arts. Music dies on the air, or at best exists only as a memory; oratory ceases with the effort; the painter's colors fade and the canvas rots; the marble is dragged from its pedestal and is broken into fragments. (170)

13. How would a blacksmith look wearing white kid gloves at a reception perfunk? (p. 172)

14. Please bear in mind that the greatest dietetic sinners are not the poor and ignorant, but the so-called educated class. We all realize the dangers from strong drink, but strong meat that sets up its ferment after you eat it, is quite as bad as the product of the grain that is fermented first and swallowed afterwards. (p. 172)

15. Already we say, "That man is the best educated who is the most useful," and the true test of education will be in its possessor's ability to serve. (p. 181)

16. Personality first reveals itself in the hat. Woman lures with her hat—a bonnet beckons. The hat is a purely secondary sex manifestation. What the comb and wattles are to the cock o' the walk, the hat is to the man. With the hat we signal, apologize, or defy. Strong men do not allow Mrs. Grundy to dictate when they shall have their hair cut, nor to select their hats. (p. 183)

17. "public opinion"—The judgment of the incapable many opposed to that of the discerning few. (p. 188)

18. "perfume"—Any smell that is used to drown a worse one. (p. 188)

19. "vacation"—A period of increased pleasurable activity when your wife is at the seashore. (p. 188)

20. "litigation"—A form of hell whereby money is transferred from the pockets of the proletariat to that of lawyers. (p. 187)

21. The Suffrage for woman means freedom—freedom from her own limitations. It means a better education of women. And woman needs education for three reasons: First, for her own happiness and satisfaction. Second, so she may be a better mother, and add her influence to racial education. Third, so that she may be a better companion for man, for all strong men are educated by women. (p. 74)

22. Among the world's great workers—and in the front rank there have been only a scant half-dozen—stands Fra Junipero Serra. This is the man who made the California Missions possible. In artistic genius, as a teacher of handicrafts and industrial leader, he performed a feat unprecedented, and which probably will never again be equaled. In a few short years he caused a great burst of beauty to bloom and blossom, where before was only a desert waste. The personality of a man who could not only convert to Christianity three thousand Indians, but who could set them to work, must surely be sublimely great. Not only did they labor, but they produced art of a high order. These missions which lined the Coast from San Francisco to San Diego, every forty miles, were Manual Training Schools, founded on a religious concept.

    Junipero taught that, unless you backed up your prayer with work, God would never answer your petitions. And the wonderful transformations which this man worked in characters turned on the fact that he made them acceptable and beautiful. Here is a lesson for us! He ranks with Saint Benedict, who rescued classical art from the dust of time and gave it to the world. Junipero is one with Albrecht Durer, Lorenzo the Magnificent, Michelangelo, Leonardo da Vinci, Friedrich Froebel, John Ruskin and William Morris.

These men all taught the Gospel of Work, and the sacredness of Beauty and Use.

Junipero was without question the greatest teacher of Manual Training which this continent has so far seen. Without tools, apparatus or books, save as he created them, he evolved an architecture and an art, utilizing the services of savages, and transforming these savages in the process, for the time at least, into men of taste, industry, and economy.

This miracle of human energy and love could not endure, and after Fra Junipero had passed out, there being none to take his place, the Indians relapsed into their racial ways. (76)

23. I have a profound respect for boys.

Grimy, ragged, tousled boys in the street often attract me strangely. A boy is a man in the cocoon—you do not know what it is going to become—his life is big with many possibilities.

He may make or unmake kings, change boundary-lines between States, write books that will mold characters, or invent machines that will revolutionize the commerce of the world. Every man was once boy: I trust I shall not be contradicted: it is really so.

Wouldn't you like to turn Time backward, and see Abraham Lincoln at twelve, when he had never worn a pair of boots? The lank, lean, yellow, hungry boy—hungry for love, hungry for learning, tramping off through the woods for twenty miles to borrow a book, and spelling it out, crouched before the glare of the burning logs! (p. 78)

24. The daily newspaper the educator of the people! God help us, it may be so! It educates into inattention, folly, sin, vacuity and foolishness. It saps concentration, dissipates aspiration, scrambles gray matter and irons convolutions. Watch the genus commuter rush for his Dope when he reaches the station in the morning. He may be a Sunday School Superintendent, a college graduate, a man of social standing, but he must have his matin-mess of rottenness or he would die of fidgets. He reads how a man in Manitoba elopes with another man's wife, with consuming interest. He scans the advertising pages with their columns of fakery and filth, and it never occurs to him that a certain amount of the slime that slides into his brain must stay there and line the vacuum. At night when he goes home he buys the last edition, reads the whole thing over again written 't other end to. He does this for ten years, twenty—does it not make him what he is? Would you like to go to Heaven with him? (p. 81)

Samples

Here is some information about three important people students should know something about.

Josh Billings

I've included some examples of Billings (Henry W. Shaw) in appendix 2, but you might want to work up more material for longer assignments. One of the best sources of such material is *The Complete Works of Josh Billings* (Chicago: M. A. Donohue, 1919). Imagine a whole book full of such pieces as "What I Kno About Pharming":

What i kno about pharmin, iz kussid little. Mi buzzum friend, Horace Greely, haz rit a book with the abuv name, and altho i haven't had time tew peerose it yet, i don't hesitate tew pronounse it bully.

Pharmin, (now daze) iz pretty much all theory, and therefore it aint astonishing, that a man kan live in New York, and be a good chancery lawyer, and also know all about pharming . . .

Even now it aint unkommon, tew see three, or four, hired men, on a farm, with three, or four, spans ov oxen, all standing still, while the boss goes into the library and reads himself up for the days' ploughing. If i was running a pharm, (now daze) i suppoze i would rather hav 36 bushels, ov sum nu breed ov potatoze, raized on theory, than tew hav 84 bushels, got in the mean, benighted, and underhanded way, ov our late lamented grand parents.

Pharmin, after all, iz a good deal like the tavern bizzness, ennyboddy thinks they kan keep a hotel, (now daze,) and they kan, but this iz the way that poor hotels cum tew be so plenty, and this iz likewize what makes pharmin such eazy, and proffitable bizzness . . .

or "Duk":

The duk is a foul. Thare aint no doubt about this—naturalists say so, and kommon sense teaches it.

They are bilt sumthing like a hen, and are an up-and-down, flat-footed job. They don't kackle like the hen, nor kro like the rooster, nor holler like the peakok, nor scream like the goose, nor turk like the turkey; but they quack like a root dokter, and their bill resembles a vetenary surgeon's.

They have a woven fut, and kan float on the water az natural az a sope bubble. They are pretty mutch all feathers, and when the feathers are all removed, and their innards out, thare iz just about az mutch meat on them az thare iz on a krook-necked squash that haz gone tew seed . . . (p. 179)

The writer of the introduction to Josh Billings's collected works (I don't know the name of this introducer) tells us that someone has said (I don't know who) of Josh Billings, "His wit has no edge to betray a malicious motive; but is rather a Feejee club, grotesquely carved and painted, that makes those who feel it grin while they wince. All whom he kills die with a smile upon their faces." Certainly, the whole notion of this "Feejee club" is worth having students explore.

This introduction also provides some other interesting assertions worth exploring in more depth:

Take a little of Martin Farquhar Tupper, and a little of Artemus Ward, knead them together, and you may make something which approaches to a *Josh Billings.* That Mr. Shaw aspires to be a comic Tupper is evidenced in the various chapters headed "Proverbs," "Remarks," "Sayins," and "Afferisms." That he has had Artemus Ward before him is demonstrable by comparing the chapter in which "Josh Billings Insures his Life," with Artemus Ward's celebrated paper entitled "His Autobiography." But Artemus is great in telling a story, having an imaginative power to conceive an accident, plan the action of a piece of drollery, invent an odd character, and describe his creation with infinite humor and force. The talent of Mr. Shaw is of another kind. He is aphoristically comic, if I may use the phrase. He delights in being ludicrously sententious—in Tupperizing laughingly, and in causing an old adage to appear a new one through the fantastic manner in which it is dished up. He is the comic essayist of America, rather than her comic story-teller.

All that sounds good—especially if you know a little about Artemus Ward and Martin Farquhar Tupper.

Artemus Ward

According to Albert Jay Nock, in his preface to the *Selected Works of Artemus Ward,* (New York: Albert & Charles Boni, 1924):

Ward puts his finger as firmly as Mr. Bertrand Russell and Mr. H. L. Mencken have put theirs, upon all the meanness, low-mindedness, greed, viciousness, bloodthirstiness and homicidal mania that were rife among us—and upon their exciting causes as well—but the person of *Intelligenz* turns to him, and instead of being further depressed, as Mr. Russell and Mr. Mencken depress him, instead of being further overpowered by a sense that burdens put upon the spirit of man are greater than it can bear, he is lifted out of his temporary despondency and enervation by the sight of the long stretch of victorious humanity that so immeasurably transcends all these matters of the moment. Such is the calming and persuasive influence of the true critical temper, that one immediately perceives Ward to be regarding all the untowardness of Baldwinsville *sub specie aeternitatis,* and one gratefully submits to his guidance towards a like view of ones own circumstances. (15)

Just think what you can do with those ideas.

Martin Farquhar Tupper

For what it's worth, Farquhar Tupper may be the worst writer of moral poetry since we discovered Mars. Check out *Proverbial Philosophy: A Book of Thoughts and Arguments, Originally Treated* (New York: Wiley

& Putnam, 1846). For those interested in understanding the relationship of "Tupperizing" and Josh Billings, here's a sample:

Of Love

LOVE:—what a volume in a word, an ocean in a tear,
A seventh heaven in a glance, a whirlwind in a sigh,
The lightning in a touch, a millennium in a moment,
What concentrated joy or woe in blest or blighted love!
For it is the native poetry springing up indigenous to Mind,
For heart's own country music thrilling all its chords,
The story without an end that angels throng to hear,
The word, the king of words, carved on Jehovah's heart!
Oh! call thou snake-eyed malice mercy, call envy honest praise,
Count selfish craft for wisdom, and coward treachery for prudence,

Do homage to blaspheming unbelief as to bold and free philosophy,
And estimate the recklessness of license as the right attribute of liberty,—
But with the world, thou friend and scholar, stain not this pure name;
Nor suffer the majesty of Love to be likened to the meanness of desire:
For Love is no more such, than seraphs' hymns are discord,
And such is no more Love, than Aetna's breath is summer

LOVE is a sweet idolatry, enslaving all the soul,
A mighty spiritual force, warring with the dulness of matter,
An angel-mind breathed into a mortal, though fallen yet how beautiful
All the devotion of the heart in all its depth and grandeur.
Behold that pale geranium, pent within the cottage window;
How yearningly it stretcheth to the light its sickly young-stalked leaves.
How it straineth upward to the sun, coveting his sweet influences,
How real a living sacrifice to the god of all its worship!
Such is the soul that loveth; and so the rose-tree of affection
Bendeth its every leaf to look on those dear eyes,
Its every blushing petal basketh in their light,
And all its gladness, all its life, is hanging on their love.

If the love of the heart is blighted, it buddeth not again;
If that pleasant song is forgotten, it is to be learnt no more; Yet often will
thought look back, and weep over early affection; And the dim notes of that
pleasant song will be heard as a reproachful spirit,
Moaning in Aeolian strains over the desert of the heart,
Where the hot siroccos of the world have withered its one oasis.

If nothing else, I love the name Martin Farquhar Tupper, and I love the
notion of "Tupperizing"—a term that ought to be significant to someone besides the makers of Tupperware. (Tupperizing may be the exact
opposite of "Gibsonizing," if you know what I mean.)

Further Inspiration

H. L. Mencken

Mencken wrote some good material about marriage, zoos, politics, and farmers that's worth writing about. See, for instance, his *Minority Report* (New York: Knopf, 1956) and *A Mencken Chrestomathy* (New York: Knopf, 1949). There's also a good collection of some of the nasty things people said about him—*Menckeniana: A Schimpflexikon* (New York: Knopf, 1928). Among other things, in the *Editor and Publisher,* Marlen Pew says:

Mr. Mencken plays a very safe game in his journalism. He is the cagiest editor of the hornblowing type the country has seen since Elbert Hubbard. His specialty is attacking groups that cannot, or will not, fight back. His shield is the festive generality. He bawls for "freedom," but persecutes those who do not subscribe to his views. His journalism is cowardly, cheap, blatant, crooked and horribly wordy.

Charlie Poole

Take a look at Kinney Rorrer's *Rambling Blues: The Life and Songs of Charlie Poole* (London: Old Time Music, 1982) and see if you can decide whether Charlie was "larger-than-life" as Rorrer claims. Poole was a rambler, a gambler, a liar, a cheat, an alcoholic, a perfectionist, and the leader of one of the most popular and influential string-bands of the 1920s. As a bonus, Rorrer provides the words to all his songs.

Theodore L. Shaw

Shaw wrote *Hypocrisy about Art: And What You Don't Gain by It* (Boston: Stuart Publications, 1962). I'm particularly taken by chapter 1 ("Art's Sleep Walkers")—a chapter in which he tries to explain why art is not eternal and chapter 3 ("No One-Best-Way in Art").

Dowsing

While there are many good books on dowsing, I particularly like the material from the *Journal of the British Society of Dowsers.* One collection of this material, *Site and Survey Dowsing,* edited by Clive Thompson (Wellingborough, Northamptonshire: Turnstone, 1980) is full of good information about dowsing rods, angle rods, color, map dowsing, dowsing and ghosts, dowsing and mineworking, and proxy dowsing.

Chickens

I'm convinced that we can learn something important if we get to know chickens well. Take a look at Page Smith and Charles Daniel's *The Chicken Book: Being an Inquiry into the Rise and Fall, Use and Abuse, Triumph and Tragedy of Gallus Domesticus* (Boston: Little, Brown, 1975). Recently, I've been interested in the fate of a Harvard professor who had her students adopt a live chicken for a day, take it to be slaughtered, and make a sculpture from the bones. (If you're interested, you might check the papers around November, 1987.)

Joe Louis

Over the years, I've been collecting small "tributes" to Joe Louis—the pieces that famous writers wrote about him right after he died. Such pieces make ideal assignments of the "Which one is the best?" kind because they contain roughly the same information, just processed a little differently. You can find some of these pieces right around 1981. Chris Mead has also written a decent biography called *Champion Joe Louis: Black Hero in White America* (New York: Scribner's, 1985). Chapter 11 ("Swan Song") gives you more about the context of Louis's death than you'll ever need.

Astronauts

In 1969, American astronauts landed on the moon. The *New York Times* in July contains many quotations by famous people about the significance of the landing—people like the Dalai Lama, Pablo Casals, Robert Jay Lifton, Eric Hoffer, Pablo Picasso, Charles Lindbergh, Vladimir Nabokov, Arthur Koestler, Henry Ford, Russell Baker, and James Reston. There are other quotations in 1979, too—on the ten-year anniversary of the event. I don't know what to do with the material, but you can probably find something to do with it besides "compare and contrast the responses in 1969 to 1979."

Rapunzel

Fairy tales are popular right now. There's a good collection of material on whether fairy tales are "Benign or Pernicious" in Anderson and Forrester's *Point Counterpoint: Eight Cases for Composition* (New York: Harcourt, 1987), and there's another collection on Cinderella in Behrens and Rosen's *Writing and Reading Across the Curriculum* (Boston: Little, Brown, 1985). There's also a great collection of material on Little Red Riding Hood in Jack Zipes's *The Trials & Tribulations of Little Red Riding Hood* (South Hadley, MA: Bergin & Garvey, 1983). I, myself, am partial to Rapunzel—because I think it is the worst fairy tale ever written. If you're interested, you might want to explore the implications of hair growth on the height of Rapunzel's tower. (See, for instance, Charles W. Whitmore and William H. Young's *A Complete Guide to Skin and Hair* [Lynchburg, VA: The Education and Research Foundation for the Health and Beauty Care of Skin, Hair and Nails, 1972].)

Burma-Shave

Frank Rowsome, Jr. has put together *The Verse by the Side of the Road: The Story of the Burma-Shave Signs and Jingles*. I don't know if you remember Burma-Shave signs—small signs set up on the highways to advertise shaving cream. The first would read something like "PRICKLY PEARS" and it would be followed by several more signs: "ARE PICKED . . . FOR PICKLES . . . NO PEACH PICKS . . . A FACE THAT PRICKLES." The final sign read, "BURMA-SHAVE." The appendix to the book is wonderful: a collection of all the Burma-Shave signs ever put up on the highway—hundreds and hundreds of Burma-Shave signs loaded with Americana and sometimes questionable taste.

The Humanist

Every year, *The Humanist* magazine publishes the winners to its essay contest. Take a look at some of those winners sometime. They're full of some strange things.

Insults

Louis A. Safian has written a "hilarious book that will make you a master of the perfect squelch"—*2000 Insults for All Occasions* (New York: Pocket Books, 1966). I got my copy at the Goodwill last semester (along with one of Bill Leary's *Graffiti* books, a book by Lenny Bruce, a book called *1000 Beautiful Things,* and Felton and Fowler's *Famous Americans You Never Knew Existed.*) I understand Safian has a sequel to his book (*2000 More Insults*). In his introduction he says, "Edged with the sharp barbs of truth, this thesaurus of sizzling flipquickies, mad-libs, bright slayings, and tongue-whippers offers you a well-stocked arsenal for the fullest expression of your critical faculties." Such material is barbaric in a useful way.

Bob Edwards Dempsey

I got Bob Edwards Dempsey's book at the Goodwill, too. His editor, Hugh A. Dempsey, describes Bob as a Canadian "best remembered as a humorist who had an aphorism for every occasion" (*The Best of Bob*

Edwards [Edmonton: Hurtig, 1975]). In this collection, Dempsey writes about the fair sex, religion, sticky fingers, Peter J. McGonigle, Booze, Life & Death, City Life, and Pure Philosophy. According to Hugh Dempsey, Bob was an off-color storyteller, a writer of one-liners, a man with a "social conscience," and an "angry man lashing out at the inequities of Canadian society."

The Journal of Irreproducible Results

There's a good collection from this journal in *Selected Papers of The Journal of Irreproducible Results: A Selection of Superb and Irreproducible Research from the Illustrious and Irreproducible Archives of the Society for Basic Irreproducible Research,* edited by George H. Scherr (Dorset Press, 1986). Some of it is valuable for something. There's also another journal called *The Journal of Polymorphous Perversity.*

Dolls

I collect information about dolls, mainly through advertisements in *Better Homes and Gardens* and *Smithsonian Magazine.* I especially like the Princess Diana Royal Wardrobe Collection—you buy the collection of the Princess Diana Doll's clothing and get the Princess Diana Doll for free from the Danbury Mint. The Danbury Mint also sells a Rapunzel doll capturing "the beauty and enchantment that won the heart of her Prince." And I suppose because of my interest in dolls, I'm rapidly becoming interested in babies, too. Marie Winn has edited a good collection of baby literature—*The Baby Reader: 56 Selections from World Literature about Babies and their Mothers, Fathers, Admirers and Adversaries* (New York: Simon and Schuster, 1973).

Carp

My friend Ron says, "*Koi ga odoreba dojo mō odoru.*" The carp is the queen of fish—and certainly the best fish in the United States. Those who know nothing about carp could check out Hur Lampman's *The Coming of the Pond Fishes* (Portland: Binfords & Mort, 1946); Wesley Marx's "Plug-ugly Minnows or 'Living Jewels,' Carp Stir Emotions" (*Smithsonian,* May, 1980); and A. J. McClane's "The Enigmatic Carp" (*Field and Stream,* September 1968); and Nathan Pritikin and Patrick M. McGrady, Jr.'s *The Pritikin Program for Diet and Exercises* (New York: Grossett & Dunlap, 1979). (Pritikin and McGrady clearly show that the carp is much better nutritionally than salmon or trout.)

Telephone Books

Margie Boulé in the July 17, 1988 *Oregonian* (section B1, col. 1) tells us:

There is no book more telling than the phone book, particularly when you're really studying the yellow pages.

I spent an afternoon at the downtown library a few days ago, poring over the familiar, several-pound November 1987/1988 edition we all know so well, and the far smaller, more friendly 1948 edition of the Portland yellow pages. I highly recommend the exercise to all elected officials. If ever one wanted to know the city of Portland, and the county of Multnomah, and the surrounding masses, there is no better source than the place where we list ourselves.

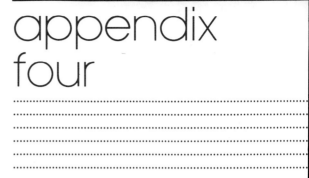

appendix four

··
··
··
··
··
··

Things to Read in Class

· ·

                        I've never heard many people talk about reading things in class, but over the years, I've collected many small pieces that I read out loud at the beginning of the hour. Reading out loud can provide a different kind of feedback that many of us don't explore. Here, for instance, is a piece by Vic Braden, the famous tennis teacher:

What tennis actually comes down to—stripped of the trick shots, the weird, sensual body movements, the best in equipment and clothes, the search for the latest theory—is a dedication to those fundamentals supported by physical laws. You may think, "Yeh, but I want to have fun out there, I want a little variety. I want to try lots of different shots, move the ball around, keep my opponent guessing." Well, *losers* have tons of variety; their shots fly all over the court— and often beyond—simply because they fail to swing the same way twice in a row. Champions are those who take great pride in just learning to hit the same old boring winner.

    The only problem with playing a "straight down the middle and deep" system is that you need a high frustration-tolerance threshold because you're not trying anything fancy to end a point quickly. Most people don't have the patience to try to outsteady their opponent. They say, "Jeez, the ball's gone over the net three times. I've got to come in and do something *big*." So they try to hit a drop shot or they go for the lines and that's when they die. It's not easy to hit those big-time shots, so just be happy to keep the ball in play. Stick to the fundamentals and try to master them first, then you can get fancy. But you'll probably find an interesting thing happening along the way: *the better you play the more simplistic you become in your approach*. You find you don't need to get fancy. It's usually the players who just can't win who feel they have to showboat.

This type of player hangs around every club in the country, scoffing at regular forehands and backhands, while saying, "Man, I just want to serve, volley, attack, and hit the overhead smash." He glories in hitting the cover off the ball and has very little respect for the common shot. But that "common shot" is what makes Chris Evert the queen of them all. . . . [Vic Braden with Bill Bruns, *Vic Braden's Tennis for the Future* (Boston: Little, Brown, 1977) 24–25.]

Well, Chris Evert isn't Queen anymore, but the point is still clear. Losers have "tons of variety." Champions hit "the same old boring winner." And the better students play and the better they get, the more simplistic they become in their approaches. This may look like just another form of exhortation, but the notion of playing tennis gives me a *vocabulary* to use when talking to students—as well as a way to show students that metaphors are not simply things we use to embellish dead prose or say things indirectly.

Here's another passage, this time from Thalassa Cruso, a gardener:

Old gardens are sometimes overgrown, and new owners cut back fiercely, for they feel smothered. If shrubs and vines are tapping at your windowpanes, some trimming is in order, but at first keep it light. Big shrubs, even when overgrown, represent a plus on any piece of property. Before grubbing out a bush or cutting down a tree, wait and see how selective you can be. . . .

Forest trees that were misguidedly planted as foundation material are a pest in old gardens. They look out of place and block out light and air. Often they can't be cut back without mutilation, so a new homeowner grubs them out. We inherited just such a clutch of overgrown foundation plantings, including arborvitae, false cypress, hemlocks, and old-fashioned rhododendrons. I was all for taking them down then and there, before we made any changes to the house. But my husband objected, he can't bear cutting anything down—ever. So we waited until the alterations to the house were finished. By the time some windows had been enlarged and the interior lightened with fresh paint, those shrubs did not look so bad. Some still had to go, but our interior changes had made such a difference that it was possible to leave big bushes at the corner of the house, where they have since been pruned into large, distinctive specimens that I now would be sorry to lose. [Thalassa Cruso, *Making Things Grow Outdoors* (New York: Alfred Knopf, 1972) 14–15.]

Too often, students want to rip out their gardens, prune their hedges, and kill the weeds—when they should be letting the old trees grow in the back of the yard while they work on enlarging the interiors of their houses.

Here's a small passage from the *Livestock Judging Handbook* by Julius Nordby, W. Malcolm Beeson, and David Fourt (Danville, IL: Interstate, 1953) 8:

Only in so far as a man forgets himself and turns his mind to the keen analysis of livestock, is he able to progress toward perfection in livestock selection. You must become livestock-minded and be aware of the perplexing problems that confront the breeder who is selecting and culling to improve his livestock. Allow your mind to dwell on the imperfections as well as the perfections of the breeds of livestock. Study groups as well as individuals.

Convert your attitude to such an extent that the problem of livestock judging becomes a real and living task, rather than a means of attempting to place four animals in the order in which you expect the judge to place them. The desire to know intrinsic values in livestock puts the mind in a very receptive state for the most effective learning of livestock selection.

This becomes part of Pep-Talk Number Seventy-two: how to get students to understand the difference between thinking about composition and learning to "place four animals in the order in which you expect the judge to place them." (The longer I teach, the more convinced I am that we could profit from the notion of "livestock-mindedness.")

Finally, here's the substance of Pep-Talk Number Seventy-six: how to get students to understand my worries when I mess with their paint:

About this time I walked up Riverside Drive one clear moonlight night with two or three other students. Up near the Soldiers and Sailors Monument we sat down on the grass. When I looked about at the night I saw two tall poplar trees breathing—rustling in the light spring air. The foliage was thick and dark and soft—the grass bright in the moonlight. The river, near—with the twinkling lights from the other side, far away. I studied the outlines of the trees carefully. The openings where the sky came through—the unevenness of the edges—the mass of the trees, dark, solid, very alive. Next morning I tried to paint it. I was fairly satisfied with my trees and water but the sky and grass baffled me. However, I covered the canvas as best I could and thought the trees particularly beautiful. I showed the painting to a student whose paintings I liked. He immediately told me that there was no color in my trees—that they should be painted with spots of red and blue and green like the Impressionists. I said I hadn't seen anything like that in my trees the night before. He insisted that it was there and I just hadn't seen it, that I didn't understand. And he took my painting and began painting on it to show me. He painted on the trees—the very part that I thought was so good. He tried to explain to me about the Impressionists. I hadn't heard of anything like that before—I didn't understand it and I thought he had spoiled my painting. I took the painting and worked on it again. I couldn't get it to be like the beautiful night I had seen and when I painted over what he had done, the whole thing was sticky and much worked over and dried very badly—but I kept it for years. It represented an effort toward something that had meaning to me—much more than the work at school. [Georgia O'Keeffe, *Georgia O'Keeffe* (New York: Viking, 1976), n.pag.]